OKLAHOMA *TRACKMAKER* SERIES

OKLAHOMA TRACKMAKER SERIES

Oklahoma Heritage Association,
Inc.

Trackmaker Committee, 1978

PANHANDLE PIONEER

The James K. Hitch Homestead

Painting by Augusta Metcalf, reproduced through the courtesy of Donald A. Brown, Farm Credit Banks of Wichita, Kansas.

OKLAHOMA **TRACKMAKER** SERIES

Panhandle Pioneer

Henry C. Hitch, His Ranch, and His Family

By Donald E. Green

Odie B. Faulk, Series Editor

Published for the Oklahoma Heritage Association by the
University of Oklahoma Press

Also by Donald E. Green

Land of the Underground Rain: Irrigation on the Texas High Plains, 1910–1970 (Austin, 1973)
The Creek People (Phoenix, 1973)
(editor) *Rural Oklahoma* (Oklahoma City, 1977)
Fifty Years of Service to West Texas Agriculture: A History of Texas Tech University's College of Agricultural Sciences, 1925–1975 (Lubbock, 1977)
Panhandle Pioneer: Henry C. Hitch, His Ranch, and His Family (Norman, 1979)

Library of Congress Cataloging in Publication Data

Green, Donald Edward, 1936–
  Panhandle pioneer.

  (Oklahoma trackmaker series; v. 7)
  Bibliography: p. 269
  Includes index.
  1. Hitch, Henry Charles, 1884–1921. 2. Ranch life—Oklahoma—Texas Co. 3. Texas Co., Okla.—Biography. 4. Pioneers—Oklahoma—Texas Co.—Biography. I. Title. II. Series.
F702.T4H574   976.6′135′050924 [B]   78-21390

To Mrs. Henry C. Hitch
A Panhandle Pioneer in her own right

Contents

Illustrations

MAPS

Preface

This book is both the history of a cattle ranch and a biography of three generations of one family that established and molded that ranch from the days of the open range to the era of computerized feedlots. The story covers a century of human drama in terms of hardships, happiness, business and agricultural activities, and the close relationship of a remarkable family. This is also an account of how one cattle-raising enterprise made the transition from the nineteenth century to the present. Our story is also in many ways a history of the Oklahoma Panhandle from the vantage point of Texas County. Last, but far from least, the reader will discover that the cement that holds this history together is the Henry C. Hitch family's faith in their region and its land, and the hold that land has on its people.

I owe a tremendous debt of gratitude to many people who assisted me in this work. First and foremost, I am eternally grateful to all members of the Hitch family, especially to Christine (Mrs. Henry C.) Hitch, Ladd Hitch, Paul Hitch, Joyce Hitch Gray, and Marjorie Hitch Price. The family allowed me complete access to private and business papers and records in the attic and basement of the stone house on Coldwater Creek that James K. Hitch had built in the early 1890s. During this process, I assembled and organized the Henry C. Hitch Papers. In addition, Ladd Hitch took time from his very busy schedule and with his good humor, sense of history, and hospitality provided me with a number of interviews, a tour of the ranch, and much encouragement. Most of all, I am indebted to one of the loveliest women I have ever met: Mrs. Henry C. Hitch. Although advanced in years and ill with arthritis, she gathered materials and photographs for me, met me at her office for interviews, accompanied me on several occasions to interview others, and never hesitated to provide me with any needed assistance.

Other helpful people and institutions who aided this project in many ways include Mrs. Roberta Hambleton, of Schenectady, New York, who provided me with correspondence between her late mother, Erma Walker Monesmith, and Mrs. Hambleton's aunt Mrs. Henry C. (Christine Walker) Hitch, as well as with family photographs; Mary ("Lit") Hitch Hall and Willie Neathery Hitch for permission to use photographs in their possession; Joe Fitzgerald, for flying me over the ranch and Texas County and pointing out several significant features of the terrain (observations that I have incorporated in this book); O. C. ("Cotton") Furnish, for showing me around the Hitch Ranch during haying season; Linda Landess, of the Hitch Ranch offices, for aiding my research; Harold and JoAnn Kachel, curators of No Man's Land Museum, for opening the museum's files to me; James L. Rogers, of Central State University, for drawing the maps for this book; Don Brown, of the Farm Credit Banks, of Wichita, Kansas, for permission to use his excellent photographs; Garry Nall, of West Texas State University, and Paul Bonnifield, of Yampa, Colorado, for sharing their research with me.

I am also indebted to Dottie France, of the District Court Clerk's Office of Texas County; Del Gittinger, of the public library at Liberal, Kansas; the Guaranty Abstract and Title Company, of Guymon, Oklahoma; Ellis Freeney, of the Oklahoma Cattlemen's Association; Jane

Hensley, of Guymon, Oklahoma; Mildred Chamberlain, Emmett Sanders, and Johnny Lee, all of Spearman, Texas; Lois Filbeck and Dorothea Ray, both of the interlibrary loan desk at Central State University; Jack Haley, of the University of Oklahoma Western History Collections; Alene Simpson, Mack Harris, Vicki Sullivan, Manon Atkins, Mary Moran, Martha Blaine, and Mary Lou Ervin, all of the Oklahoma Historical Society; and Ann Hall, my typist.

Very special thanks are also in order for the organization and the personnel responsible for initiating and publishing this work: the Oklahoma Heritage Association; Paul Lambert, Executive Director; Jack Conn, President; and especially the editors of the association's Trackmaker Series and my good friends, Kenny Franks and Odie B. Faulk.

Edmond, Oklahoma   DONALD E. GREEN

PANHANDLE PIONEER

1.   No Man's Land

The young cattleman from Tennessee relaxed to a slump in his saddle as he pulled up his horse at the edge of a valley on the High Plains. Pausing on the northern rim, he stared at the lush, sub-irrigated pasture in the bottomland that extended for miles to the southwest and northeast. He spurred his horse down a trail over the yellowish rim of the Cap Rock outcropping, a trail perhaps first laid down by buffalo feeding off the natural hay meadow. As rider and horse approached the middle of the valley, James Kerrick Hitch made a mental note of the clear stream with deep pools that cut through the region sandwiched between the Texas Panhandle and southwestern Kansas, known as the Neutral Strip, the Public Land Strip, or No Man's Land.

As the horse began grazing the short but thick buffalo grass, the lean figure dismounted. Hitch removed his wide-brimmed hat, revealing a thick shock of black hair with no hint of baldness. He lay on his belly and stretched forward to bury his mouth in the cool waters of the creek. They tasted sweet and cold, indicating a nearby spring. Rising to his feet, he wiped his mouth and drooping mustache on the back of his shirt sleeve. As he surveyed the landscape, he saw neither cattle nor settlers. Jim Hitch had reached his promised land—a land he had been looking for since leaving his native Tennessee a decade earlier.[1]

The Coldwater Valley was one of the few well-watered

James Kerrick Hitch, ca. 1890. Unless otherwise noted, all the photographs in this book reproduced through the courtesy of the Hitch family.

areas in the region. Like Palo Duro Creek on the east, the northeastward-flowing Coldwater was a tributary of Beaver River. The Beaver, called the North Canadian River after it flowed out of the "Strip," was the primary stream of the region.

Before white men began driving their herds into the Neutral Strip, this was a borderland for native Americans. Comanches and Kiowas and their northern enemies, the Cheyennes and Arapahoes, hunted the abundant buffalo along the Beaver and Cimarron Rivers and their tributaries. The first white men to pasture their herds on this grass were Mexicans from the west. As early as the 1860s, José Baca from Las Vegas, New Mexico Territory, pushed as many as 25,000 sheep into the area around present-day Kenton. Others followed, such as the Bernal brothers, Juan and Ramon. These sheepmen employed herders, many of whom, like Juan Cruz Lujan, eventually settled in the western part of the Strip. In the summer, herdsmen sheared their animals, loaded wool sacks onto wagons, and freighted the fleeces up the old Santa Fe Trail to Missouri. In the late 1870s the Anglos—cattlemen from the East and South—began arriving, and they pushed the sheepmen back into New Mexico. The cattlemen may have used threats and coercion, but many herdsmen believed that some sheepmen were paid by the cattlemen to leave. Juan Cruz Lujan recalled in later years the story that José Baca was given $25,000 to remove his 25,000 sheep. Carl Coke Rister, author of *No Man's Land,* was told that both Baca and the Bernal brothers were paid off.[2]

By the late 1870s a number of ranches had sprung up in the region. The original 101 Ranch first appeared in the vicinity of present-day Kenton on tributaries of the Cimarron River. Owned by an English group known as the Western Land and Cattle Company and managed by

Ruins of the OX Ranch house on the Beaver River.

Ruins of the OX corral and barn.

T. H. Burnett, the 101 eventually spread its operations into the pastures of Nebraska, Wyoming, and the Kansas Flint Hills. Farther east on the Goff Creek tributary of the Beaver River was the OX, owned by a partnership known as Towers, Gudgell, and Simpson. Its manager was Major "Hi" Towers.[3]

John ("Hooker") Threlkeld, a Kentuckian who came to the region as a cowhand in the 1870s, was the OX foreman. The origin of Hooker's name has long been a disputed subject. Some old-timers contended that the name came from the famous Union general of the Civil War Joseph ("Fighting Joe") Hooker. Others believed that Threlkeld took the name from some early cattleman. Harry Chrisman, historian of the region, has described him as having "the appearance of an eagle." If so, a hook-shaped nose could have been the source of the nickname. But Chrisman believes it probable that the name was given to him by admiring cowhands who coveted his extraordinary skill in "hooking" calves with a rope. It was said that Threlkeld could ride into a herd and quietly drop a small loop over the head of any calf, no matter how close the animal stood to its mother.[4]

One of the largest cattle outfits in the Strip was the CCC Ranch, owned by the concern of Vickers, Wells, and Gates, of Tombstone, Arizona. Its twenty to thirty thousand head ranged over a half-million acres and grazed deep into the Texas Panhandle. Another of the better-known ranches of the central Strip was the Anchor-D whose more than thirty thousand head pastured on 1,500 sections (960,000 acres) of land extending from Kansas to Texas. Its headquarters was about twenty miles west of the present Guymon. E. C. "Anchor-D" Dudley, a Boston businessman, was the founding owner. His first brand was the Double-X, but cowboys too often referred to it as the

Double-Cross, so the Bostonian changed it. The Anchor-D was dotted with forty-seven windmills pulling water from hand-dug wells.[5]

One of the more popular cattlemen in the region, who would become a neighbor of James K. Hitch, was Colonel A. J. ("Jack") Hardesty, a man as much at home in Dodge City as in the Strip. He was principal owner of the Half Circle S, whose vast herds spread up and down Chiquita Creek. Hardesty was an amiable soul, and he was known as a good man to work for. According to Chrisman, one cowboy characterized him in this way: "Colonel Jack don't expect a man to do anything he cain't do from the back of a hoss."[6]

In addition to the large ranches, there were many smaller cattlemen when J. K. Hitch arrived in the middle 1880s. Pasturing herds on the bottomlands and uplands of the streams were "Old Man" Ludwig Kramer, Charley Grimmer and his son, the Healy brothers, Fred Taintor, Tom Connell, Jesse Evans, John Steel, and others too numerous to mention.[7]

By 1885 cattlemen reigned supreme over this rectangular region, but they could hold no legal title to the land. In neighboring southwestern Kansas a man or single woman could file on a homestead claim of 160 acres on any creek bottom not already taken and perhaps buy another quarter of a section under the provisions of the Timber Culture Act. In addition, a cattleman might have his cowhands file individually on a number of other quarter sections in a checkerboard pattern up and down the creek in order to control a maximum acreage of land still in the public domain. After his hands had lived on the land for six months, he could supply them with the money to purchase the land for $1.25 per acre. They could then deed the property to their boss. Of course, the new owner

The Charlie Grimmer Ranch headquarters and family, ca. 1890.

was not without gratitude, and some token in cash generally served to express his appreciation.

In the Neutral Strip, however, cattlemen could not own even 160 acres. All the land there was public domain not yet officially opened to settlement, and the unwritten law of the range determined control of land and water. Prior water control dictated grazing rights. The first cattleman to drive his herds to a stream grazed his cattle to the watershed divide, or approximately half the distance to the next parallel stream.[8]

The Strip constituted that land between the 100th and 103d meridians and between 36° 30′ and 37° north latitude. To the south was the Texas Panhandle, to the west New Mexico, and to the north Kansas and Colorado. To the east was the Indian Territory. Before 1885 the Cherokee Nation claimed the Strip as an extension of its so-called

9

Outlet and occasionally tried to collect lease payments from cattlemen in the rectangular area. In truth, however, this vast, level piece of short-grass country belonged to no one—hence the name given it by most Americans of the day: "No Man's Land." It was believed that because no state or territory exercised jurisdiction over it, the "Strip" had become a haven for outlaws and a place of violence.[9]

As with all such stereotyped concepts there was some truth in this popular notion. Kansas law by 1881 prohibited the sale of liquor, thanks to the crusade of Carry Nation and her Anti-Saloon League. The proximity of the Neutral Strip offered numerous opportunities for satisfying the illegal thirst of Kansans, as well as that of local cowboys and the settlers in southwestern Kansas. The economy of Beer City and its Elephant Saloon, situated just south of the Kansas boundary, was grounded in Kansas prohibition. One exceptionally large still was located on Hog Creek, near Gate City, in an earth-covered lean-to. Using corn meal and sugar freighted from Dodge City, the brewers apparently conducted "a flourishing business night and day." According to the recollections of one contemporary observer, the distillery's business "extended and developed to as far west as mankind was known."[10]

The making of whiskey was not the only illegal activity in the region. Some outlaws found the absence of law compatible with their interests for a time. Writers have often cited the infamous Coe gang to show that the region must have been full of outlaw hideouts. This lawless group, led by one Cyrus Coe, had a stronghold on Carrizo Creek near Black Mesa. By the end of the Civil War the gang was preying on wagons along the Santa Fe Trail and exacting tribute in the form of mutton and wool from poor Mexican shepherds. The bandits finally pushed the Bernal brothers too far one day when they killed three shepherds and drove off 3,400 sheep. Ramon Bernal took four men, pursued the outlaws, and caught them at night asleep. Before they awoke, he had their guns and horses, and they were left to walk back to Black Mesa.

Other Mexican sheepmen sought the aid of a United States Army detachment at Fort Lyon, Colorado. According to one account, Lieutenant Colonel William H. Penrose led an attack on the "robbers' roost," captured Coe, and reduced the stronghold to rubble with a six-inch cannon. The surviving outlaws dispersed like a covey of quail. A different account was given in 1913 by L. A. Allen, a former sheriff in southeastern Colorado. According to Allen, who was also in the cattle business, he got word that the Coe gang was on its way to Colorado to steal cattle. He rode with a group of Colorado militiamen and found the desperadoes asleep one night in an abandoned adobe hut. Allen and his men dismounted some distance away. With his rifle in one hand and six-gun in the other, the sheriff burst through the door. The gang surrendered without reaching for a gun. Coe was not there, but one of the bandits told Allen where to find him. The posse hanged all eleven of the outlaws to the limbs of convenient cottonwoods along a river, then set out after the elusive leader. They captured Coe that same night, tied him to a horse, and turned him over to the sheriff in Pueblo. The same night, Allen said, Coe was locked in the Pueblo jail, but a mob broke in and lynched him.[11]

Harry Chrisman, in his *Lost Trails of the Cimarron*, tells of only a few gangs of outlaws in the Strip, besides the Coe gang. One of them consisted of two men known as Bill Williams and "Big Jim." In the late 1880s, as these two men were returning drunk from Neutral City to their shack near Gate, they decided to shoot up the sod house of a settler named Ira Norton. With six-guns blazing in the middle of the night, the drunks yelled and galloped around the soddy, firing into its sides and through its windows. Norton was alone. He had only a muzzle-loading double-barreled shotgun, some powder and caps, but no pellets. In desperation he hammered an old cast iron teakettle into small pieces and rammed them into both barrels. He waited patiently. When the carousers paused for another drink from the crock jug on "Big Jim's" saddle, Norton pointed his long gun out the window. Two loud booms tore open the night air. When the smoke cleared, Bill Williams was dead on the ground; "Big Jim" was still on his horse, but was bleeding from his neck and shoulder. The lone survivor raked his spurs into his horse and never again was seen in that country.[12] Being an outlaw in the Neutral Strip seems to have been a riskier occupation than it was in neighboring Kansas or Texas, where the accused might at least have had a chance to stand trial.

Another group, a gang of horse thieves operating about 1885, was led by Bill Chitwood and his two brothers. Their headquarters were on Coon Creek near Sodtown. Chitwood, though, was not all bad. As one early settler related, Chitwood once stopped a vigilance committee from hanging an old drunk. The Chitwoods later left the region and settled in Idaho, where Bill eventually was elected county sheriff.[13]

Much of the violence in No Man's Land had nothing to do with outlaw gangs, but rather was the result of political anarchy. A close observer, the first legally elected sheriff of Beaver County, Jim Herron, believed that "most of the killings were over personal grievances, usually associated with cattle theft and quarrels over range and water." One small rancher shot a neighbor he suspected of maliciously killing some of his stock. The son of a sheepman was murdered in a conflict over range rights. Two families, in a dispute over pastureland, started a feud that ended with the killing of two young men, one from each family. And, of course, there were the inevitable saloon fights and killings.[14]

Cattle rustling, especially the stealing of a few head at a time, usually was done not by organized gangs, but by one or two individuals, often cowboys. This was a major problem for cattlemen. Oliver Nelson, one-time cowhand in the Strip, claimed that winter joblessness was the most important cause of such thefts. The ranches employed most of their cowboys only from the spring through the fall months, retaining few hands through the winter. A cowhand might be fortunate enough to find a winter job for himself, as did "Brushy" Bush when he became marshal of Beer City, or he might "ride the grubline," simply going from ranch to ranch and staying a day or two at each one for a few free meals. Still others sought refuge in abandoned soddies and butchered a few beefs from some rancher's herd. This "slow elk" sustained them through the winter.[15]

Another problem that created still more friction was the very location of the Neutral Strip. It lay astride cattle trails, including the Jones-Plummer Trail, used by Texas Panhandle ranchers in driving their herds to market. One of the worst scourges of the cattle industry in those days was "Texas fever," which was brought into the Neutral Strip, Kansas, and the Indian Territory by tick-infested Texas longhorns that were immune to the disease but acted as carriers. The disease was spread by the ticks. It was perhaps in the mid-1880s that Colonel Jack Hardesty and "Old Man" Ludwig Kramer decided to take it upon themselves to divert the Texas cattle drivers away from their ranges. They laid out a circuitous route for the drovers to follow, but not without some conflict with the Texans. When tough trail-boss Ab Blocker drove his herd into the Strip, he encountered the best-armed group of cowboys he had ever seen. As Blocker put it:

The cow outfits up there . . . had organized to fight rustlers and to keep their stock from mixing with trail herds. We heard of this down the trail, even before we got to Fort Worth, and we found that these men meant business. It looked like every man had a Winchester rifle in his saddle boot and a six-shooter or two strapped on him. And even the *boys* were dressed that way! The way I remember it was that it looked like a place where the kids teethed on forty-five caliber cartridges![16]

Since virtually every man carried a gun, when tempers flared between cowboy and cowboy, or neighbor and neighbor, with no authorities to answer to, the outcome occasionally was an unpremeditated killing. An editor for the Kansas City *Live Stock Record* understood this phenomenon in a region whose absence of law offered many opportunities for conflict over grazing rights, water rights, and land claims. He wrote: "It is absurd to strap a brace of revolvers and a belt full of cartridges about a young man and expect him to exist any great length of time outside the limits of savage life."[17]

The most important cause of violence in the region was a problem that appeared time and again on America's frontier: conflicting land claims. Settlers and cattlemen were preoccupied with this problem. Even the children knew that "claim jumpers" were a bad lot. James K. Hitch's son Henry in later years recalled playing only one game as a child. In this game he drew a square on the ground and called it his claim. When on one occasion a toad jumped into the square, Henry accused it of being a claim jumper and clubbed it with a stick.[18]

Claim jumping became an issue when in 1885 the Secretary of the Interior handed down an opinion that the Cherokee Outlet ended at the 100th meridian. No Man's Land was thus officially declared to be part of the public domain. According to one account, the secretary's decision was first relayed to southwestern Kansas by Commissioner of the General Land Office A. J. Sparks in a letter to a citizen of Englewood, Kansas. The letter was received October 13, 1885, and news spread rapidly from the town through the region.

Although the Strip could not be opened immediately to settlers under the Homestead Act because it had not been surveyed into 160-acre units, a trickle of squatters in traditional frontier fashion began moving from Kansas primarily into the eastern part of No Man's Land along the Beaver River. The central and western portions remained, for the time being, in the possession of the cattlemen. Seeing an opportunity to create the first town to serve the squatters, promoters in Wichita, Kansas, organized the Beaver City Townsite Company. A man named McLease was president. On March 6, 1886, William Waddle, agent for the company, and Ernest A. Reiman, a surveyor who formerly had been with David Payne's colony of Oklahoma "boomers," arrived at a "road ranch" at the point where the Jones-Plummer Trail crossed Beaver River. Road ranches were supply stations located along trails. They usually combined in one operation a saloon, general merchandise store, and campground. Jim Lane's establishment was no exception. It also served as a stage-coach station for a line running from Dodge City to Mobeetie, Texas. It was built in 1879 or 1880, and by 1885 it consisted of a barbed-wire corral, a stable covered with prairie hay, and two sod houses. Lane kept his store and post office in one of the soddies and lived in the other. He claimed 160 acres as a squatter, but aside from squat-

ter's rights he had no legal paper for the land. Nevertheless, he agreed to cede his "claim" in exchange for two
blocks in the proposed town of Beaver City.[19]

According to J. R. Spears, a correspondent for the *New
York Sun* whose story "No Man's Land" received national
publicity in January 1889, it was the Wichita Townsite
promoters who first coined the phrase "No Man's Land,"
to indicate that the lands were vacant and to attract settlers.
When the Spears article appeared in the edition of January 20, 1889, the issue also contained an editorial entitled
"God's Land, But No Man's." The editorial emphasized
the conflict and violence in the Beaver City area.[20]

Although the General Land Office refused to recognize
the validity of the townsite, a number of businesses were
established within the next year or so as a result of the
publicity the company received in Kansas newspapers.
George Blake built a hotel, while O. P. Bennett and the
Tracy brothers constructed a dance hall of sod slabs adjacent to the livery stable. D. R. Healy excavated a large
dugout, erected a front wall of logs, and laid a sod roof on
the structure to complete the town's livery stable. No
frontier town was complete without at least one grog
shop. Jim Donnelly, a fat, ruddy-complexioned fellow,
met that need with his saloon. Other businesses soon included a general merchandise store, a dry goods store,
a blacksmith shop, several grocery stores, a hardware
store, and a lumber yard. When a boot-and-saddle maker,
two or three doctors, a couple of ministers, two druggists,
and a newspaperman set up shop, Beaver City began to
take on all the trappings of a civilized community.[21]

By the spring of 1886 scores of farmers and their families were erecting sod houses along the eastern Beaver
and its tributaries. According to George Rainey, in his
No Man's Land, much of the sod was sliced by a wooden

sled made of two- by six-inch runners, with a horizontal steel blade some twelve to sixteen inches long bolted between the runners. The driver occupied a seat on the sled, which cut the sod into bricks one and a half to three feet long. The builder used these bricks to erect the walls of his soddy. Boards served for ridge poles and roof. Tar paper, if available, covered the roof boards, and sod was laid over the boards. Both the outside and inside walls were finally smoothed with a sharp spade. Occasionally settlers made a gypsum plaster with which they whitewashed the interiors. Hard-packed dirt sufficed for the floor.[22]

A few of the sod houses were large, some even elaborate. The Overton house, for example, built in 1887 south of Beaver City on Clearwater Creek, was twenty-five feet square, divided into four rooms, and had a pine ceiling. Most were more modest, less than half that size, with no ceiling except possibly a piece of canvas.[23]

All kinds of sod towns sprang up in the Strip in 1886 and 1887 as potential promoters looked toward profits to be made from town lots. Carter Tracy and a couple of associates founded Gate City at the eastern edge of the Strip. A group from southwestern Missouri founded Neutral City four miles west of Gate. Sod Town, on Kiowa Creek near the Texas line, was a wide-open assortment of saloons and a frequent hangout of the Chitwood gang. Benton sprang up in 1886 on Mexico Creek. Rothwell was established on Willow Creek. Among the more permanent settlements were Hardesty, named after rancher Jack Hardesty, at the mouth of Coldwater Creek; Optima, northwest of Hardesty; and Carrizo (later Kenton), near Black Mesa. More ephemeral towns included Mineral City (south of Carrizo), Nevada, Alpine, Riverside, and others whose sites are difficult to find today. Even towns with such grandiose names as Grand Valley, near the mouth of Fulton Creek, and Paladora, on Palo Duro Creek, no longer exist. The leaders of each town entertained thoughts of their settlement becoming the metropolis of the plains, despite the fact that only about 3,000 people inhabited all of No Man's Land by 1886.[24]

Settlers who flowed into the region, primarily from southwestern Kansas between 1885 and 1888, staked out squatter's claims in valleys and uplands that had neither been surveyed into units smaller than six-mile-square townships nor been opened to settlement by the government. The initial survey of the Neutral Strip was made by John H. Clark after the United States General Land Office commissioned him to establish the boundaries of West Texas under provisions of the famous Compromise of 1850. Clark drew the southern boundary of the Strip in 1860. Two deputy surveyors named Chaney and Smith, who appeared on the scene in 1881, drew the Cimarron Base Line. They then used that base line to survey the region, dividing it into traditional six-mile square townships. Unable to find Clark's survey markers, they made another survey of the southern boundary, but erroneously drew it a few hundred feet north of the actual line. The final survey and division of the region into 160-acre, or quarter-section, units was not made until 1890–91. When Carter Tracy, a founder of Gate City, arrived in the fall of 1885, he noticed the pot-shaped stakes of zinc marking the township corners erected by Chaney and Smith. Squatters had to approximate their160-acre claims from those markers.[25]

In the absence of any legal right to own land, quarrels and violence over land claims threatened squatters' rights to their lands. On August 26, 1886, a group of thirty-five farmers and townsmen met at the sod school house in Beaver City and formed a "Respective Claims Committee." Its stated purpose was to "discourage claim-jumping and avoid discord among settlers over claims to town lots and homesteads." A board of directors of prominent Beaver City men—Dr. O. G. Chase, Dr. J. A. Overstreet, and J. C. Hodge—was commissioned by the group to draw up "a code of laws" and a quitclaim deed form "for our common use in the transfer of claims from one party to another." All settlers with claims in the region were admonished to join the organization for a fee of one dollar. Members could then have the Respective Claims Board investigate and validate their claims.[26]

This extralegal organization convened for another meeting on October 16 and adopted the following rules to govern the validation of claims: (1) any person at least twenty-one years of age could hold a 160-acre claim if at least five acres of the land had been put into cultivation by April 1, 1887, or some other equal improvements had been made by that time; (2) the same person could also establish a claim for absentee members of his own family who were of age if he also made improvements on those claims by that date; (3) any person who made such improvements but left his claims was given four months to return; and (4) the organization asserted its right to punish claim jumpers by "measures sufficiently severe."[27]

The Respective Claims Committee was similar to other "claims clubs" formed in a number of areas of the frontier midwest before and after the Civil War. These clubs were also squatters' associations attempting to protect their members from conflicting claims through force. In Iowa a number of these organizations were dominated by land speculators, both large and small, who sought to protect the right of their members to buy and sell claims.[28]

Like the Iowa claims clubs, the Respective Claims Committee attempted to protect squatters' rights not recognized by United States land law. Some of the Iowa groups stated that members could hold an additional 160 acres for an absentee friend, and they protected the right of minors or the children of claimants to hold claims. In similar fashion, the rules of the Neutral Strip group allowed a claimant to hold other claims for absentee relatives. Usually the person guarding the claims built a sod house and broke out a small piece of ground on each of the vacant claims.

Much of the claim jumping in early Iowa was caused not by someone contesting a claim already occupied by a settler, but rather by contestants quarreling over the unoccupied lands of absentee or minor claimants.[29] Not enough is known about claims contests in the Strip to state that this was the most important cause for such conflicts, but it was certainly the cause for the most celebrated instance of vigilante justice at Beaver City. On March 2, 1887, the Respective Claims Board reached a decision against Frank Thompson in a contest involving George Scranage (or Scrange). Thompson, a gambler, was not the most popular man in Beaver. Scranage, who was a land speculator and the townsite developer for the abortive town of Grand Valley, had come to the Strip in quest of a fortune. He claimed several parcels of land around Beaver City and Grand Valley. By 1887, Scranage was advertising himself in midwestern newspapers as a land "locator" and promising the settler "titles clear and terms easy" in the Neutral Strip. His activities were known to the extent that one United States Congressman denounced him as "a thief and a robber."[30]

Scranage bought a claim on the south edge of Beaver from Noah Lane, Jim Lane's brother, reportedly for his brother-in-law W. J. Kline. A businessman named O. P. (or possibly F. E.) Bennett and Charley Tracy, who owned a dance hall and a feed store, backed Thompson and furnished him with materials to build a crude shelter, probably a dugout, on the claim. Both the Thompson and Scranage factions were known for their land-grabbing tendencies, but the Thompson group represented the gambling and saloon element in town. When the committee announced its decision against Thompson and ordered him to vacate the claim, he refused to do so.

A grudge already existed between Thompson and the town marshal, Addison Mundell, who also served as an agent for Scranage. In what apparently was a classic case of evidence-planting, Mundell accused Thompson of stealing his Winchester rifle and sent deputies to search the sod dugout of the accused. It came as no surprise when the rifle was found there. Rather than react in a defensive way, Thompson angrily threatened to shoot Mundell on sight. The marshal did not try to arrest him for the theft. When the two men happened to meet each other in front of the post office, Thompson got the drop on Mundell, but a bystander grabbed his gun hand, and Mundell hastily retreated. On another occasion Mundell got the drop on Thompson and began firing at his feet. With raised hands, Thompson did a stomp dance around a well curb in the middle of the street until a "spooked" mule across the street diverted the marshal's attention for a moment, and Thompson got the drop on him. Mundell then did his dance. According to Oliver Nelson, who witnessed the bullet dances, "That's where Mundell got so he didn't like Thompson."[31]

When Thompson refused to give up the claim, a vigilante committee composed of Mundell, Scranage, Kline, J. C. Hodge, Lee Harlun, L. N. McIntosh, and others was formed. Mundell acted prematurely, however, and ambushed Thompson on a Beaver street. A bullet shattered the gambler's knee, and Mundell failed to finish his work.

Thompson managed to make it to his dugout. There he lay on his bed while the vigilance group encountered Bennett and told him that Thompson was badly wounded and needed him. While the vigilantes accompanied Bennett to the dugout, Charley Tracy fled town on his horse. Bennett entered the dugout first and approached the bed of the groaning Thompson. When Bennett heard the crisp clicks of gun hammers being cocked, he wheeled in time to meet a volley of bullets. As Bennett lay dead on the dirt floor, the men turned their weapons on the helpless Thompson and blasted him with twenty-three shots. The committee then went to the Tracy store and told the younger brother of the absent Tracy to close down and get out of town in a few days. An inquest was held with Drs. J. A. Overstreet and O. G. Chase, among others, serving as a "coroner's jury." In its report, the "jury" pointed out that the dead men had been accused of "stealing and receiving stolen property, some of which was found on their premises after they were killed," driving away settlers, and "holding a dozen or more claims." The conflict with Scranage was not singled out. Along with other reasons for the executions, the report stated: "The deceased were bad citizens—one having run a house of prostitution and the other living in open adultery in our town."[32]

Oliver Nelson, a local cowhand whose squatter's claim Scranage would later attempt to jump, rode into town the day after the killings and found a number of townsmen visibly shaking with fear. Only one person would talk to him about the incident, a man named Norton who worked at the Tracy feed barn. Norton was a cowhand whom Nelson had first met at the roundup of '85. Norton told Nelson that it was "the cold-bloodedest murder I ever seen, and I ben in Abilene 'n Hays 'n Dodge 'n Caldwell."[33]

Vigilance committees sprang up in many of the early towns. They spread their brand of justice to varying degrees. Some vigilantes simply frightened horse thieves. In one instance, after a kangaroo court was assembled, the accused were quickly found guilty and given ten days to leave the Strip. In other instances there were no trials, only speedy executions by rope or gunfire. One early observer, Judge Fred C. Tracy, believed that about one-third of the homicides actually were vigilante executions.[34]

Jim Herron, the first sheriff of Beaver County, recalled a number of instances of vigilante justice. In one, Herron and a friend broke up an attempted lynching of an old man in a grove of cottonwood trees on Mexico Creek. When asked what the fellow had done, a member of the group replied, "Why he's a damn old drunkard an' he's bin feedin' them outlaws." On another occasion Herron found two bodies hanging from a ridge pole at the big distillery on Hog Creek. The owner, a "Judge Sutter," explained that two strangers openly bragged in Beaver City that they would rob him of both his liquor and his money. A vigilance group promptly apprehended the pair and hanged them before they could do any harm. Vigilantes even attempted, unsuccessfully, to get cattlemen to screen all strangers coming into the region by inquiring about their past, a practice which no cowhand would have liked. Herron later reflected: "Them Vigilante groups that organized to maintain 'law and order' got as bad as the outlaws."[35]

Vigilante justice did not last long in the Strip, only three or four years at the most. Yet it was long enough for newspapermen like J. R. Spears, of the *New York Sun,* to spread the word of lawlessness in No Man's Land throughout the nation. To counterbalance that unfavorable treatment, Elmer E. Brown, an early newspaperman of Beaver

City, a few years later wrote the governor of Oklahoma Territory:

> Factions existed in the village of Beaver, as they exist in all small towns. The factions grew out of quarrels over cats, dogs, chickens, cattle and children, just as factions start when a code of laws governs. . . . The truth is that the government of No Man's Land, prior to the extension of law over the country, was a tame, rosy affair. Outlaws did not operate there, and did not rendezvous there. Petty thieving was practically unknown.[36]

Brown reflected a changing political and social climate in No Man's Land by the 1890s. The Respective Claims Committee members took the initiative in calling for a mass meeting of the citizenry for November 29, 1886, at Beaver City. Dr. O. J. Chase was chosen chairman, and rules were adopted laying the machinery for electing delegates from three districts to form a territorial council to meet at Beaver on March 4, 1887. The three districts were separated by the 101st and 102nd meridians, the boundaries that would later divide the three Panhandle counties. Seven of the nine elected men showed up for the meeting and adopted a resolution, drafted by R. M. Overstreet, that called for the creation of Cimarron Territory, recognized the sovereignty, Constitution, and laws of the United States, and acknowledged "Almighty God to be the Supreme Ruler of the Universe." Other resolutions further divided "Cimarron Territory" into seven districts and provided for electing nine senators and fourteen delegates to the Territorial Council. Thus began an attempt to obtain territorial status from the federal government, primarily through the efforts of leaders at Beaver City. Many squatters in the central and western parts of the Strip did not receive word of the new "government." Dr. O. G. Chase was sent to Washington as "delegate." Of course, he was not seated in Congress, for only Congress, under the Constitution, can create territories. But he made friends with several of the more radical members of Congress who already were strongly pressing the issue of opening the Unassigned Lands of Indian Territory to settlement, men such as James B. Weaver, of the Greenback Party and future Populist Party, and Senator William Springer, of Illinois. On December 12, 1887, Springer presented the Cimarron Council's petition to Congress, where it was referred to the Committee on Territories and tabled.[37]

By 1889 a cosmopolitan population from twenty-two states and six nations inhabited the old Neutral Strip. The next year Oklahoma Territory was created by the federal government and the Strip became that legally constituted territory's seventh county, later named Beaver County with Beaver City as the county seat. A federal land office was established at Beaver City in 1891 after the government finally completed surveying the area into quarter-section units. By act of Congress, settlers who had been on their claims for at least three years had to wait only two more years before receiving patents for their lands (the Homestead Act of 1862 required five years residency).[38]

Local boosters such as R. B. ("Dick") Quinn, editor of the *Hardesty Herald,* believed that the trickle of home-steaders would soon become a flood and that cattlemen would fade from the scene. In an editorial on August 16, 1893, he wrote:

The joyous cowboy of yore is fast fading away—he's no more. He used to be gay, naturally restless and very emphatic when he was bowling up. He wore $7 pants for everyday, used silver mounted bridle bits, a pearl handled six-shooter, but was satisfied with beans, bacon and black coffee at the chuck wagon.

Now he wears blue over-alls, wants sugar in his coffee, demands oatmeal for breakfast and smokes cigarettes.[39]

Many of the same boosters resented the label of No Man's Land. J. C. Hodge, editor of the *Advocate* of Beaver and one time vigilante, insisted, "Call us 'McGinty' if you choose, but in the name of your protection from an idiot's asylum, don't call us 'No Man's Land.'"[40]

However, the cattleman was not yet on his way out. The Unassigned Lands (central Oklahoma) were opened to settlement in the famous Run of '89. Accompanying the thousands of homeseekers that day were numbers of settlers who departed their claims in No Man's Land because of an extended drouth. Of the nine members elected to the abortive Council of Cimarron Territory, only one, R. M. Overstreet, still lived in the region in 1890. Other land openings in Oklahoma Territory, particularly the Cherokee Outlet Run of 1893, attracted still other settlers from the more arid western area. Settlement would not begin to flow into the old Neutral Strip again until after 1900. In the meantime, cattlemen dominated the region. In 1893, Beaver County shipped more cattle to market than any other county in Oklahoma.[41] There was still time for an aggressive young man, such as James K. Hitch, to put together an impressive ranch from the rich pastures of No Man's Land.

2.   Tennesseans in No Man's Land

When Jim Hitch first entered No Man's Land in 1884 or 1885, the western frontier already had been romanticized in the mind of the nation and a new West was gradually emerging. The Indians had been pushed onto reservations. Railroads constructed into Fort Worth, Texas, and southwestern Kansas had all but ended the necessity for the long cattle drive of several hundred miles. And herd law, which made it necessary for ranchers to fence their pastures, went hand-in-hand with the ever-increasing number of farmers settling on the ranchers' open range. But dime novels embodying the fictitious adventures of both real and mythical heroes, as well as popular wild West shows, were keeping the romanticized image alive.

The contrast between the myth and the reality of the plains was obvious in the Kansas of 1886. In February that extraordinary entrepreneur of the wild West show, "Buffalo Bill" Cody, opened his new melodrama "The Prairie Wolf" at the Grand Opera House of Topeka. The star of the play was William Levi ("Buck") Taylor, a tall Texan whom Cody made into the first cowboy actor, literally setting the stage for such later arrivals as Tom Mix, William S. Hart, Buck Jones, and Gene Autry. The same month Cody's play opened at Topeka, G. J. Coleman, of Mound Valley, Kansas, was arrested and charged with cruelty to animals because he had dehorned his cattle! The charge was dismissed by the court, and a few years later dehorning became as commonplace in the ranching industry as dipping for tick control.[1]

The world of cattleman James Kerrick Hitch was more akin to that of G. J. Coleman than to that of Buck Taylor. Hitch was born near Maryville in the mountains of Blount County, eastern Tennessee, on February 15, 1855. The Hitch family originally had migrated from England to settle in Maryland and Virginia before the American Revolution. Christopher Hitch, who leased a farm from Lord Fairfax in Fauquier County, Virginia, had four sons. One was Elias, born on November 24, 1783. Sometime between 1800 and 1810, Elias and his three brothers, Loyd, Leven, and Archibald, moved west into the Appalachian Mountains and made their way down the Shenandoah Valley to the frontier of eastern Tennessee. Elias married Nancy Kerrick in about 1810 in Blount County. A son named Stephen was born to this union in 1829; he married Charlotte George in the early 1850s. Stephen and Charlotte were the parents of James Kerrick.[2] (The spelling of the surname was changed to Karick by some of the descendants.)

Like many other young eastern Americans after the Civil War, Hitch viewed the west beyond the Mississippi as the land of economic opportunity and adventure. In about 1875, as the nation prepared to celebrate its Centennial during a dismal economic depression, the twenty-year-old Tennessean slipped quietly away from the family home one night with ten dollars in coin taken from a kitchen container that held the family savings. He wrote a long goodbye note on both sides of a slate and left the message on the kitchen table. He made his way to Knoxville, sixteen miles away, and bought all the railroad ticket he could get for ten dollars. The next morning when James's younger brother Charlie awoke, the house was almost afloat with tears. Charlie first thought some member of the family had died.

Jim Hitch was bound for Springfield, Missouri, because his Aunt Arminda George had often told him about a youthful beau who once had courted her and now lived in the southwestern Missouri town. His name was Bob McElhany, formerly of eastern Tennessee, but now a successful Springfield banker. Arminda was so certain that McElhany would give Jim some kind of financial break in life that she encouraged him to go. When his railroad fare played out, he worked at odd jobs and even walked much of the way. At one time he had only twenty-five cents in his pocket and no friend in sight. As he later recalled, the woods were "getting thick" and the sun was setting when a friendly black man pulled up in a wagon. The man offered the boy a ride and took him to his employer who, in turn, gave him a job.[3]

When Hitch finally arrived in Springfield, McElhany was out of town, but he got a job as a roustabout in a local wagon factory. When the banker returned, he befriended the lonely young man. Some time later a farmer named Henry Westmoreland stopped by the bank to conduct some business. Like Hitch and McElhany, the Westmorelands also were from eastern Tennessee. Westmoreland had been born in North Carolina in about 1825, but he had moved to Bradley County in eastern Tennessee as a young man. There he married sixteen-year-old Zilpha Clark on August 16, 1847. Sometime between 1850 and 1854 the Westmorelands moved to Missouri. There they reared their six children: Hirum H., Sarah, Benjamin E., William, Mary Frances, George, and Josephine. Although not rich by any measure, Westmoreland had become an established farmer. According to the United States Census of 1870, he owned real estate valued at two thousand dollars.

Henry and Zilpha Westmoreland.

More important, he had good credit at McElhany's bank.[4]

Perhaps sensing Jim's homesickness, McElhany introduced the youth to the bearded fellow Tennessean. Westmoreland took Hitch into his home as a farmhand and paid him twice the wages he was earning in the wagon factory. This fateful encounter proved a major turning point in Hitch's life. During the next few years he demonstrated that McElhany's confidence had not been misplaced. He could handle either a plow or a horse with equal skill. Moreover, he demonstrated both a capacity for hard work and good judgment.

Mary Frances Westmoreland took special note of the quiet, slender young man with the thick shock of coalblack hair and piercing blue eyes. As the family sat through supper night after night for the first few weeks, Jim smiled a great deal at her, but spoke only when she asked him questions. Mary mistook his natural reserve, bordering on shyness, as an attempt to ignore her. She was ready to suggest to her father that he fire Hitch before she finally realized that he was simply too shy to talk to girls. During the next few months Mary's anger turned to fondness as she finally got Jim to talk.[5]

About the same time that Custer met his defeat at the Little Big Horn in 1876, Henry Westmoreland laid plans to go into the range cattle business. Perhaps he had long been thinking of taking the plunge. In 1866 the growing demand for beef in expanding Eastern cities had led to the opening of the first of the famous cattle trails stretching from Texas to loading pens on a railhead. The trail that terminated at Sedalia, Missouri, passed just west of Springfield. It is tempting to believe that an early contact that year with longhorn cattle and drovers may have planted the thought in Westmoreland's mind. But he may also have been among those Arkansas and Missouri farmers who resented the passage of the Texas cattle across their lands. In 1867 an innovative cattle dealer from Illinois named Joseph G. McCoy turned Abilene, a new railhead on the Kansas-Pacific Railroad, from a small insignificant village into the first of the Kansas cattle towns. During the spring of that year he kept a crew of workers busy building stockyards, loading chutes, barns, and even a hotel for drovers. The first head of Longhorns arrived in Abilene over the Chisholm Trail late that summer. Throughout the next decade the range-cattle industry, spurred by reports of good profits, spread across the public domain of the Great Plains.[6]

Westmoreland announced to his family in 1876 that he would soon buy a herd of Missouri cattle, drive them to the unsettled open range of southwestern Kansas, and become a rancher. Why he made that decision is not known. The economic depression may have made him desperate enough to try it, or he may have talked to someone who had enjoyed some success in that business. Still another possibility is that he may have read a glowing account of the ranching business in a newspaper or book. The same Joseph McCoy of Abilene fame wrote a book entitled *Historic Sketches of the Cattle Trade and Southwest,* published in Kansas City in 1874, only a couple of years before Westmoreland made the plunge. If he had read that book, or some account of its contents in a newspaper, he might have been greatly encouraged.[7]

McCoy's book contains a number of biographical sketches of men who migrated to the Great Plains to become well-to-do cattlemen. Had Westmoreland read the book, he might have been motivated by the story of John Hittson, a fellow Tennessean who first moved to Palo Pinto County, Texas, to become a rancher, and by 1874 had become a wealthy cattleman with herds from Texas

Cattle roundup scene in southwestern Kansas, ca. 1880s.

to Colorado. McCoy had suggested to his readers that profits in cattle could be enhanced by "finishing" herds driven up from Texas on the grasses of western Kansas and Colorado prior to sending them to market. Moreover, a rancher who fattened his herds in southwestern Kansas had only a short drive of less than a hundred miles to the new railhead at Dodge City. Indeed, the first Texas cattle began arriving at Dodge along what became known as the Western Trail in 1875.[8]

Whatever the reason, Westmoreland became a rancher. He acquired a herd of 1,500 head of cattle, and branded them with his LV on the left hip and a 6 on the right hip. Two of his sons, Ben and Billy, along with son-in-law Howard Langston and two or three hired hands, left Springfield and began the drive across southern Kansas in 1876 or 1877. For the time being they left behind young Hitch; the oldest son, Hirum, and his family; the women; and the younger children. During the long drive a cowhand named John Scott arose one morning, glanced out over the sea of horns, and announced, "Well boys, there is one gone!" The statement became an early-morning standing joke for the duration of the drive. When Westmoreland reached

Medicine Creek in Barber County, he halted the herd and constructed a crude dugout. During the next three or four years Henry Westmoreland returned to Springfield only about once a year for a short visit, probably after accompanying his steers to market in Kansas City by rail.

In that same span of years, Jim began courting Mary Frances. They were married March 6, 1879, at Springfield. On one of Westmoreland's visits, perhaps after the birth in 1880 of Mary's first child, Della (named for Jim's oldest sister), Henry asked his new son-in-law if he would like to buy some cattle and join the men in Kansas. Indeed he would, but he had neither money nor livestock. Of course, Westmoreland knew that he had no assets and asked Jim if he would like to sign a note at McElhany's bank for a loan to purchase two hundred cows. Again Hitch answered yes. Thus with the help of borrowed money and his father-in-law, James K. Hitch went into the cattle business.

The next year when Jim returned to buy five hundred more cattle and drive them to the Westmoreland Ranch, Mary Frances pleaded with him to take her and Della with him. Jim tried to dissuade her by enumerating the hardships, including living in a dugout. But the strong-willed young mother insisted, so Hitch took her along.

Her new life was indeed primitive. Among her other duties she became the cook for the LV cowhands. The sod-covered roof of the dugout leaked in wet weather. She moved her choice household goods from corner to corner to keep them dry. During roundup season the men were away for a week or two at a time. On one occasion, as Jim and Mary sat down to dinner during a hard winter storm, cattle drifted on top of the dugout. The roof timbers gave way and a big calf landed on top of their supper table. Mary Frances adjusted to the harsh life without complaint. By 1882 the remainder of the family, with the exception of the oldest son, Hirum, had probably joined the LV outfit, so her isolation was ended.[9]

As the tide of westward-moving settlers flowed into south-central Kansas and filed on the quarter sections of the public domain that cattlemen had been using, the LV outfit moved farther west, driving their herds before them. They next stopped on Crooked Creek, near Meade, Kansas, and in 1883, a year or two later, they pushed their cattle into Seward County. There they built their first sod houses on the "dry" Cimarron River, and Jim Hitch filed a homestead claim on a quarter section of land on September 5, 1883.

For the next few years James K. Hitch prospered during the flush times of the range-cattle business. Market prices were good, and the rainfall was adequate for growing the thick turf of short buffalo grass common to the High Plains. He continued to use the LV brand on the left hip, but added his own circle on the right hip in place of the Westmoreland 6. A "swallowfork" earmark further distinguished his stock from the Westmoreland animals. Each year after the traditional roundups in which each cattleman, in cooperation with his neighbors, sorted out his stock and branded his fresh calves, Hitch, the Westmorelands, and Howard Langston drove their three- and four-year-old steers some seventy miles to the Dodge City stockyards. In March, 1886, Charlie Hitch arrived from Tennessee in time to join his brother's annual roundup.[10]

In later years Charlie Hitch vividly remembered the drive of 1886. By this time the Missouri cattle were well mixed with Longhorn blood. According to Charlie, "Their horns were so long they almost scared me." They were "fat . . . and wild." The first night on the trail to Dodge, the restless cattle were bedded down in a dry camp (no water). During the day the drive crossed a number of creeks, but most night camps were dry. "Every night or two we would have a little trouble with these steers, but none got away," Charlie recalled. The last day before reaching the railroad loading pens, the drovers allowed the cattle to drink their fill on Mulberry Creek, near a road ranch ten miles south of Dodge. Loading began the next day, and by four o'clock the last steer had been driven into the cattle cars. As the train pulled out, Howard Langston swung aboard the caboose to accompany the cattle to Kansas City.

Jim and Charlie Hitch tied their horses to the mess wagon and drove the last two miles into Dodge, where Jim had some business to conduct. Before they reached the town limits, they heard shooting and yelling. Although a prohibition law had been passed in Kansas, wide-open saloons continued to operate in Dodge until about 1886. As the men approached, they saw drunken cowboys galloping their horses up and down the main street, firing their six-guns into the air, occasionally shattering a window with a wild shot. Painted dance-hall girls and "soiled doves" were mounted behind some of the men, riding the horses astraddle. Some drunks had fallen off their horses and lay in the street while their mounts, frightened by the shooting, continued to dash back and forth. This was certainly the wild West of the cattle towns, but it was not the world of James K. Hitch, who neither drank nor smoked and did not carry a six-gun. The Hitches stayed in town two or three days. According to Charlie, a number of Jim's cowhands "tied into some of these girls," but the older Hitch did not let his younger brother "out of his sight."

One of Jim Hitch's few disputes with farmers, or "grangers" as cattlemen often referred to them, occurred during

Charles A. ("Charlie") Hitch with his favorite saddle horse, ca. 1890. Courtesy of Mary Hitch Hall.

the return trip from Dodge. Jim, Charlie, and their cook camped on Crooked Creek in Meade County at the point where the Jones and Plummer Trail crossed the stream. Between the time that Hitch had driven his cattle to the railhead and returned, settlers had occupied the tract. That evening, as the Hitch brothers sat around a campfire eating their supper by light from a kerosene lantern, two "hard-looking" men rode up and told the party that they would have to move out that night. Jim informed them that he would gladly pay for the horses' overnight grazing, but the men insisted that the cowmen vacate the camp-ground. Jim then simply turned his back and refused to listen. The strangers rode on. The next morning they returned, riding by the camp without saying a word. They carried a hatchet and a bucket of fencing staples. Charlie recalled, "We knew then that we probably would have hell."

Breaking camp, the Hitches continued south with their mess wagon and remuda. Half a mile down the trail they were stopped by a new four-wire fence. There was a wide wooden gate there, but the two grangers had nailed and wired it to posts. Jim, who was not feeling well, was riding in the wagon. The strangers were standing on the other side of the gate when the cattleman got out of the wagon carrying an axe. Again he offered to pay for the grass, but the farmers evidently carried a grudge for ranchers in general and refused to budge. Hitch finally exploded. As Charlie put it, "Jim then got mad, the maddest man I ever saw, and said, 'Watch these men, boys. We are going through.'" He swung his axe at the gate, but changed its direction in midair and brought the blade down hard at the nearest man, slicing through the brim of the stranger's hat. The farmers retreated. A few swings of the axe cut the gate down and the party passed through. The grangers brought charges against the Hitches over that confrontation. Jim and Charlie remained in Meade for the ten-day trial, which ended in their acquittal.[11]

By 1884 a number of Kansas cattlemen, possibly including Jim Hitch, were grazing their herds in No Man's Land. In the spring of that year the primary problem discussed at the convention of the Western Kansas Cattle Growers Association, held at Dodge City, was that of settlers moving into the area. During the annual roundup in May a cowboy named Jim Herron noticed for the first time a number of sod dugouts and tents on claims in the eastern part of the Neutral Strip. He also observed the sod houses of a "granger town" named Benton.[12]

Although only a small number of squatters began moving into No Man's Land, a tide of new settlers began pouring into southwestern Kansas in 1885. A Methodist circuit minister, one Jeremiah Platt, described the scene: "It beats all the world. Language can hardly tell it. The Children of Israel going into the 'promised land' don't equal it."[13]

Where they were numerous, settlers brought in "herd law" which ended the open range. Doubtless, it was this settler pressure and the need to find new grazing land that brought James K. Hitch to Coldwater Creek in central No Man's Land in either 1884 or 1885. He ran cattle there for perhaps a year or two before settling in the valley. On March 1, 1886, he laid claim to a short quarter section (containing 150 acres) on the north side of Coldwater Creek about ten miles above Hardesty. When Charlie Hitch arrived from Tennessee the same month, Jim and two of his hired hands were already down on the Coldwater slicing sod from the valley floor with a team and cutting the material into bricks two feet long. They erected a number of sod houses at intervals along the Coldwater for the Westmorelands and the Hitches, and probably for hired hands as well. By April the LV outfit had six or eight soddies in the valley. Jim put young Charlie in one of the houses with some supplies and told him to stay there and hold the claim. The boy remained there for weeks without seeing a soul. Because it was illegal to hold more than one homestead claim, Jim canceled his application for the Kansas claim in Seward County on May 6, 1886.[14]

The year 1886 not only marked the permanent settlement of J. K. Hitch on the Coldwater, but it also began a transitional period for the ranching industry. Better cattle prices in the early 1880s had attracted more cattlemen to the open ranges. The result of this increase in cattle was overgrazing. A drouth that began on the southern Texas plains in 1885 created a shortage of grass, and cattle went into the winter of 1885–86 without adequate forage. Few ranchers put up even prairie hay in those days. Conditions were ripe for catastrophe when a three-day blizzard struck the plains beginning on January 6, 1886. The temperature plunged to twenty below. When the weather cleared, perhaps as many as half the cattle in the region were dead. Carcasses lined the east-west drift fences. When spring finally arrived, the stench of rotting flesh filled the air for weeks.

Jim Hitch and Henry Westmoreland, still in Seward County, were hit hard by the disaster, but they were determined to stay. With characteristic vigor, Hitch skinned 500 carcasses and sold the hides to help offset his losses. Charlie Hitch recalled that Jim was "a fast worker—would skin a cow or two while the average man was sharpening his butcher knife." He probably used the same technique as Jim Herron, who also skinned out dead cattle in the aftermath of the same blizzard. The dead animal's neck was tied to a post. After peeling the hide back from head and feet, the skinner made a shallow slit down the belly, tied onto a "knot" of neck hide, and attached the rope to a doubletree hitched to a pair of mules. A driver urged the mules forward, thus pulling the hide off while the skinner had only to slash gently here and there with his curved blade.[15]

The blizzard may have been partly responsible for J. K.'s decision to settle on the Coldwater. The north wall of the valley offered a windbreak for cattle and the valley floor contained natural hay meadows. Determined never to experience that kind of death loss to his stock again, Hitch returned to the valley in September with a haying crew. He, Charlie, and his hired hands cut and stacked eighty to a hundred tons of prairie hay from eighty acres, enough forage to get him through another hard winter.[16]

The LV men then turned to building a twenty- by forty-foot sod house for Jim's family about half a mile north of the stream, just below the valley's rim. In October the Westmorelands moved Mary Frances and her children down from Kansas. Meanwhile, Charlie had staked a claim several miles up the Coldwater near the Texas line. The Westmorelands moved into sod houses between J. K.'s and Charlie's claims. Howard Langston, incidentally, did not move his family to the Coldwater. He settled in the northern part of No Man's Land, near present-day Hooker, and later went into the hardware business.

Jim and Mary now had three children, all of whom had been born in Springfield. Della had been born before leaving Missouri. Mary Frances had subsequently returned to live with relatives, possibly her oldest brother Hirum's family, before the birth of the other two babies in order to use the services of the family physician. The children and birthdates were: Della A., April 10, 1880; Josephine Lee, September 2, 1882; and Charles Henry (Henry C.), December 13, 1884. The girls were named after Jim's sisters, while the boy's namesakes were Jim's brother and his grandfather Henry Westmoreland. The next year, Mary gave birth to her youngest child, George Clark, in the sod house on September 23, 1887. The year George was born, Jim built an eighteen- by twenty-four-foot addition to the soddy, using limestone quarried from the north side of the valley.[17]

A number of J. K.'s relatives arrived from Tennessee in the next few years to work for him and/or to take up claims. His sister Della came out in 1887 to stake a claim adjacent to J. K.'s. She helped Mary Frances with cooking and household chores, and, in turn, Hitch helped her build a sod house, a chicken house, a calf pen, a cellar, and a stone addition to her house. On Christmas Day 1891 she

The children of James K. and Mary Frances Hitch, ca. 1896. Left to right: Henry, Della, George, and Josephine.

married a local cowhand named George Wright. Jim's sister Nanny and her husband, James N. Byerly, arrived a short time later. By 1892 Jim's nephew Bill George (grandson of his Aunt Arminda, who had been instrumental in his decision to go west) was also working for him. In the 1890s the oldest Hitch brother, Elias, moved to neighboring Hansford County, Texas, where Jim also acquired ranching interests. There, Elias was elected county treasurer. When Guymon was founded in 1901, he moved there and became county surveyor.[18]

J. K. Hitch added a number of improvements to his claim. He dug a well and began planting a grove of cottonwood trees around the house. Using the abundant limestone from the upper part of the valley, he built a twenty-by eighty-foot barn and added a corral made from hackberry poles. The first year he broke out five acres and planted the sod ground in some crop, possibly corn. The experiment proved unsatisfactory, and in 1887 he planted the acreage in fruit trees. By 1893 he had an orchard of 150 trees producing an abundance of fruit. The primary crop of the valley remained prairie hay. Hitch stated in 1893: "The land is what is known as hay land. I have mowed 80 acres of it each year for 6 years, yielding from 80 to 100 tons to a season."[19]

Another severe blizzard struck in February, 1887, but thanks to the hay crop Jim's losses were minimal. The drought, which began in Texas in 1885, spread over the Great Plains and lasted, off and on, until about 1896. To make matters worse, a severe economic depression settled over the nation from 1893 to 1896. Indications of hard times in No Man's Land could be seen in the changes in ownership and consolidation of many of the ranches. A Texan named T. C. Schumaker bought out the vast Anchor-D from E. C. Dudley in the early 1890s. Schumaker then added to the Anchor-D the holdings of Charlie Grimmer and "Little" Charlie Grimmer, W. D. Vaughn, Mervin Harp, Billy Brown, the Thomas and Stevens outfit, Harry Clark, and Court Brown. When Schumaker's operations reached their zenith, he controlled much of the central Beaver River, with holdings stretching as far south as Frisco Creek near J. K.'s ranch. But by the late 1890s, Schumaker was in financial difficulties, and he sold out to H. M. Stonebraker.[20]

One of the early problems the Hitches and Westmorelands faced was pure and simple isolation. Because they had moved to the region as a large family unit (one is tempted to use the word clan), they never really lonely. But isolation from the outside world was pronounced for some time. The nearest postoffice at first was Hardesty, about ten miles downstream. On February 12, 1891, a postoffice was officially opened at Eubank, two miles north of J. K.'s headquarters. Named for rancher and neighbor Jesse L. Eubank, the postoffice remained in business until 1902. A few miles farther upstream, a postoffice was established on the Charles Westmoreland place on July 25, 1894. Charles was a younger son of Henry. Charles's wife, Clara, was designated the first postmaster, and she named the place Roy after her young son. For years the mail was carried from Hardesty to Eubank to Roy in a hack by a carrier named T. J. Creel. When Creel died, he was buried in the Roy cemetery.[21]

Mary Frances Hitch felt an even more destructive isolation than lack of mail service. At first the family had neither church nor school. The Hitches and Westmorelands were Methodists, and in 1887, Mary began holding Sunday school in her large sod house. On February 15, 1888, she penned a letter to the Reverend A. P. George, a presiding officer of the church in Kansas:

Dear Brother in Christ:

Will you and your Bishop listen to the plea of a mother who lives with her family, 140 miles from the railroad. Reared in a Christian community in Missouri, I am trying to rear my children with Christian teachings. Having a little Sunday school on the Coldwater Creek we would like very much to have a minister. We keenly feel the need of a spiritual shepherd and counselor. Of course, we can give little by way of a salary, but our home will be his home. We will do our best. The minister closest to us is at Fargo Springs, Kansas, and occasionally comes to Laflette, 50 miles from here. Could your mission board help us to have a pastor out here in No Man's Land. Awaiting an early reply, and praying God's blessing on your work, Your sister in Christ.[22]

The Macedonian Call from the Neutral Strip did not fall on deaf ears. Young, zealous Reverend E. F. Reser, fresh from an eastern seminary, volunteered his services. He arrived later that same year as a circuit rider and moved his new bride into a dugout at Optima, north of the Beaver River. He conducted the first service in Mary Frances' home. At first the church was established in an abandoned claim soddy east of J. K.'s place. Two or three years later, it was moved into an abandoned rock house about half a mile downstream. Finally, the church found a home upstream at Roy, where it remained until Guymon was established. The first baptisms after Reser's arrival were those of the four Hitch children. Using the Coldwater mission as his base, Reser rode a circuit once a month from Boyd City, about thirty miles east, to Kenton, near the northwestern corner of No Man's Land. At the end of his first year the minister reported to his mission board that he had twelve members and thirty-one enrolled in Sunday school. He was paid ninety-six dollars for the year's work. The mission board supplied fifty dollars of that amount, and the Roy church paid the remainder.

The difficult frontier ministry created an almost annual turnover in preachers. Between 1888 and 1901 there were eight different ministers. Reser was succeeded in 1891 by the Reverend C. T. Mellor from New York City, who brought his well-educated wife and his sister, a physician, with him. The Reverend David J. M. Jones replaced Mellor in 1892 and settled on a relinquished claim adjacent to J. K.'s claim on the southeast. Hitch paid a local craftsman to build a four-room stone parsonage for the large Jones family.[23]

No school had been established on the Coldwater by 1889, but a four-room brick school had just been constructed in the new railroad town Liberal, Kansas, about forty-five miles north. Mary moved to Liberal with the children in the fall of 1889 to enroll the older three in school. Della was nine, Josephine was seven, and Henry was five years old. They remained there until March, 1890, when the children became ill with whooping cough. Mary then moved them back to the ranch.

In the fall of 1890 the Hitches, Westmorelands, and some neighbors, including the Eubank, Halenstein, and Hanklie families, formed a subscription school and hired a teacher. The school, like the church, began meeting in a claim shack. Situated about one and a half miles east of the Hitch headquarters, the shack was owned by a cowhand named Harry Reeves. The children's first teacher was Dyke Ballinger, who also had a claim in the immediate area. Ballinger taught school for more than four years before being elected county clerk in the middle of the school year. When the young schoolmaster announced his resignation to his students and told them he would not be back the next day, Henry misunderstood. The child ran home at noon and happily told Charlie: "Uncle Charlie, Uncle Charlie, school's out for good. I don't have to go no more." The joy was short-lived, however, for a young lady showed up the next day to take Ballinger's place. Henry's school career was not yet over.[24]

George Westmoreland lived six miles up the Coldwater. When his children were old enough to enter school, a larger building, and one not so far away, was needed. To meet that need, J. K. bought a vacant store at Hugoton, Kansas, for seventy-five dollars. He and brother-in-law Jim Byerly jacked up the small frame building, put it on wagon beds, and hauled it down to the Coldwater. The building was put on a rock foundation about halfway between the homes of Westmoreland and J. K. Hitch.[25]

Until 1888, Hitch got most of his supplies by wagon from Dodge City. On those infrequent occasions when he drove to Dodge, he usually filled his wagon with buffalo bones along the way. These were remnan of the great buffalo hunt of the 1870s. The bones sold for $6.00 a ton, and were shipped east to be ground into fertilizer. In 1888 the railroad was extended southwest of Dodge. At the time, a county-seat war was raging between Springfield and Fargo Springs. That conflict furnished the Rock Island Railway with a convenient excuse to bypass both and plat its own town. Thus the railroad opened the townsite of Liberal on April 13 and sold $180,000 worth of lots the first day. By April 21 there were eighty-three wooden buildings in town. Among the businesses was one bearing the sign The Star Grocery. The owner was Ed T. Guymon, who brought his grocery stock with him on the first freight train to arrive after the plat was opened. For the next thirteen years, Hitch traded primarily at Liberal and frequented The Star Grocery.[26]

A wagon road running as far as Hansford, Texas, crossed the Coldwater near the Hitch house and wound across the broken plains to Liberal. After 1902 the road curved north-westward toward Guymon, and the old Liberal branch fell into disuse, and was soon covered with buffalo grass. Once the road left the Hitch pasture, there were no gates to open between there and Liberal. J. K. frequently fell asleep after he closed the last gate because the mules knew their way to town. On one such occasion, after he fell asleep on the spring seat, the mules turned the wagon around and headed back to the ranch. George Westmoreland, who was on his way to town, encountered the southbound wagon with its team of eager mules and the dozing passenger. Westmoreland awakened Hitch, but even then it was not easy to persuade J. K. that he was headed in the wrong direction across the flat, unmarked plains.[27]

By the early 1890s the Tennesseans from Missouri had become well established in the Coldwater Valley. The Circle brand of J. K. and Charlie's 7 had become well known in central No Man's Land. J. K. had found his promised land on the treeless plains so far from the wooded mountains of his native Tennessee. Over the next decade and a half, availing himself of every possible opportunity, he would build an empire of buffalo grass and water.

3.   The Beginnings of an Empire

Those early years on the Coldwater were marred by tragedy in 1891. Mary Frances became ill in May. A doctor was summoned, but could do nothing. When the children returned from school the afternoon of May 22, someone emerged from the house and told the children, "Come in if you want to see your mother before she dies." About 5:30 that afternoon, Mary Frances breathed her last. Neighbors and relatives prepared the body for burial in a simple pine box. The nearest cemetery was in Hardesty, ten miles away. J. K. made the decision to bury his wife on the ranch. The next day a grave was opened west of the house, and with appropriate readings from the Bible at a graveside funeral the body was interred in the serene valley she had come to love.[1]

Josephine ("Josie") Westmoreland, Mary's younger sister, moved in to take care of the children. She and J. K.'s sister Della cared for the children and did the household chores for the next few months. Later that same year, on Christmas Eve, Charlie Hitch married Josie and took her up the Coldwater to his 7̄ ranch. The next day Della married a cowboy named George Wright, and the couple took up housekeeping on her claim.[2]

The next few years were lonely ones for J. K. He occupied himself primarily with long days of hard work, and he concentrated on expanding the LV Circle holdings in cattle and land. Within a year or so after Mary's death, he tore down the soddy, leaving the rock addition standing. Using the same kind of native stone, he built a two-story house attached to the rock room. Its dimensions were twenty by forty feet, the same as the original sod structure. Rock houses were replacing many sod houses and dugouts along the Beaver River and its tributaries in the 1890s. Most of those along the Beaver were constructed by a stonemason named Virgil Hockett. Among these homes were the Faught (later named the Casto) Ranch, which raised sheep and had rock corrals, and one belonging to a man named Calvert. The J. M. Myers Ranch, like the Hitch Ranch, had an impressive two-story house. Other stone houses along the Beaver belonged to George Malicoat, John Glenn, the Bradley family, whose home was noted for its low "ranch-style" construction, W. D. Crane, and the OX Ranch, which Jim McQuillen now owned.[3]

J. K.'s house was built by a mason called "Dad" Morris, who was well known in Seward County, Kansas, for his handiwork. He had constructed the early school building that the Hitch children first attended at Liberal. Morris also had built a number of rock houses to the east of the Hitch headquarters, including one on Palo Duro Creek for a "Judge" Tyler and another for a man named Pearson. J. K.'s nephew Bill George quarried the stone from the upper part of the valley back of the house. A hired hand named Louis Williamson hauled plain black mud from the creek for mortar, while Morris and his son Jim shaped the stone and fitted the pieces together to form walls two feet thick. A carpenter named Haskell did the woodwork for the roof, windows, doors, and interior. The entire job cost about eighteen hundred dollars. Henry Hitch remembered his father sitting at his desk one night peering at bills and receipts by the light of a kerosene lamp. Finally he looked up at the children and exclaimed, "Well, you don't need

The stone house on the Coldwater, ca. 1900. Henry Hitch is the dismounted rider at the right.

to tell me that a rock house has no lumber in it. The lumber in this house cost six hundred dollars!"[4]

The new house symbolized the expansion of the ranch. Beginning in about 1889 or 1890, a severe, extended drought in New Mexico and northern Mexico gave Hitch the opportunity to buy several hundred Mexican cows at seven dollars a head. In a quest for new pasture for their growing herds, Jim and Charlie rode southeast one day across the Coldwater. Just beyond the Texas line they came upon a large playa lake full of water and bristling with waterfowl. Neither cattle nor settlers were to be seen. Within a few days, the Hitch brothers drove almost a thousand cattle over to "Texas Lake." In the next few weeks, they bought still more of the thin New Mexican cattle. Then a local cowman named Huff Wright became general manager of a large ranch in Mexico called the Carletis and began flooding the Panhandle with cheap

Mexican cattle. The Hitch brothers also bought "quite a few" of those.

By the late 1890s, J. K. had about 5,000 head of mother cows, and Charlie was running another 2,000 head on the same range. Using a big wall tent, they established a line camp at Texas Lake and began pushing their expanding herds farther southeast across Hansford County until they reached another large playa known as Farwell Lake. There they encountered Texas cattlemen who had pushed their herds from Palo Duro Creek to Farwell Lake. By mutual agreement, the lake served as a dividing line between the two groups. At that time there were virtually no settlers in northern Hansford County. The only settlement was a hamlet named Farwell, a few miles east of present-day Gruver. The Hitch brothers drilled several wells and erected windmills between the two "lakes."

At Texas Lake they erected a twenty-strand barbed wire corral that could "hold a jack rabbit," according to Charlie. A drift fence running from the corral northwest to the Coldwater served to keep Coldwater stock and the Texas cattle separated. To replace the wall tent, J. K. built a large split-level board-and-batten bunkhouse for the hands at the line camp.[5]

The later 1890s were flush times for the Hitch brothers despite the low price of cattle. Adequate rainfall during most years kept the playa lakes full and the buffalo grass thick. Charlie recalled in later years that the discovery of Texas Lake "was the spark that kindled the fire that made us quite a little money." By 1900 the LV brand of the Hitches and Westmorelands marked ten thousand cattle. J. K. and Charlie alone pastured their part of the cattle on forty to fifty thousand acres.[6]

There were other young cattlemen in the area who took advantage of the settler exodus (mentioned in the previous chapter) to establish ranches. One was Boss Neff, who first came to the Neutral Strip from Ohio in 1883. For a few years Neff worked as a cowhand and trail drover for several outfits. In 1887 he and his brother Ira built a dugout on Palo Duro Creek in Hansford County, fenced two sections of land, and the next year bought eighty-three head of cattle that Boss branded NF. He left Hansford County in 1889 and bought a relinquished claim complete with sod house on the Beaver River, one and a half miles north of Hardesty. Like J. K. Hitch, he filed on his 160-acre claim when the land office was opened at Beaver City in 1891 and expanded his control over the surrounding grassland. In 1898 he built a ranch house. By that time he was running about fifteen hundred cattle on three leased sections and forty-five other sections of public domain that he fenced for pasture.[7]

Another ambitious young rancher was Otto Barby, who first came to the Panhandle in 1894 to work on the Fred Taintor Ranch. Barby had left the family homestead in Kansas as a boy of fifteen to work as a cattle drover. In 1896 he bought a 160-acre relinquishment, which became his headquarters, east of Beaver City.[8]

Life was not all work for the Hitches and their neighbors. It was not uncommon for cowboys to ride ten or twenty miles to attend a dance, even during a roundup. The author was told of an instance in which a young cowboy rode to a dance thirty miles away and returned home the same night. Needless to say, neither horse nor rider was capable of much work the next day. Charlie Hitch recalled that while working on a round up before he met Josie, he attended a dance in Beaver City when his outfit got within ten miles of town.[9]

The most popular family entertainment in the area was the annual three-day Fourth of July celebration at McDer-

mott's Grove on Frisco Creek, a few miles due west of
J. K.'s headquarters. The picnic ground was owned by
Myra McDermott, whose 160-acre claim included the
beautiful cottonwood grove. Myra came from Liberal,
where her father had owned a hotel. Like Della Hitch, she
also filed on land before her marriage. Families began
arriving at the grove on July 3, camped there that night,
and did not leave until the fifth. Steers were butchered
and barbecued. Ice was hauled in by wagon. The central
event was a competition (later called a rodeo) featuring
local stock and local cowboys. In later years Henry Hitch
recalled that concessions also operated there. Tommy
McQuillen, for example, had a little glass case enclosing
a model racetrack with seven metal horses. It was mounted
on a pedestal. McQuillen took bets at ten cents per horse.
After all bets were down, tough cattlemen and cowboys
crowded around the little glass dome. The suspense was
heightened by McQuillen's racetrack descriptions:
"They're at the quarter! They're at the half! They're at the
three-quarter! And the winnah is . . . ! Who's got the lucky
card?"[10]

The rodeo became an important entertainment for spectators as well as participants. Jim Herron recalled that in
the mid-1880s, after the annual roundup, he and a group
of cowboys were standing at the bar of a saloon in Benton
when "someone mentioned the wild West show of Buffalo
Bill, popular at that time. One cowboy had ridden in
Cody's show and he said there were just as good cowboys
there [in the saloon] . . . as in the show. That set us to thinking about putting on a Wild West Show of our own." The
primary objective, according to Herron, was to put on a
show for the "the grangers and especially for their pretty
daughters, for the range men wanted to get better acquainted with them." Consequently, what may have been the

first rodeo, although the word was not used at the time, in the Oklahoma Panhandle was held at Benton, complete with bronc riding and steer roping. The bronc-riding event featured six two-men teams who, at a signal, all rushed into the wild-horse remuda. Each team had to rope a horse, throw a saddle on him, and bridle him, all without his co-operation. While one man forced the horse's head down by the ears, the other had to climb aboard and ride the bronc to a finish line about 100 yards away. A tough cow-hand named Irish McGovern won first place riding a mustang named Soda Biscuit. Other shows were held from time to time in the summer after roundups. The best-known of the earlier events was held at Hardesty in 1891 when a well-known top steer roper named Pomp James, foreman of the Diamond Tail outfit in the southeastern Texas Panhandle, rode up to the Strip to compete with the local boys. Boss Neff, riding his favorite roping horse, Pocket, beat James that day and became something of a local legend. Decades later, old-timers were still talking about that contest.[11]

Although roping skills were highly prized by cowhands, the range-cattle industry that spawned them was coming to a close by 1900. In 1901 the final land opening in Oklahoma occurred when the unallotted lands of the Comanche-Kiowa Reservation were distributed by lottery. A new crop of settlers once again became interested in acquiring the last free, or cheap, arable lands on the Great Plains. Rising prices for both agricultural commodities and land throughout the United States attracted thousands of newcomers into the short-grass country. In the neighboring Texas Panhandle, land speculators with large holdings, such as William P. Soash, organized special excursion trains in the Midwest to bring land "prospectors" to the region. It was reported during the late summer of 1904 that half a dozen wagons a day, loaded with families, were passing through Canadian, Texas, bound for the Oklahoma Panhandle. The *Guymon Herald* announced in the summer of 1908: "Land is available as low as $10 per acre. There are many relinquishments that can be bought. The prices ranging [sic] from $1,600 to as high as $8,000 for a quarter section."[12]

In order to stay in the cattle business, J. K. Hitch could no longer rely on an unsettled public domain for grazing purposes. He had to buy land, preferably as much as possible of those tracts that joined his. From the mid-1890s to about 1910 he selectively purchased tracts along the Coldwater and land extending out onto the "flats" (High Plains) from the watered area. In a similar fashion he acquired grassland bisected by Hackberry Creek in Hansford County, Texas. Moreover, he also managed to block out a sizeable holding in Seward County, Kansas.

The first step was receiving a patent to the homestead on the Coldwater. In 1890, No Man's Land was included in the act of Congress which created Oklahoma Territory. Henceforth the region, officially designated at first as County Seven (7) of the Territory, was more and more referred to as the Oklahoma Panhandle. Like settlers in the rest of Oklahoma Territory, settlers in the Panhandle could acquire land only under the Homestead Act of 1862, which required the claimant not only to make "improvements" such as building a house and planting crops, but also to live on the claim for five years before receiving a patent, or title to the land. The only exception to the residency requirement was contained in the "commutation" clause of the law. According to that provision, the claimant, after living on the land for six months, could purchase the property directly from the government for $1.25 per acre. The maximum acreage that could be so acquired under the law was a quarter section (160 acres).

Another federal law of 1890, however, allowed "old settlers" in the Panhandle up to three years of squatter occupation to count toward the five years. In 1891 the final survey that determined the division of the region into quarter sections was completed, and a land office was opened in Beaver City. On June 13, 1891, less than a month after the death of Mary Frances, J. K. and his sister Della rode into the land office and filed on their claims for a fee of fourteen dollars each. Both received patents in June 1893 after "proving up" their claims. Proof was furnished by the testimony of two witnesses, David C. Davis and Thomas F. Murphy, who affirmed that the length of occupancy and kinds of improvements were as stated by the claimants.[13]

Homestead units of 160 acres were too small for most settlers to survive on in the semiarid western Great Plains. When the Homestead Act first became law, it was applied to the more humid regions immediately to the east, such as western Minnesota, eastern Kansas, the eastern Dakotas, and eastern Nebraska, all of which had annual rainfalls of twenty-five inches or more per year. But as settlers moved beyond the 98th meridian into an area of cyclical drought and rainfall that often was too scant for the survival of farm crops, the basic law was not changed. In 1878 scientist and explorer of the West John Wesley Powell suggested in his classic work *Report on the Lands of the Arid Region of the United States* that the law be changed to allow a maximum of 2,560 acres with water rights on a stream as the homestead unit. Stock farming rather than raising crops would be stressed. Congress chose to ignore Powell's plea.[14]

In a recent study of homesteading on the High Plains (the western flatland part of the Great Plains), historian Paul Gates observed that although the federal law appeared to restrict land holdings to unrealistically small units, those individuals who were innovative, more acquisitive, and had a little cash and credit were sometimes able to put together large ranches.[15]

J. K. Hitch was obviously cut from that cloth. He put his earnings from Mexican cattle into land. Beginning in the mid-1890s, as neighbors and relatives received their patents, he began buying parcels that either adjoined his or were nearby on the Coldwater. After Della "proved up" her claim in 1893, she and her husband sold the land to Hitch and moved to Missouri. In 1896 and 1897, J. K. bought other adjacent tracts from his brother-in-law James Byerly, former schoolteacher Dyke Ballinger, and Methodist minister David J. M. Jones. Over the next few years he purchased land from a number of others, some of whom were doubtless his hired hands. He picked up other grassland from mortgage companies and at sheriff's sales. School lands placed on the market by Oklahoma also became part of the expanding Hitch empire. It is impossible to establish the average price that J. K. paid per acre. From deeds in Hitch files it appears that in 1896 he bought land for as little as $3.30 per acre, while in 1905 he paid between $9.00 and $10.00 per acre.[16]

Texas land policy, distinct from the federal Homestead Act that applied to Oklahoma and Kansas, offered still other opportunities for land acquisition. Under the Texas Land Act of 1895, a settler could file on a maximum of four sections (2,560 acres) at a price of $2.00 per acre for the first section (classified as agricultural land) and $1.00 per acre for the remainder (grazing land). An amendment of 1897 reduced the price of agricultural land to $1.50 per acre. The most important part of this law of 1895 was that the land could be bought from the State of Texas on credit with only one-fortieth, a maximum of $80.00, down payment. The remainder of the principal could be spread out in payments over the next thirty-nine years. Interest on the loan was only 3 percent.[17]

Under that law a number of Texas County cattlemen filed on land in adjacent Hansford County. Among them were J. K.'s oldest brother, Elias, nephew Mark Byerly, and brothers-in-law Charles and George Westmoreland, as well as J. K.'s brother and sometime partner Charlie. J. K. himself filed on four pieces of land, totaling 1786 acres, but relinquished the property, possibly in a trade, to Jack Flanagan. Ultimately he acquired relinquishments on 4,522 acres. In addition, he and Charlie were partners on another 960 acres of relinquished land. Charlie himself patented 2,536 acres. Some idea of the price paid for relinquishments in this part of Texas may be had by observing that J. K. obtained two sections from H. O. Chappell for $2,500 (about $1.95 per acre) in 1905. Outright purchases from patentees were more expensive. One such transaction of a quarter section in 1909 cost Hitch $15.62 per acre. Moreover, land on a stream such as Hackberry or Coldwater brought a higher price than upland tracts.[18]

Kansas offered still other opportunities. There he bought a number of land parcels from mortgage companies, at sheriff's sales, and directly from patentees, all in Seward County. In the winter of 1898, J. K., his new son-in-law Brice Keating, who had married Della, and Brice's brother Burt fenced a large block of land that included not only their own but also a number of sections of the public domain west of Liberal. This operation lasted only two or three years, but it was long enough for the three to make some excellent profits on cattle in the closing days of free grazing on public land. J. K. doubtless used money made on that operation to buy more Kansas land.[19]

By 1921, James Kerrick Hitch had amassed an estate of 30,223 acres, including 12,080 in the Oklahoma Panhandle, 9,440 acres in Seward County, and 8,703 acres in Hansford County. Although much of the money for investments in land came from his Mexican cattle profits, other sources of his capital should not be overlooked. First, he had entered the cattle business through his wife's family. Henry Westmoreland probably countersigned his first note at McElhany's Springfield bank. More important, J. K. doubtless bought cattle, and perhaps land, with money given to his wife by her father upon her marriage. A grateful James K. Hitch noted in his will that "the foundation of my fortune has been the money and property of the mother of my children by my first marriage."

Hitch also secured both short-term and long-term credit from various sources. Credit was not readily available in the Panhandle itself. The first bank near the area, at Liberal, was not established until 1900. Guymon was not established until 1902. Even with the establishment of a bank in that new town, there was no financial institution to furnish long-term credit for land purchases. The same was true at Beaver City, Liberal, and Hardesty. J. K.'s life insurance policies constituted a modest credit resource. On a number of occasions he borrowed against those policies, usually for only five or six hundred dollars at a time.

A more substantial source was needed to complete the purchases of large blocks of land over the fifteen-year period from 1895 to 1910. Hitch found the most convenient financial market to be Kansas City, which was the only metropolitan area linked directly (via the Rock Island Railway) to the Panhandle. The ribbons of steel over which Hitch cattle were carried to market conveyed funds for

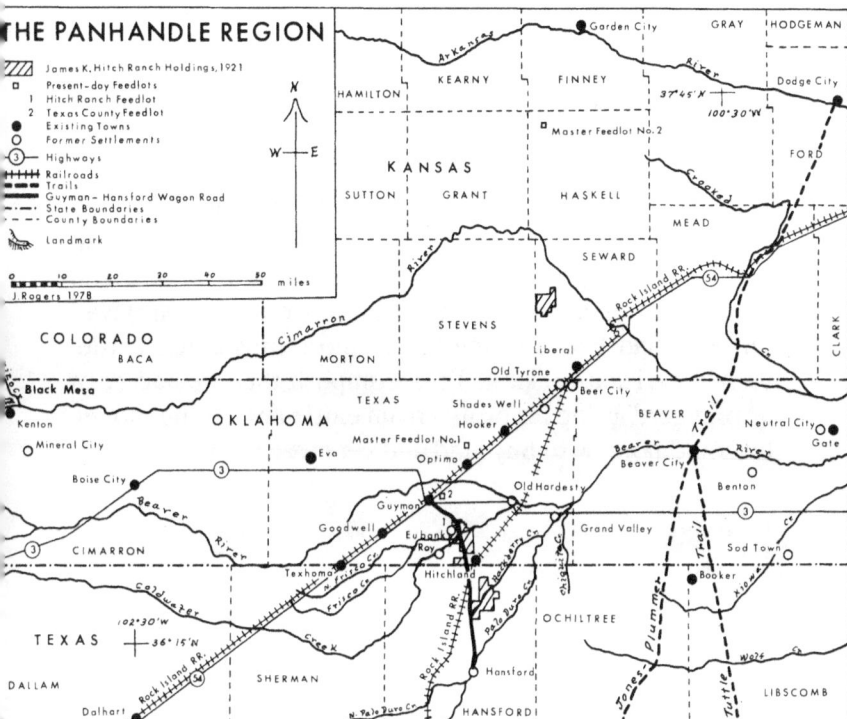

THE PANHANDLE REGION

James K. Hitch Ranch Holdings, 1921
Present-day Feedlots
1 Hitch Ranch Feedlot
2 Texas County Feedlot
Existing Towns
Former Settlements
Highways
Railroads
Trails
Guymon - Hansford Wagon Road
State Boundaries
County Boundaries
Landmark

J. Rogers 1978

The Oklahoma Panhandle and James K. Hitch Ranch holdings.

investment back to the cattleman. Kansas City mortgage financiers began loaning money to J. K. at least by 1906, possibly earlier. That year the rancher borrowed $31,160 from J. D. Robertson of Kansas City, using Seward County land as collateral. Hitch's largest creditor was Charles Baird, also of Kansas City. By 1920, J. K.'s debts to Baird amounted to more than $90,000. In addition to arranging loans from mortgage companies, J. K. also borrowed several thousands of dollars from friends and relatives through unsecured promissory notes. Among those creditors were rancher Frank Lindsay, businessman W. N. Fletcher, Charles and George Westmoreland, and most important of all, J. H. Langston, who was doing very well in the hardware and implement business.[20]

By 1920, J. K. Hitch owned an empire of well-watered grassland. Unlike some of his contemporaries who had been unable to make the transition from the range-cattle industry to enclosed ranching, he not only had survived but also had become one of the most substantial cattlemen in a tri-state region. To accomplish that, he had been a "plunger," using his profits from cattle and all the money he could borrow to buy land and yet more land.

4.   Henry and Christine

If any man ever grew up in the cattle business, it was J. K. Hitch's oldest son. Born on December 13, 1884, and named Charles Henry, he so admired Grandfather Henry West-moreland that he reversed the order of his given names. When he started to school, he told his teacher that his name was "Henry Westmoreland." By the time he was a young man, he was signing his name "Henry C. Hitch."[1]

His Uncle Charlie Hitch and the hired hands called the child "Boss." When he began riding a horse, his first saddle was made from a piece of tarpaulin or wagon sheet with stirrups made from pieces of rope. His first job was tramping hay on wagons when he was ten or eleven years old. J. K. paid him five cents a day for that job. In later years Henry recalled that he got his first job as a cowhand when he was about eleven years old. Uncle Charlie needed help in rounding up and moving some cattle. Henry begged his father to let him go along. Jim told Charlie, "Well, if he can do a man's work, he can go." Henry worked for three days. He got wet in a downpour and got lost one night riding home, but the experience was worth it. He had proved that he could "make a hand." The thirty cents his uncle paid him for the job was evidence enough.

He began working for his father as a horse wrangler, a position usually reserved for the "kid" or youngest member of a ranching outfit. By age fourteen he was indeed doing a man's work, and his younger brother, George, became the horse wrangler. That year, 1898, Henry and George accompanied their father and a few hired hands on a drive of twelve hundred cattle from a place west of Dodge City to the Coldwater. During the drive a cowhand asked Henry what Jim Hitch was paying him. The boy replied, "My boarding and clothing." The boys were rewarded that fall, however, when their father cut out thirty heifer calves worth about fifteen dollars each for them. Henry and George were in the cattle business.[2]

About the same year, J. K. decided to send the boys out by themselves to drive back a couple of stray cows some distance from the ranch. At the breakfast table one morning he told each of the boys to bring back a stray from some fifteen to thirty miles away on different ranches. George was sent down the Coldwater beyond Hardesty for his cow, while Henry rode farther east toward Palo Duro Creek to find his. The distance was so great that Henry had to spend the night at a ranch house before driving the cow back the next day.[3]

By the late 1890s, Jim and Charlie Hitch were shipping as many as ten thousand steers and heifers per year to market in Kansas City by way of a new town named Tyrone. The Rock Island Railroad had built southwestward across Seward County, Kansas, in 1888, and Liberal had been platted as a railroad town. The track was extended a few miles farther southwest of Liberal to the Kansas line. Tyrone sprang up there and became the major cattle-shipping point for the Panhandle. Because of a cattle quarantine law enacted by Kansas in 1885, the railroad built Tyrone's loading pens on the Neutral Strip side of the line. The purpose of the law was to protect the livestock of Kansas settlers from the fever ticks carried by Texas longhorns. Consequently, cattle from south of the

Kansas line could be driven into the state only from December 1 to March 1.

Neither the quarantine nor Kansas prohibition (now being enforced in Dodge City) existed at Tyrone. The loading pens were built with seven chutes to load a like number of cars at the same time. Catch-wing fences extended 200 yards onto the plains to funnel the wild cattle into the pens. Livestock were loaded night and day during the fall market season on trains of twenty-five to thirty cattle cars each.

Tyrone earned a reputation as a wide-open town. It contained two large saloons, three dance halls, two card-rooms, a hotel, a couple of restaurants, a boot-and-saddle shop, a post office, and a red-light district. It was not as large as Dodge, but could be just as lively with a hundred or more cowboys in town at night. One important difference, however, was that Tyrone had more cowboys than it had "black leg gamblers," as Charlie Hitch once put it. As the cowboys got drunk, the gamblers sneaked away to the safety of nearby sandhills to avoid trouble.

Seven miles south of Tyrone, J. U. Shade, a livestock agent for the Rock Island, constructed a cattle-holding area by drilling a well seventy-five feet deep and erecting a large wooden overhead tank. Shade also built a number of long, wooden watering troughs twenty inches high and eighteen inches wide. As many as two thousand cattle could drink from the facility at the same time. Shade's Well, as the cattlemen called the place, was first pumped by a large windmill. The mill proved inadequate and was soon replaced by a steam engine. Zack Cain managed the well, serviced the pump, and repaired the engine. He also kept cowboys happy by means of his wife's home-style meals served at twenty-five cents each.

J. K. and Charlie, accompanied by Henry, George, and a number of cowhands, made the drive into Shade's Well and Tyrone in October and November. It usually required a week to round up the livestock and another three days to drive them to Tyrone. The first day's drive brought cattle and crew about half a day beyond the Beaver River. From there it took another day and a half to get to Shade's Well.[4] The well provided more than water. It also offered opportunities for cattlemen and cowboys to renew old acquaintances, discuss low cattle prices and high freight rates, and recall the good old days of the open range.[5]

After an afternoon stay at the well, the Hitches drove their cattle north during the night to Tyrone. The cowhands liked to be at the railhead on Sunday afternoon because in fair weather a group of girls from Liberal usually rode down atop the cattle cars for the occasion. Leader of this group was Myra McDermott, daughter of the manager of the Rock Island Hotel in Liberal. She later became the owner of McDermott's grove on Frisco Creek, southwest of the Hitch Ranch. In later years Charlie Hitch said that the reason the men liked the drive to market so much was, "They would meet half the cowboys in the world at Shade's Well and half the good-looking girls in the world at the end of trail—Old Tyrone."[6] When not pushing the wild longhorns up the chutes and into the cars, the cowhands were milling around the cars talking to the girls on top. For most of the men this was one of the more important social occasions of the year.

After the last fall drive Henry Hitch returned to school. After completing the elementary grades at the school on the Coldwater, Henry, George, and his sisters went to high school in Liberal. Because of his responsibilities at the ranch Henry went only half a term each year after he was twelve. In all, he attended high school for three and

The tall
windmill tower
at Hitch Ranch
headquarters,
ca. 1900.

Hitch Ranch headquarters, ca. 1900.

Hitch cattle on the Coldwater, ca. 1900.

Cattle on the Hitch Ranch, ca. 1900.

a half "half-terms" (one school year was a "term"). In the fall and winter of 1901–02 he completed his formal education by enrolling in a business college at Winfield, Kansas, where he remained for three months. By the early spring of 1902 he was back on the Coldwater. As he neared his seventeenth birthday that fall, he asked if J. K. would pay his expenses to continue the business college course. J. K. first said, "Yes, I guess so." A few days later, however, when Henry was hitching a team to J. K.'s buggy, the older man turned to his son and said, "Well, a boy who is 17 years old, he's too old to go to school. I think you'd better stay here and run this ranch."[7]

J. K. was not unfeeling about his son's desire for more education. Henry was a bright, quiet, sensitive student who would remain an avid reader throughout his life, devouring books and magazines in his little leisure time. But Hitch's ranching operations had grown too large for a single manager, particularly one who now had other interests. He had married twenty-eight-year-old Josephine B. Brown, sister of Court Brown, a cattleman and business associate, on December 18, 1899. Their first child, Robert, was born on November 12, 1900. Josephine gave birth to a daughter, Catherine, on August 8, 1902, and the last child, Harry Kerrick, arrived on October 22, 1905.[8]

Wishing to devote more time to his new family, J. K. built a spacious frame house on north Academy Street in the new town of Guymon. The neighbors of J. K. and Josephine were the Langstons. Howard Langston and his wife, Sarah, had sold their farm and moved into Guymon about the same time that J. K. did, and built a house on the same street. Howard and his son Edward opened a hardware and implement store, which established the Langstons firmly in the business world. Another son, Jack, also moved into a house on Academy and went into business. The Langstons did well financially. Still another son, W. H., received his degree from Washington University medical school in St. Louis and, after practicing medicine first in Hansford County, Texas, moved to Guymon to become the town's first physician. In a few years Academy Street was dominated by the houses of Hitch and Langston.[9]

While J. K. continued to operate the Coldwater ranch and to oversee his Hansford County holdings, he sent Henry to manage his Kansas ranch in Seward County. Henry managed those operations for the next several years. J. K. at first paid him sixteen dollars a month, but later raised his salary to twenty-five dollars. That was less money than J. K. paid the hired hands working under the young man. In addition, the older Hitch informed the new ranch manager that there was no cook in the deal. Henry would either have to hire a cook from his own wages or do the cooking himself for the four cowboys working under him. Of course, J. K. would supply food for the outfit. During the next six years Henry learned much about the cattle business. He rose at half past three in the morning to cook breakfast for his crew, usually a meal of fried steak, biscuits, and flour gravy. After a hard day he still had to cook supper. It was a strenuous life for a young rancher, but he never complained. His energy seemed to be inexhaustible. He even found time to file on an unclaimed quarter section of Seward County land and raise some livestock for himself.[10]

Henry Hitch was not only the manager, but also he became his own "top hand" as well. The highest praise that a cattleman could bestow on another man was, "He *knows* cattle." Through experience and observation Henry acquired an intuitive as well as a rational expertise about livestock. The early Texas cattleman Shanghai Pierce

Young Henry C. Hitch as manager of J. K. Hitch's Kansas ranch, ca. 1902. Photograph taken in Liberal, Kansas.

once boasted that he was "Webster on cattle, by God, Sir."[11] If young Hitch was not yet "Webster," he was on his way to becoming "Funk & Wagnalls" on cattle. He knew their behavior patterns, their usual diseases and how to treat them, their eating habits, and the best feeds. He could also hold a large number of cattle in a bunch while working them individually with branding iron and knife, throw a rope over a head or around the back hooves, and cut (separate) animals from the herd. Moreover, he knew most if not all of his mother-cow herd as individuals, not by name but from some quirk of appearance such as color-markings, size, horns, or any one of a thousand details that the uninitiated would never notice.

The primary tool of the cowhand was his horse, and his efficiency was related to his ability to pick horses with "cow sense" and stamina. A good horse and rider could cover more ground in a day than a mediocre horse and rider. Henry Hitch was known for his ability to get the most out of a good horse. During the busiest part of the year, from spring to fall, he rode six horses a week—one for each work day. A horse needed six days to recuperate from a Hitch workout. John Knight, one of the Tennesseans who came to work for the Hitches, recalled in later years, "Whenever you rode all day with Henry Hitch you knew you had been riding." Henry left the corral at dawn at a "lope" and returned at dusk at a "lope." Holding the bridle reins in his left hand, he held the end of his lariat rope in the other. Every time the horse's hooves touched the ground, Henry lightly pecked his mount with the rope. If that pace did not wear out a cow pony, it often wore out the cowhands riding with Hitch.[12]

The Kansas experience was a lonely life for Henry the first few years. He never really regarded any place as home except the stone house on the Coldwater. Even the howl of coyotes on a still night sounded lonesome to Henry, whereas the same howl on the Coldwater was simply part of the environment. There was little leisure time. He was never fond of gambling and, like his father, did not drink or smoke. Incidentally, his grandmother, Zilpha West-moreland, was leader of the temperance committee of her Methodist Church. Henry never attempted to enforce his values on others. His hired hands gambled, and like most cowboys they were always short of cash. Playing poker at night by kerosene lamp between paydays was usually the method of dividing up the six eggs laid by the dozen hens on the ranch each day.[13]

Henry occasionally found time to hunt coyotes with his two greyhounds. He killed enough to make a lap robe, but he did it with some regret. Years later in Amarillo, Texas, he found a verse that impressed him so much that although it was about the wolf, he applied the poem to the coyote and copied it down on a piece of hotel stationery. When he was past eighty, he could still recite the piece from memory.

> Born to be a cattle killer
>   thief & general all round pest
> But I hate to kill you partner
>   cause you are part of our old West.
>
> You and I are sort of brothers
>   with our backs against the wall
> In an act that's almost over
>   and the curtain's bout to fall.[14]

The act was indeed almost over. The movement of more settlers into western Oklahoma after 1900 caused perhaps the last conflicts between cattlemen and farmers on the Great Plains. Settlers who could not afford to fence their fields were sometimes grazed out by the livestock of cattlemen, who continued to use any unfenced land. In 1902 a number of farmers in the western part of Oklahoma Territory complained to Governor Thompson B. Ferguson and Dennis T. Flynn, the territorial congressional delegate. A farmer from Antelope, Oklahoma, wrote: "The cattle men say they are going to let their stock run just the same as they have been doing. . . . Will our government stand and not protect us? . . . I am just a young man getting on a claim of my own. I am not able to fence and lots of the claims taken are in the same shape." At Woodward, settlers got together after having fields destroyed by open-range livestock in 1901 and petitioned Flynn for Congress to pass a closed-range law or herd law that would require cattlemen to restrain their stock.[15]

The pressure by settlers caused the Oklahoma Territorial Legislature to pass a herd law in 1902. Under its provisions the region east of the Panhandle became a closed range. Any part of a county could become open range if by popular petition the county commissioners decided to divide the county into stock districts and if the majority of voters in a stock district opted for open range. But under the same law the Oklahoma Panhandle was declared an open range unless the same kind of procedure was used to adopt "herd law." In other words, east of the 100th meridian the burden of election was placed on the cattlemen, while west of the 100th meridian farmers had to carry the burden. The law simply recognized the continued predominance of cattlemen over settlers in the Panhandle.[16]

Within two years the renewed tide of settlers into old No Man's Land brought threats of violence. In a mass meeting held at Beaver City early in 1905, farmers printed a circular that warned cattlemen to restrain their stock after May 20, 1905, and they called on the legislature to extend "herd law" to the Panhandle. C. W. Stewart wrote to President Theodore Roosevelt, "Our county . . . is now on the verge of a fierce and bloody war!" He suggested that the President declare martial law.[17]

No new law was passed, and martial law was avoided. But settlers succeeded in 1906, under the law of 1902, in closing the range in the central Panhandle (the area that would become Texas County in 1907 when Oklahoma became a state). That movement ended for all time the last vestiges of open range for the Hitch Ranch and its neighbors. To reinforce that act, another herd law referendum was conducted on April 29, 1911, and it passed overwhelmingly in all fifteen stock districts of the county.[18]

Herd law was but one of many indications of the rapidly changing world of the Hitch family. In 1907 the last three wild mustangs in the Panhandle were run down, roped, and captured by two Texas County cowboys, Perry Brite and "Con" Jackson. In 1911 another cowhand named Carl Ragland reverted to a once popular Saturday night prank and rode his horse into Harrison Pool Hall in Guymon before leaving town for the Anchor-D Ranch. Ragland was awakened and arrested early the next morning in the bunkhouse by Deputy Sheriff J. V. Farr. Even the Beaver River showed the effects of a closed range. The editor of the *Guymon Herald* recalled in 1910 that at one time the Beaver was a deep stream with grass running to the water's edge. He reasoned:

When cattle could go into the streams at any point, the grass was not worn away, but with the advent of fences and narrow water gaps, cattle tramped the ground bare at such gaps and it was at the watering places that the sand started to washing when dashing rains and high waters came. The banks of the stream were cut away and the stream widened and the deep water became a thing of the past. Down near the mouth of the Coldwater where the Beaver is now a sand bed 100 yards wide, twenty years ago it was an easy matter to run and jump from one bank to the other.[19]

Cattle, mustangs, cowboys, streams—the closing of the range had changed them all.

The agrarian attitude working to change the economy

was echoed by the editor of the *Guymon Herald* in 1911 when he wrote: "The ultimate development of this country must be the development of our farms. The country is changing and must eventually evolutionize [sic] from the cattle country of a few years ago to a stock farming community and possibly to a straight farming community."[20]

J. K. responded by diversifying his operations. He began to grow alfalfa on some of his Coldwater hay meadows for seed as well as for forage. He sold the seed to local farmers. Poverty-stricken settlers who could not afford to fence their lands sometimes lacked work animals; J. K. Hitch often met that need by loaning out teams of bronc mules for a year at a time. In this arrangement settlers broke the animals for Hitch, who then loaned the farmers another team of unbroken mules for yet another year. It was a mutual business deal advantageous to both parties, one that could go on indefinitely. J. K. sold the broken mules locally or shipped them to the thriving market in his native Tennessee.[21]

There was more to life for Henry Hitch than adapting ranching operations to changing times. In 1908 he attended a meeting of the local literary society at the Pleasant Valley school about six miles southeast of the Kansas ranch headquarters. The "literary," as it was commonly called, was a cooperative effort between school and community. Literary societies were to be found all across the frontier of the rural Great Plains. They usually met on Friday nights about once a month and sometimes more often, although one was being conducted in Guymon on Saturday nights in 1910. Programs varied, but usually both children and adults took turns standing on makeshift stages and reciting poems, engaging in debates, singing, and declaiming famous addresses. Such recitations might run the gamut from "Mary Had a Little Lamb" to "Spartacus' Address to the Gladiators," to "The Face on the Barroom Floor." Examples of debates conducted by the Guymon literary in 1910 included: "Resolved, that high license is a better means of controlling the liquor traffic than state wide prohibition," and "Resolved, that a man should not marry on an income of less than $500 per year." The literary society played an important role in the social and cultural life of the community that could not be satisfied by the usual round of church services, parties, and dances. It offered an opportunity to exchange ideas, to defend one's political or economic views, and to engage in general intellectual stimulation. What made the literary even more interesting was that the newly arrived homesteaders from across the nation and Europe were often well-read and represented myriad viewpoints. Such meetings must have been a unique learning experience.[22]

In later years Henry could not recall the details of that evening's program. He found it difficult to take his eyes off the tall, dark-haired teacher. She was wearing a white, high-collared shirtwaist and ankle-length dark skirt. She closely resembled the "Gibson girl" sketches created by the famous illustrator of that time Charles Dana Gibson, that appeared in many of America's popular magazines. Like the "Gibson girl," the teacher possessed poise, beauty, intelligence, and wit. Her name was Christine Walker.

After the program the usually reserved young man introduced himself to Miss Walker. She discovered him to be a well-read conversationalist, but one who used few words. Henry offered to walk her home, and she accepted. In the bright moonlight of a crisp fall night, the two walked side by side up the sandy road, with Hitch leading his horse the quarter mile to her mother's house. They talked about the evening's program. He was delighted with her pupils' performances and thought that her work with them showed her to be a gifted teacher. It may not have been love at first sight, but they liked each other's company from the moment they met. Before Henry bade her goodnight, he invited her to accompany him to a literary at another school some miles away. In a few days he called on her in a buggy pulled by a pair of horses with the colorful names of Ginger Pop and Gooseneck. During the next several months the rig became a familiar sight at the Walker homestead.[23]

Christine Arena Walker was a sensitive, intelligent, charming young woman. Born in 1890 at Sun City in Barber County, Kansas, she was the daughter of Thomas Walker and Matie Cline Walker. Matie had been born into a German family at Fond Du Lac, Wisconsin, in 1865. Her oldest sister, Hattie, once described her as "the most willful, and liveliest of all of us." The Cline family moved to southeastern Kansas about 1875, then farther west to Pratt County, and finally to Prowers County in southeastern Colorado. While in Kansas, according to the same sister, her father "married her off" at age seventeen to Thomas Walker at Medicine Lodge, "not exactly her choice." Walker was fifteen years older than Matie, but "was considered well to do, as he owned cattle and land." Thomas Walker had been born in Kentucky in 1850, the son of R. B. and Judith Walker. The family had moved to Barber County, Kansas, in 1874. Thomas had been a buffalo hunter and also a cattle drover before meeting the Cline family.

Thomas and Matie had five children: Irvin, Earl, Allen, Christine, and Erma, the youngest. In an age that considered divorce a tragedy second only to falling from grace, the couple finally decided on divorce in 1905. By then the two older boys were on their own. They eventually wound up living near Prescott, Arizona. Tom retained

Christine Walker at age fourteen and her brother Irvin, ca. 1904.

custody of the youngest boy, Allen. Matie took Christine, then fifteen years old, and six-year old Erma, and moved to Rocky Ford, Colorado, where they lived with her sister "Pet" for a year. The next year Matie moved her family to Seward County, Kansas, where she filed on a 160-acre homestead just over the hill from where the Pleasant Valley school would be built.[24]

While in Colorado, Christine was graduated from high school and secured a teacher's certificate. After the move to Seward County she was hired at a salary of forty-five dollars a month. The school first met temporarily in the living room of neighbor O. L. Cain's home. Then Christine moved her sixteen to eighteen pupils into a recently built, low-ceilinged frame structure that measured fourteen by twenty-eight feet. It was used later by Cain as a chicken house. Like those who attended the literaries, her students were from many cultural roots. She was amused one day at the expression of an English boy who, in describing his grandmother making a dessert, said, "The old hen gave over and we had a bonny custard." Another student was a gifted German boy who "sang like an angel." During the next couple of summers Christine attended the Emporia State Normal College at Emporia, Kansas, to complete work on her Kansas teaching certificate.[25]

Although their values were identical, Christine Walker and Henry Hitch gave ample evidence that opposite personalities may be attracted to each other. Henry, like his father, was quiet and reserved but a keen observer of people and nature. He was amiable but tended to be introspective and engaged in very little small talk. He could be drawn into a conversation, however, to discuss an important matter. Beneath his stoic exterior lay the talents of a master storyteller, and occasionally his dry humor cropped out. An old cowboy named Allen Walker, who was given

Christine Walker, her students, and her first school, which was in the living room of this private home. Her younger sister Erma is standing on the far right of the front row.

to exaggeration, once remarked that a ranch he worked for at one time drove herds of cattle to market so large that when the lead cattle were entering Dodge City, the drags were just leaving Hackberry Creek in the Panhandle! Henry grinned. He knew of one bigger than that. This larger ranch had so many cowhands that the sourdough for breakfast biscuits had to be mixed in a canyon![26]

If Henry was largely an introvert, Christine was a charming extrovert and individualistic in her own way. She had large expressive eyes and the sensitivity of an artist. She had come from a family of independent-minded women,

Christine and Erma Walker on their mother's homestead claim in Seward County.

many of whom had been in business. Her aunts Hattie and Ella owned a millinery store in Rocky Ford. Aunt Opal had become a buyer for Bullock's Wilshire, a prestigious lady's wear store in Los Angeles. Another aunt, Debby, had made a small fortune in real estate while operating both a boarding house and dairy at Trinidad, Colorado.[27]

Christine also possessed an independent turn of mind. While she and Henry were courting, the young rancher was shocked to learn that she did not ride a sidesaddle as did his Aunt Josie. An excellent horsewoman, Christine had always ridden horses astride in a man's saddle, and she informed her beau that she never intended to ride side-saddle. Henry did not argue with her. He was charmed rather than threatened by that soft, eloquent voice, her ready smile, and her sharp sense of humor.[28]

Wedding picture of Henry Hitch and Christine Walker Hitch.

By the summer of 1909, Henry and Christine were engaged, but Henry was needed back at the Coldwater to assume more responsibilities for J. K. Thus the couple parted for a year. Christine returned to school during the spring and summer terms at the normal college before going to a better-paying job at Isabel, Kansas, near her birthplace of Sun City. But they continued to correspond. Henry was able to get away from the ranch to visit her

Henry and
Christine
in Colorado.

once in Emporia. On that occasion he gave her a long
stole made from the fur of an Alaskan Cross Fox that he
had obtained through his brother-in-law Lyman Savage,
a veteran of the Alaskan gold rush.[29]

They set their wedding date for June 22, 1910, Christine's twentieth birthday. On June 21, Henry rode a big
bay horse named Old Dewey (after the Spanish-American
War hero) into Guymon and boarded the train for Liberal.
He spent the night with his sister Della and her husband,
Brice Keating. Early the next morning Henry rented a
surrey from the livery stable and drove out to the Walker
homestead. He returned to town with Christine, Matie,
and Erma. The wedding was held in the Keating home
with James J. Ballinger, minister of the Methodist Episco-

pal Church of Fowler, Kansas, officiating. After the simple ceremony Henry and Christine boarded the Gold State train at Liberal for Dalhart, Texas, switched trains, and continued their honeymoon trip to Colorado. They stopped at Trinidad and Pueblo to visit Christine's relatives, climbed Fisher's Peak and Simpson's Rest near Trinidad, and arrived in Denver in time to celebrate the Fourth of July. They returned by way of a marble quarry in which Henry had invested some money near Colorado Springs.[30]

When the couple returned from Colorado, Christine saw her new house—the stone house on the Coldwater—for the first time. In comparison with the houses of other rural neighbors, it had an impressive domestic water system. A wood-vaned Fairbanks-Morse Eclipse windmill stood high on the slope behind the house pumping water into three large metal storage tanks that stood about twelve feet high. A pipe carried water to the house by gravity, not only for the kitchen but also for the stone springhouse that had once been the addition to the original sod house. Along one wall of the springhouse a shallow masonry trough about three feet wide collected the water for cooling the fresh milk, cream, and butter kept in stoneware crockery; from there the water flowed south of the house to a large cement tank for the livestock.[31]

The structure was not Christine's dream house. After J. K. had moved into Guymon, the building was used as bunkhouse, feed bin, and storage area. The drab interior walls were covered with dark paper and the woodwork was equally dark. The floor was dry and cracked, and the whole place needed a thorough cleaning. Christine went to work with a vengeance. To brighten the interior, she covered the walls with "oatmeal" paper, so called because of its color. She and a painter coated the dark woodwork

with an ivory paint only to discover that the mahogany
showed through. Everything had to be redone with another
paint. She filled the cracks in the floor with a mixture of
papier-mâché, but pieces of the hardened substance occasionally broke loose and boards popped up. Despite such
difficulties Christine made the house into a home for
Henry, a veritable refuge to sustain them through both
the lean and good years of the next half century.[32]

5. The Hitch Family of Coldwater Valley

When Henry Hitch moved his bride into the Coldwater headquarters, the region was still young. Oklahoma had been a state less than three years, and Texas County was the same age. At statehood in 1907 old Beaver County, covering the entire Panhandle, was broken into three parts: Beaver County in the east, Cimarron County in the west, and Texas County in the middle. Guymon, the county seat of Texas County, was only nine years old. The Rock Island Railroad ran diagonally across Texas County, with cattle-loading facilities in almost every town along its route. Consequently Tyrone was no longer the primary cattle town for the Panhandle. Within a few years, that town and Shade's Well would all but fade from the plains.

Guymon at first had some characteristics of the rough cattle towns of the past. One of the first buildings in town was a shack that served as a saloon. It was opened by an old cowboy/cook named Jimmy, who became his own best customer. Henry Hitch once recalled that old Jimmy "drank up all his profits." A higher class establishment named the Senate Saloon replaced Jimmy's shoestring operation after a few years. When Oklahoma became a state, prohibition came with it, and the saloons were closed down. Oklahoma, thanks to its bootleggers, did not dry up, but towns like Guymon and Beaver City took on a new, more respectable look without their saloons.[1]

Only a quarter of a century had passed since James K. Hitch had first viewed the Coldwater Valley and driven his cattle onto its open range. Yet because of the many changes, including the end of the open range, the arrival of the railroad, the appearance of automobiles on Guymon's streets, the influx of thousands of farmers, and other such developments, the old days seemed to belong to a remote time. Symbolizing the end of that era was the death of the white-haired, bearded patriarch of the Hitch, Westmoreland, and Langston families, Henry Westmoreland, on April 18, 1908, at the age of ninety. The citizens of Texas County, however, were not yet ready to turn their backs on the past. They were already growing nostalgic about that earlier period. A "Cow-Boy Reunion and Frontier Days Celebration" was held in Guymon from March 31 through April 2, 1910. The main event was a rodeo, which featured a "cow pony race, . . . barrel race, cigar race, potatoe [sic] race, hat race, ladies horse race, roping contest, riding contest, wild horse race, steer riding, . . . and a fancy and trick roping exhibition."[2]

Although Panhandle folks might have been sentimental about the colorful past of their region, they showed a greater interest in utilizing the material progress of an industrialized America for their present needs. Dr. W. H. Langston, Henry Hitch's cousin, bought one of the first automobiles in Guymon. By April, 1908, there were sixteen motor cars in the town with "new ones . . . coming in almost every day." More automobiles required better streets. By February, 1910, W. C. Ondler, pulling a road grader with a gasoline traction engine, completed the grading of ten miles of Guymon streets. The *Guymon Herald* boasted, "There is not a low spot anywhere and there is not a high place or big jump off all over town. If a man decides to start across the street anywhere, whether

The main street of Guymon after a "gully washer" in the spring of 1908.

there are electric lights at the place or not he will have the satisfaction that he will not bust up three or four bones in making the attempt."[3] C. Summers and Sons, a dry-goods store, proudly opened the doors to its "new brick building" on March 1, 1910. The merchants of Guymon were planning to put in a septic tank for the business section and to pipe its overflow to feed the trees in a proposed park on the west side of town. A good indication that running water and bathrooms were in greater demand in town was that an "expert plumber" from Salt Lake City, D. Z. Stewart, opened a shop just north of the Texas County Bank in October, 1910.

Advertisements in the *Guymon Herald* furnish an insight into the town's thriving business district in 1910. J. G. McLarty, Grocer, had "Good groceries and plenty of them." The Langston Hardware Company offered "Stoves All Kinds." The City Meat Market, owned by

C. A. Booth, had "fresh and cured meats on hand." The Savage Drug Company, owned by Henry Hitch's brother-in-law, advertised "Dr. King's New Discovery Quickest, Safest, Surest Cough and Cold Cure and Healer of All Diseases of Lungs, Throat and Chest." Dr. Lightner, a dentist, had his office over the First National Bank. Doc Ross & Fletcher operated a feed, seed, and coal store next to its wagon yard. William Dutch, Baker, made "bread, pies, cakes, buns, etc. that stand the test." The Star Lumber Company informed consumers, "You pay for what you get, and you get what you pay for—nothing less." The Star Mercantile Company, founded by the town's namesake Ed Guymon but now owned by George Ellison and Guy Baird, advertised Monarch brand canned goods and White House Coffee. A competitor, the North Main Street Grocer, asked, "Do you Have Trouble Getting Groceries with the Right Taste?" The Westland Hotel, recently remodeled, not only was "the best hostlery up and down the line," but also was "a good place to take your Sunday dinner."

Ennis & Dale took out a full-page advertisement for Buick Motor Cars. Langston & Lyons Automobiles sold EMFs (ancestor of the Studebaker) and Maxwells, "the swellest movers in the automobile line of today. They are the cars that make the record, the cars that stand the service—in short the quality cars. No road too long and no hill too high—the cars that go and come back." Other businesses included: Ennis & Dale Real Estate, which advertised homestead relinquishments for sale at $1.50 to $5.00 per acre and improved farms for $6.50 to $7.50 per acre; Farmers' Co-Operative Milling Company; Lon Holland, a blacksmith; J. C. Sheil Dry Goods and Clothing; Latham Dry Goods; and Hazleton & Langston, Bonded Abstracters with offices in Beaver as well as Guymon.[4]

Latham Dry Goods had a sale in January in which every purchaser of a $20.00 suit, the most expensive sold, was given a "free" $5.00 Stetson hat. The Star Mercantile Company sold Red Turkey Flour at $2.80 for a fifty-pound sack, potatoes for $0.90 a bushel, ten pounds of Golden Glory Syrup for $0.45, Calumet Baking Powder for $0.20 a can, and sixteen pounds of beans for $1.00. Even dentists advertised prices; Dr. F. O. Keifer in his office above the post office would put in a twenty-two-carat gold crown for $4.50, a gold filling for $1.00 and up, a platina filling for $0.50 to $1.00, and pull an offending tooth for $0.50.[5]

For those with some leisure time, Guymon offered varied entertainment. The Nickelodeon had already been replaced by The Dime, which showed "a big Western" such as "Arizona Pete or The Bad Man's Last Deed" every Saturday. On weeknights patrons might see such silent thrillers as the double-bill program "Indian Girls Romance" and "His Hunting Trip," or "The Lost Trail" and "The Surgeon's Visit." Guymon also boasted an opera house frequented by theatrical touring companies. "The Two Orphans" opened there on October 12, 1910. The management billed the show as a "great French melodrama" set in the age of Louis XV and boasted that this six-act, costumed production would satisfy the most demanding critic.[6]

The Guymon Dancing Club was one of the more active organizations in town. The group sponsored periodic ballroom dances. The new brick Summers Building was the scene of a large ball on February 24, 1910, in which "music of the best talent" was employed. An invitation to the event was sent to President William Howard Taft, but he failed to respond.[7]

Christine and Henry Hitch were not members of the

dancing club. Henry did not dance, and Christine had been reared as a Baptist. She had been taught that dancing and card-playing were "cardinal sins." The emphasis by her church on those shortcomings had convinced her as a child that those were "the only sins." Even if the couple had been interested in Guymon's social whirl, they had little time for leisurely activities. Soon after Christine arrived at the Coldwater, while she was in Guymon shopping at the dry-goods store, proprietor Louis Latham asked her what she and Henry did for entertainment. She replied with her usual sense of humor, "We don't have any." With a grin, Latham responded, "Well, when you are first married you don't need a German band on every street corner."[8]

J. K. increased Henry's salary to fifty dollars a month after his son's marriage. Christine, aided the first few years by a domestic servant provided by J. K., cooked for a hired crew that ranged from four men in the winter to eleven or twelve during the summer haying season. J. K.'s cowhands originally had slept in a wooden frame structure called the "dog house," a short distance from the main house, but the building was cold in the winter. After Christine came, the four all-year hands were housed in a large unused downstairs room of the stone house. In the summer the additional work crew slept in the large wooden barn that J. K. had recently built. Henry continued to rise early and cook breakfast for the men and his family. Long after he had no more hired hands to cook for, he continued to prepare his favorite breakfast of fried steak, biscuits, and gravy for the family. Christine cooked the larger meals and took care of the house. Food was prepared on a large wood-burning range that had a twenty-gallon hot-water reservoir on the side and warming ovens on top.[9]

Meals consisted of various dishes, including hot bread, chicken and dumplings, Irish stew made of beef cut from the carcass that hung on the back porch during the winter, potatoes, onions, greens from the garden, and fruit from the orchard. The stew was a winter staple for supper. In the summer Christine cooked a lot of chickens. Her favorite Sunday dinner dish was chicken loaf prepared the day before from a hen or rooster. It was made by boiling the fowl until the meat dropped off the bones, adding boiled eggs to the meat and thick broth, seasoning the mixture, and chilling it like souse. Another dish was made by soaking salt pork in a shallow dish of water and rolling it in egg and cracker crumbs before frying. Still another popular dish was boiled wheat, which made a tasty cereal when mixed with heavy cream.

The hired hands ate at the same table as the family, but usually at different hours because of the work schedule. The men had an early breakfast at 5:30 or so, a late dinner in the middle of the afternoon and a late supper. They ate heartily. One man always piled his plate high and then poured sorghum molasses over the pyramided food only to have the syrup overflow the plate and drip on the oil cloth covering. Christine Hitch remembered in later years that the sight almost made her sick.[10]

Henry and his brother George remained close socially as well as in financial matters. George also married in 1910, on November 23. His bride was Willa Neathery, of Stevens County, Kansas. In the process of settling Henry Westmoreland's estate, George bought the Westmoreland Ranch, situated five miles up the Coldwater, from the rest of the heirs. As J. K. and Charlie had been partners in a number of cattle deals, so were Henry and George. Each young man had his own cattle and interests, but they were partners in land in Hansford County and in some cattle.

The Hitch Ranch camp (Texas Camp) at Texas Lake, ca. 1910. The split-level bunkhouse is in the background.

They were even partners in the buggy which Henry had used to court Christine. Their partnership in cattle originated when J. K. gave the two young "hired hands" thirty heifer calves in 1898. In 1907, when Henry was still in Kansas and George was on the Coldwater, each was still looking after the other's interests. When one of Henry's mares on the Coldwater foaled an excellent mule colt, George found a "mate" for it among J. K.'s young mules so that his brother would have two matched teams of mule colts.[11] The brothers and their wives often visited each other's homes for Sunday dinner. Frequently Henry and Christine and George and Willa drove out to Texas Camp on the big playa lake for outings as well as for work.[12]

Although Henry had little time for leisure, he managed to pursue some hobbies. As a young man he occasionally had hunted water fowl at Texas Lake or on the Coldwater and rabbits in the pastures. Christine or the children sometimes accompanied him. The game wound up on

Christine Hitch and Willa Nethery (Mrs. George) Hitch at the Texas Camp bunkhouse.

the Hitch table to feed family and hired hands. As Henry grew older, his favorite hobbies were sedentary ones. He was an enthusiastic collector of stamps and Indian artifacts. His collection of hundreds of flint points, which he had been gathering since he was a boy, ultimately filled several display cases.

His stamp collection became one of the most complete of its kind and worth a small fortune a few decades later. But the hobby that this physically active man enjoyed most, both for professional reasons and pleasure, was reading. As a boy he had devoured the poor-boy-makes-good novels of Horatio Alger, which so influenced the youth of his day. As an adult, when he found the time to sit down at home by the light of a kerosene lamp, he almost always had a book, magazine, or newspaper in his hand. He not only read those farm and ranch magazines that were standard fare in the region, such as the *Oklahoma Farmer-Stockman,* the *Cattleman,* and *Progressive Farmer,* but also devoured publications of the United States Department of Agriculture, especially the *Yearbooks* and bulletins from the Oklahoma Agricultural Experiment Station.[13]

Henry was fascinated by the frontier of Alaska, possibly because his brother-in-law Lyman Savage had gone to Fairbanks soon after the turn of the century in pursuit of gold. He read a number of books and articles about the territory and even seriously considered going there, but he contented himself by buying a share of a mining claim on Little Eldorado Creek near Fairbanks.[14]

The rancher was also very fond of history. Included in his library were early editions of such works as Theodore Roosevelt's classic *Winning of the West,* John Clark Ridpath's multivolumed *History of the United States from Aboriginal Times to Taft's Administration,* Edward Eggleston's *A History of the United States and Its People,* and Anna M. B. Marti's *A Story of the Cuban War.*[15]

If Henry's hobbies were intellectual, Christine's were aesthetic. She had the soul of an artist. Instead of seeing only grass, water, and cattle on the ranch, she viewed "A type of gallardia, a bronze plant with a yellow and black center . . ., clumps of white marguerites . . ., prolific gray-green sage . . ., sunflowers that seemed to be different by years . . ., the soapweed bell-like flower of the yucca . . ., the winecup flowers of Indian root . . ., the purple flower of the loco weed . . ., and yellow flowers that made carpets on the slopes whose botanical name I never knew." She even thought that the tumbleweed "had its good points. It has a nice bloom."[16] Until 1912, however, she had never thought of herself as an artist.

Her mother and a local art teacher helped to remedy

Christine Hitch holding her first child, Marjorie, in 1911. Corral is in background.

that oversight. When Christine was expecting her first child in 1911, her mother had just proved up her Kansas claim and no longer had to live on it. She and Erma decided to join Christine on the Coldwater in order to be of some help. Matie assumed much of the household work and remained with Christine for more than two years after the birth of Marjorie. In the meantime, Guymon had acquired an art teacher. In 1910 a homesteader's wife named Claudia Moore, who had studied at a Chicago art institute, formed an art club in Guymon to paint china. Charlie Hitch's wife, Josie, and Dr. W. H. Langston's wife were among the club members. By early 1911, Mrs. Moore had students working in oil, pastels, watercolors, charcoal, clay, tapestry, woodcarving, and cartooning, as well as china at her studio. By then, her many students included Charlie's daughters Dot and Mary.[17]

Matie reminded Christine that two of her aunts had been artists and encouraged her to take lessons. Christine said that there simply was no time for such things, but Matie insisted that she learn to paint. Besides she and Erma would take care of the household chores in her absence. Christine finally agreed to take lessons. Getting to town, however, posed a small problem. Although Henry and J. K. jointly owned an automobile, Christine had not yet learned to drive. Besides, J. K. would not have approved using the automobile in that way. It was used only for going to church, family outings, and business. Consequently, once a week Christine hitched a black mare named Old Doll to the family buggy and drove the ten miles to Claudia Moore's studio in Guymon.[18]

She learned quickly and began painting landscapes on tapestries, china, and pillow cases, as well as on canvas. She found a local market for her pillow cases and sold them for $2.50 each. In fact, she sold enough of the vel-

Christine at her easel with some of her paintings, ca. 1914. Courtesy of Roberta Hambleton.

vet pillow tops to buy Henry a Christmas gift of a minia-ture golden steer with tiny diamond eyes; he wore it for years as a watch fob. Christine loved to paint landscapes, but Henry persuaded her to start putting livestock into her pictures. Thus she began to paint scenes on the Cold-water of Hereford cattle, horses, and buffalo. A visiting banker from Kansas so admired one painting that he paid Christine $250 for it.[19]

The young artist had less time for painting as her re-sponsibilities grew larger. Three children were born into the closely knit family, each delivered by Dr. Langston: Marjorie Christine on May 22, 1911; Joyce Helen on Octo-ber 12, 1916; and Henry Charles, Jr., on April 5, 1918.

Henry was a devoted father. After coming home at night from his usual hard day's work, he held the babies in the family rocking chair. His son was especially fond of being

One of Christine's early paintings of the ranch's registered Herefords on the Coldwater.

rocked while Henry sang the lullaby "By low, my laddie, by low." When the father stopped singing occasionally to catch his breath, "Laddie" opened his eyes and emphatically demanded, "BYE LOW! BYE LOW!" This command performance continued until the "audience" fell asleep. After a heavy snow Henry would accompany the children up the slope behind the house, put them in dishpans, and shove them off for a thrilling ride downhill. As they grew larger, he made a sled big enough for all three children and pulled them by saddle horse with his lariat rope looped on the horn. At night he often gathered the children around a kerosene lamp to read articles and books about Alaska or the north-country novels of Jack London. As they grew older, the children assembled around the kitchen table with Henry and Christine to play dominoes or the new popular Parker Brothers games of the late 1920s and early 1930s, such a Rook or Monopoly. On Sunday afternoons Henry and the children often walked along the Coldwater looking for Indian arrowheads.[20]

"Laddie" was shortened to Ladd as the baby grew to boyhood. Both he and Joyce were climbers. On one occasion, Ladd drove large nails into a tree in order to reach an upper branch. He and his sister then climbed up the tree using the nails for toe holds, but could not get back down. Henry had to bring them down by ladder. Joyce, whom Henry called "Little Tyke," climbed to the top of the sixty-foot windmill tower behind the house when she was three years old. Henry's half-brother Robert climbed to the top and brought her down.

Ladd and Tyke loved to ride horses. When cutting cattle near the house, Henry often pulled the little girl up into the saddle behind him. With his right arm curled behind the child, he set to work gently, urging the horse into jackrabbit starts and turning sharply to separate individual animals from the herd. It was a rough ride but an exciting one for Joyce. When she was old enough for her own horse, Henry gave her a pony. She never lost her love for horses, and throughout her youth she helped Henry ride pasture and work cattle.

Marjorie never quite developed a fondness for horses, possibly because of the antics of her pony, also a gift from Henry. His name was Billy Button. He was a Shetland, little bigger than a Saint Bernard, and endowed with all the erratic characteristics that have made that breed infamous. He was stubborn, unpredictable, smart, and just plain mean at times. One cold day as Marjorie started to school on the pony, he threw her off. She later remembered, "It was too cold for him, and in an effort to change my mind, he bucked me off. He had me convinced, but not my Mother. She insisted I get right back on, and make him behave." She succeeded, but did not relish the experience. On another occasion she led the Shetland to a fence stile and climbed up the steps to get on. As she tried to mount, Billy Button turned his head toward her, grabbed her bonnet in his teeth, and yanked her off.[21]

Marjorie leaned more toward the domestic side of life rather than the outdoors. She enjoyed helping her mother with the household tasks and was constantly at her side cleaning house, making beds, washing clothes, sewing, and cooking. By the time she was ten, she was preparing family meals by herself.

The children played the usual childhood games of the time. Among their favorites were "blindman's buff," "go sheepy go," and "annie over." They especially enjoyed swimming in the deep pools of the Coldwater. On warm Sunday afternoons Henry and Christine often took the children down to the stream. Henry assumed the role of instructor, teaching them to float and to dog paddle.[22]

Marjorie started to school in a new, white, one-room frame schoolhouse built about 1916 to replace the building that J. K. Hitch had hauled by wagon from Hugoton, Kansas, for Henry and his generation. Her first teacher was her aunt Erma Walker, who had been one of Christine's students at the Pleasant Valley School. Erma lived with the Hitch family that one year and drove the two and a half miles to school each day with Marjorie in a buggy. The next year Erma left for college, and Marjorie began riding Billy Button to school. In winter the child wore a woolen bloomer outfit, designed by Christine, that fitted over her clothes. Within a few years Joyce and Ladd were accompanying their older sister to class by horseback.[23] Perhaps the most unusual aspect of the school was that most of the students were cousins of the Hitch children. They included Mary Elizabeth Hitch, the daughter of George and Willa, and Betty Pearl and Jean Stratton, daughters of Tom Stratton who had married Mae Westmoreland and had bought the ranch from his brother-in-law Charles Westmoreland.[24]

There were the usual childhood illnesses and accidents. All three Hitch children came down with scarlet fever. Ladd was only about two years old and suffered a great deal with swollen lymph glands in his armpits. One time Marjorie got hold of a big styptic pencil used to treat open wounds of horses. Thinking it was hard chewing gum, she put it into her mouth. Christine rushed her to a doctor in Guymon. He prescribed vinegar for the painfully swollen mouth, but when she drank the acetic solution, its reaction with the base compound of the styptic pencil caused a frothing which almost choked the child. On another occasion Marjorie dropped to the floor of the barn from a lower rung of a ladder onto a nail sticking through a board, completely piercing her foot. No other adult was on the place, so Christine had to pull the child's foot off the nail by herself.

The Hitches rarely called on a doctor despite the fact that Henry's cousin W. H. Langston was their family physician. Dr. Langston was usually called only to deliver Christine's babies. For the most part Christine relied on home remedies. When Marjorie landed on the nail, her mother washed the wound with hot water, soaked the foot in kerosene, and applied a poultice of fat meat to "draw the poison out."

A number of other popular remedies of the time were used as the need arose. Quinine was taken for headaches and rheumatic pains. Calomel capsules were used as purgatives and for indigestion. Because Ladd was a hearty eater, he probably was the primary beneficiary of calomel in the family. Of course, castor oil was indispensable for almost all internal complaints. Christine recalled that "if you stumped your toe, even the doctor gave you castor oil."[25]

The Hitch family continued to be active in the Methodist Church. Henry's mother had been responsible for bringing the first Methodist missionary to what became Texas County. The first church was established on the Coldwater at the town of Roy. A small frame church was built at Guymon in 1903 to unite Methodists from Roy and the new town into a single congregation called the Roy-Guymon "charge." Circuit riding ministers preached to the membership until 1905 when the church got its first full-time pastor, Innis D. Harris. By 1910 the Guymon Methodist Episcopal Church, North, had 114 members and was paying its minister A. E. Henry an annual salary of $800. The cornerstone for the new building at Fourth and Roosevelt streets was laid in 1912. The church was completed at a cost of $16,000 in the late summer of 1913 and opened with a week-long dedication.[26]

On Sundays the Hitch family would climb into its usually dependable EM&F automobile (some said that the name stood for Every Mile Fix'em), and drove into Guymon for Sunday school and church services. Although Christine was a Baptist, she chose to follow Henry to his church. He never asked her to do so, nor did he attempt to convert her to Methodism. Nonetheless, she accompanied her husband to church for fourteen years and reared their children in the Methodist faith. Christine had never really been comfortable as a Baptist. She later recalled: "As a child it worried me terribly, this once-in-grace and preordination. It worried me that somebody wouldn't get to heaven." She was attracted by the Methodist emphasis on grace and love. When Marjorie was thirteen, she became the first of the children to join the church. It was then that Christine decided to become a Methodist herself. Walking to the front of the sanctuary that Sunday morning, Christine and Marjorie, hand in hand, joined the church.

The family's faith remained an important part of their lives. Christine served on the mission committee and taught the sixth-grade Sunday School class. Henry could never be coaxed into teaching a class. Like his father, he was given more to thinking than to talking. Because of his business skills, he was appointed to the finance committee, on which he served until his death.[27]

In the cattle business Henry Hitch proved to be an excellent manager. He did not confine his activities solely to running J. K. Hitch's ranch. Before he and Christine were married, he had slowly been acquiring cattle and land of his own, and he was plowing his profits from livestock into more land and cattle. By February 1914, before his thirtieth birthday, his assets included 860 cattle, 150 horses and mules, and 2,850 acres of land. His total assets amounted to an estimated $85,750, while he listed liabilities totaling $34,500, leaving a net worth of $51,250. He was already exhibiting characteristics that would earn him the reputation of being a tenacious, fearless "plunger." Like his father, he was not afraid to go into debt in order to expand his land holdings. Besides, the steady increase in prices for agricultural commodities and land values in the period from 1900 to 1920 appeared to justify his optimism.

Among his liabilities in 1914 were notes to the City National Bank of Guymon, the Citizens State Bank of Liberal, and, largest of all, some $16,000 to the Drovers National Bank of Kansas City. In addition, again like his father, he borrowed money on unsecured promissory notes from several friends and relatives.[28]

Perhaps because of the few months he spent at the business college in Winfield, Kansas, Henry showed a tendency, unlike his father, to diversify his financial interests into areas other than cattle and land, for he bought stock in various speculative companies. His first stock venture was in the Crystal River Marble Company of Colorado in 1907 or 1908. He acquired some 3,300 shares at ninety cents a share. To make the purchase, he borrowed $3,000 from a Liberal bank. Knowing almost nothing about marble, except that it was used to make statues, ice cream parlor tables, and the decor of such prestigious buildings as banks, Henry bought the stock because Ed Guymon invested in the marble quarry. Guymon first interested Brice Keating, Henry's brother-in-law, in the proposition. Keating acted as agent and earned a commission of ten cents on each share of dollar stock sold. It was Brice who sold the stock to Henry, less his commission. During the honeymoon in Colorado, Hitch took his bride over the continental divide to see the quarry. He brought back a chunk of marble and had it carved into a small buffalo, to be used as a paper-weight, at a cost of $6.50. That was the only tangible yield he ever realized from this investment. Later he summed up that early venture with his characteristic lack of verbosity, "Well, I lost it all."[29]

Henry scorched his fingers in his investment in marble, but this did not sour him on stock issues. It only made him more cautious about putting a large amount of money into speculative ventures. During the next few years he acquired stock in a number of fruitless companies, but rarely sank more than a hundred dollars or so into each proposition. One of these was the Cannon Ball Motor Company of Texico, New Mexico, organized in 1917, and its sister concern Western Tire Manufacturing Company. President of both was James D. Hamlin, an eminent West Texas jurist. Henry bought one hundred shares of Cannon Ball and twenty-seven of Western Tire for one dollar a share. This ambitious project set out to raise $10 million for capital investments in order to manufacture automobiles, trucks, and farm tractors.[30]

The founder of Cannon Ball, C. A. Roberson, built a three-story brick office building at Texico. A few models of Cannon Ball cars were manufactured in the East and shipped to Texico. The company also began construction of a tire plant at Farwell, Texico's sister city on the Texas side of the state line. But America's entry into World War I halted the flow of money and the construction. No automobiles or tires were manufactured at Texico or Farwell. Roberson was convicted of mail fraud in Kansas, and that ended any prospects for developing an automobile industry on the High Plains.[31]

The most numerous stock issues held by the young rancher were in oil and gas exploration companies, among them The Lucky Darner Oil and Gas Company, Kay Oil Company, Lincolnville Oil and Gas Company, Beaver Oil and Gas Company, and Kansas-Oklahoma-Wyoming Petroleum Company. His largest investments were in the Beaver Oil and Gas Company of Liberal, Kansas, in which he owned 130 shares at ten dollars per share, and the Peco Producing and Refining Company of New Mexico, in which he held 1,000 shares at a dollar each. One concern, the Northwest Oil and Development Company of Denver, Colorado, sold Hitch, as well as J. B. Langston, who also acted as agent for the company, lots on which the company proposed to drill for oil in Big Horn County, Wyoming. An official of the company sent Henry a letter in 1916 congratulating him "upon being connected with at least one oil enterprise that will make good."[32]

Hitch's interest in oil investments was understandable in view of the rising price of petroleum at the time. The growing number of automobiles on the roads created a demand for fuel. Moreover, public enthusiasm about the opening of such oil fields as Spindletop near Beaumont, Texas, in 1901, Glenn Pool near Tulsa in 1905, and El Dorado, Kansas, in 1916, only whetted everyone's desire "to be in on" the next discovery field in the mid-continent region. Oil fever spread to the Oklahoma Panhandle in 1919 when the Beaver Oil and Gas Company began drilling east of the Hitch Ranch and the Home Development Company started a well north of Texhoma. Leases and rumors of leases spread like searing summer wind through the short-grass country.[33]

It was not in oil-company stock that Henry Hitch made money in this period, however; rather it was in cattle and land. As J. K. had done in the 1890s, Henry bought cheap cattle from a number of places farther west and southwest. Taking his saddle and blanket with him, he would travel by train to a terminal near prospective livestock, rent a horse for a dollar a day, and ride out to ranches for a look. Some time usually was spent with the owner of the stock, making offers and counter-offers while leaning on a corral fence or squatting nearby and scribbling in the sand while trying to reach a compromise price.

Henry heard about cheap cattle in Colorado in 1912, caught a train and returned a few days later with 300 steers that cost him forty-one dollars a head. Another time he traveled to El Paso in the hope of buying Mexican stock. There a rancher told him that some excellent cattle in Phoenix were being sold at bargain prices. Henry then went on to Phoenix only to discover that the steers were in Winslow, Arizona. Because there was no north–south railroad across Arizona, he had to go back to El Paso, change trains to Albuquerque and catch a "westbounder" for Winslow. He was weary of train rides by the time he reached his destination, but the trip was worth it. He bought 300 yearlings at thirty-three dollars a head. Henry ordered cattle cars and loaded them himself. Forty is considered the average number of grown cattle to be put in a car. Thus he would have needed eight cars for cows, but the yearlings were smaller and he may have tried to get by with seven or even six cars. As the train moved across New Mexico that night, some animals kept "getting down," which may have indicated overcrowding. To prevent them from being trampled, Henry crawled from one cattle car to another, twisting tails and pushing at the bawling mass in order to get this one or that one to its feet.[34]

The young rancher's good fortune in those early years was aided partly by the outbreak of World War I in August, 1914, which drove the prices of agricultural commodities higher and stimulated the entire American econ-

Working cattle
on the Hitch Ranch,
ca. 1912.

omy. The devastation of farm lands in Europe created new markets for American farm products, particularly meat and wheat. Between 1914 and 1918 beef exports climbed from 6 million pounds to more than 514 million pounds a year. Moreover, the annual per capita consumption of beef in the United States increased from about 62 pounds in 1915 to more than 75 pounds by 1918, despite the government's attempt to discourage beef consumption at home in order to increase supplies for America's soldiers and allies. The price of "plain" range cattle was about $7.65 per hundredweight in 1914, but the same sort of animals were bringing $14.50 per hundredweight four years later at the Kansas City stockyards.[35]

As noted earlier, Henry Hitch's net worth in 1914 had been $51,250. The next year, the number of cattle he owned was 1,445 compared to 860 the previous year. His land holdings had climbed from 2,850 acres to 5,944 acres. His total assets were estimated at $179,675, while his liabilities stood at $74,275, giving him a net worth of more than $100,000. Between 1915 and 1920 his net worth increased from $100,000 to $242,000. The increase was attributable to his acquiring more cattle and land, as well as to the increased valuation of both because of rising prices. Between 1914 and 1920, Henry bought an additional 9,240 acres in Texas County. During the same period the number of cattle he owned climbed to 1,715. Whereas in 1915 he had placed a valuation of $60 a head on his mother-cow herd, by late 1919 the market value was $75 a head. Land prices also had climbed. Hitch held a section of land in Hansford County, Texas, that would have brought $6,400 in 1914, but by 1920 it was worth $12,000, an increase of 87 percent.[36]

The increase in cattle prices encouraged Henry and J. K. to buy registered Hereford cows and bulls to improve their commercial herds. They were not the first to bring registered Herefords into the region. Pioneer rancher Fred Taintor, originally from Connecticut, was probably the first to introduce registered stock to the Oklahoma Panhandle. In about 1884 he had brought in 50 purebred Hereford cows and a few registered Hereford bulls and confined them to a fenced pasture near his headquarters on Taintor Creek, but registered beef cattle still were so rare in the region that other stockmen took note of the new Hitch livestock. By 1915, Henry had 10 registered bulls. The next year he added 15 more bulls and 45 registered cows. All were probably of the Domino strain. By the end of the war Henry alone owned 200 registered Hereford cows valued at $250 per head.[37]

The Panhandle rancher improved not only his herd but also the quality of his feeds as well. Formerly, only prairie hay cut from the Coldwater meadows had been used as winter forage. Shortly after the turn of the century, J. K. Hitch had started growing some alfalfa in the valley. By 1915, Henry was feeding not only alfalfa, but also some grain sorghums and cottonseed "cake," a high-protein product of the cottonseed oil mills bought in the bordering cotton belt.[38] Much of the cake had to be hauled by wagon all the way to Texas Camp, about thirty miles from Guymon. Those long hauls were combined with hauling wheat to Guymon during threshing season (another enterprise that the Hitch family had entered during the war). John Knight, who began working for Hitch before World War I, later recalled that he often made that wagon run with his two wheel mules Jumb and Loke and leader mules Red and Blue. One day would be spent loading the grain onto the wagons with a hand scoop, driving to the Coldwater headquarters, and spending the night there. Next day the wagons rolled into town, unloaded the grain at the elevator, put on a load of cottonseed cake from a boxcar or warehouse, and drove back to the ranch house before dark. After a second night there, the wagons headed back toward Texas Camp.[39]

One of the problems in feeding was to get the forage to the livestock during such severe winters as those of 1911–12 and 1918–19. During those winters snow began falling in November or December and lay on the ground until February or March. In 1911 several Hitch cattle were trapped against a cliff by heavy snow and died there. The deepest snowfall of this period began on December 16, 1918. By the time it let up the next day, waist-high shocks of grain sorghums in the fields were covered with snow almost as deep. During such foul weather cake and hay were loaded onto sleds and pulled by the big mules to cattle stranded in the pastures and canyons.[40]

Looking south across the Coldwater Valley in the winter, ca. 1910. Stone house is in foreground. Haystacks are in the center background.

An occasional hired hand looked for any excuse not to venture outside during such cold weather. One such man, nicknamed "Bat Eye" by the other men, usually became suddenly ill as the mercury dropped, and he remained in bed during the day. Bat Eye feigned sickness once too often one morning. Henry grabbed the big bottle of castor oil from the medicine chest, picked up a large spoon as he went through the kitchen, and marched into the bunk room. "We must do something before you get any worse," Henry said. And in his best bedside manner, Hitch poured the large spoon brimful of the concoction and forced it down his patient's throat. The man appeared to be completely cured the next day, and was never ill again as long as he worked for Henry Hitch.[41]

Despite the increased production of beef during the war, the government stressed that civilians, including the meat producers themselves, should patriotically consume less red meat. Christine recalled that a popular song of the time went like this: "My meals, they are meatless. My bed, it is sheetless. Oh! How I hate the Kaiser!" She often served chili to the cowhands and family on those "meat-less" days. Unknown to the hands, Christine made the chili from jack rabbits bagged by Henry. One cowboy, who was especially fond of the chili but ignorant of its ingredients, had often boasted that he had never eaten jack rabbit and never would. When the same man complimented her for the tasty dish, Christine's smile almost broke into a laugh.[42]

A more significant impact of the war was that Henry and J. K. diversified their operations by plowing up grass-land on the flats (the plains above the valley) and engaging in farming. The reason for such a basic change in the econ-omy of the growing Hitch empire was easy to grasp. As with cattle, the price of wheat also began climbing. Whereas in 1913 Oklahoma elevators were paying $0.76 a bushel for wheat, the price reached $2.54 in May 1917. In the spring of 1919 it had dropped slightly but still stood at $2.10 a bushel. Until the beginning of the war the Panhandle was not a part of the wheat belt. Some grain had been planted as early as 1899. In 1903 a banker from Tyrone, G. W. Riffe, sowed a few acres. The same year, or possibly the next, a Texas County farmer named "Windy" Johnson harvested twenty acres and attempted to thresh the grain, first with a chain broomcorn seeder, and then with a pitchfork. In 1912 one of the first custom threshing outfits in the Panhandle was owned by Earl and Euel Dixon.[43]

The wheat acreage in Texas County increased in direct ratio to the rise in wheat prices. The entire Panhandle had only 206 acres of the grain in 1899. Texas County had

48,000 acres of wheat in 1909, most of which had been planted by newly arrived farmers. By 1920 the county was producing 1,727,000 bushels from 151,380 acres, making it one of the largest wheat-producing counties in Oklahoma.[44]

Henry and J. K. first began planting wheat in about 1915. By 1916 Henry alone had 1,000 acres sown. At the time, the ranch had no wheat-farming implements. Local farmers were hired to sow the wheat and custom threshing outfits using steam traction engines harvested the grain.[45]

Diversification best describes the Hitch Ranch by 1920. The cattle and wheat operations were in marked contrast to the earlier days of the open range. Yet they were complementary. Winter wheat made an excellent pasture for livestock, and if cattle were pulled off the fields by early spring, a maximum grain crop would still be harvested. More important, the movement into farming operations demonstrated Henry Hitch's adaptability to changing economic conditions. In so doing, he established a tradition that would become one of the most significant characteristics of the empire on Coldwater Creek.

6.   "The First Time I Went Broke . . ."

Henry Hitch once said: "The first time I went broke, every-body knew about it. The next time I went broke, only my banker and I knew. The last time, only I knew." The early 1920s was a period when "everybody knew."[1] As Hitch had been aided by the rising price of cattle, wheat, and land—caused by the increased demand for agricultural products in World War I—he was hard pressed by an economic downturn not of his own making in 1921. The end of the war brought an economic depression that began first in the industrialized eastern part of the nation in the middle of 1919 and spread west through rural America by 1920. As unemployment increased, consumption of beef declined.

Cattle that had brought $14.50 per hundredweight in 1918 were selling for $8.80 in 1920 and $6.15 in 1921. Cows in neighboring New Mexico were bringing as little as $5.00 per hundredweight by 1922.[2] When the Charles Dixon Commission Company of Kansas City sent its week-ly report to Hitch on October 31, 1919, the market was $0.25 to $0.50 cents lower on all kinds of cattle with "the kind selling around $14.00" taking a drop of $0.75. Six months later two carloads of J. K. Hitch's steers sold for $10.10.[3]

Prices for all agricultural commodities declined sharply. Many farmers and ranchers were unable to pay either their bank loans or their taxes. According to a story circulating through the Great Plains at the time, a Montana farmer who was being pressed to pay his debts wrote his banker: "I got your letter about what I owe you. Now be patient. I ain't forgot you. Please wait. . . . If this was judgment and you were no more prepared to meet your Maker than I am to meet your account, you sure would have to go to Hell." When the Texas County tax assessor published the 1922 list of delinquent land taxes in the local newspaper, two and one-half pages of fine print were required.[4]

Because of these problems several large ranchers in the Texas Panhandle found it more profitable to sell their land to small farmers rather than to raise cattle. Ranch lands that once had pastured thousands of cattle, herds owned by such men as George W. Littlefield, C. C. Slaughter, and W. E. Halsell, were broken up into cotton farms. A similar trend occurred in the Oklahoma Panhandle. On June 21, 1921, Howard M. Stonebraker, owner of the 130,000-acre Anchor-D, stated that as a result of "bad luck and the downward trend of meat prices," he was declaring voluntary bankruptcy. He listed assets of $1,390,000 and liabilities of $1,037,618. Even before this depression the severe winter of 1918–19 had dealt him a death loss of $150,000 worth of cattle.[5]

Stonebraker and his partner E. W. Zea, an officer of the Commerce Trust Company of Kansas City, made plans to plat much of the spread into farms. Zea arrived in Guymon during January 1922 to confer with Texas County Agent J. B. Hisey, who had suggested that the land would be suitable for small dairy and wheat farms. Zea liked the idea and announced that most of the ranch would be cut into 500 farms. By August 1922 the land had been platted; the sale had been turned over to R. G. Keller and I. L. Ennis of the Oklahoma and Texas Land and Loan Company. These 260-acre farms could be purchased on credit over a span of twenty years at 6 percent interest. In lieu of a down payment the buyer could elect to build his home and make certain improvements on his land. No payment was required until the end of the first year. Diversified farming was emphasized. The Guymon newspaper editor claimed that not only "the cow, sow and hen have a natural range here," but also that, "it [cutting up the Anchor-D] will be the greatest boost for Texas County."[6] Smaller ranchers who went broke were not as fortunate as H. M. Stonebraker. They were left with little or nothing for their years of hard work.

In 1928, Henry and Christine drove to Arizona to visit her brother. They stopped in Winslow, Arizona, late one night at a rooming house only to discover that the operator was an old acquaintance. She was the widow of a cattleman who once had been foreman of the CCC Ranch and who had fallen on hard times prior to his death. The scene touched Henry to the quick. He later reminisced, "It was quite a set down for [his] widow to have to make a living running a rooming house."[7]

Like other ranchers, the Hitches fell on hard times. One day while Henry and Uncle Charlie were discussing their mutual financial problems, three-year old Ladd "loped" into the room on his imaginary horse brandishing a small quirt. "Well, how are you making it in these hard times, Ladd?" asked Charlie. Without breaking his gait, the child replied, "They ain't no hard times for me," as he whacked his leg with the quirt and trotted out of the room.[8]

In the summer of 1923, with two years of low prices behind him, Henry Hitch estimated his assets to be $448,050 while he listed liabilities of $223,500, leaving him a net worth of $224,550, or about $20,000 less than in 1920. A year later Hitch's net worth had dropped to $94,525. By the summer of 1925 that figure had declined to $32,540, a sum less than his financial worth in 1915. His liabilities remained fairly stable at about $224,000, but his assets in land, cattle, and wheat continued to slide downward.[9]

Wheat that had sold for a record high of $2.54 per bushel in 1917 plunged to $1.42 in 1920 and $0.85 per bushel in 1921. To add to the wheat farmer's woes, the cost of threshing, which had risen during the war because of inflation and manpower shortages, remained high. By 1921 custom threshing outfits were charging about 20 percent of the wheat's value as contrasted to about 10 percent before the war. Some farmers responded to this cost-price squeeze by joining with their neighbors in buying small threshing machinery that they owned cooperatively and used only for their own needs. Others, like Henry Hitch, moved toward greater efficiency and lower cost-of-acre production through the new technology in gasoline tractors and combines that had appeared in the wheat belt during the war.[10]

The first combines (a shortened name for "combined header and thresher") had appeared in southwestern Kansas in about 1914 and spread into the Oklahoma Panhandle. In 1917 an implement dealer in Tyrone reportedly sold 190 Holt combines. About 1920, J. K. Hitch bought a Holt. The machine cut a twenty-foot swath and was pulled by twelve horses or mules. Power was furnished by a "bull wheel." The price of the implement ranged from $1,800 to $2,000. But the big machine was hard on animals. John Knight recalled that it took only one day to break "bronc" mules when they pulled that combine. "It wore 'em out," he said.[11]

In the early 1920s, Henry bought a McCormick-Deering Number 3 from implement dealer J. B. Langston. The machine was brought to the ranch unassembled by wagon

Some of J. K. Hitch's mules.

from Texhoma. It took about a week to put the combine together at the edge of a wheatfield. The most important component of this new implement was the four-cylinder gasoline engine that powered the machinery. No bull wheel was necessary and only eight horses were needed to pull the combine. At first Knight hitched up only four mules. When his "skinner" mounted the seat, Knight cranked the engine. The sudden noise startled the mules, and they ran away pulling the combine in a half circle through the field. The grain wagon, which was normally driven alongside the combine to catch the threshed grain flowing from a spout, could not keep up with the spooked animals. The horses hitched to the wagon were also frightened of the noisy apparatus. Only a few minutes passed before the mules tired of their heavy load and came to a halt. Thereafter Knight had to "engine-break" all the mules in a similar way before using them.[12]

By the late 1920s, Henry owned three or four combines,

Threshing wheat on the Hitch Ranch, ca. 1916.

six trucks for hauling grain, and a number of the most modern grain drills and disc-plows. Moreover, tractors had replaced the mules. In 1929 he owned an estimated $10,000 worth of farm implements, a sizeable investment for the time.[13]

Mechanization only partly offset the trend toward low prices. Ironically, it also contributed toward overproduction, the cause of depressed prices, by giving farmers the equipment to farm even larger parcels of land. Between 1920 and 1929 wheat acreage in Texas County increased from 151,380 to 475,478, an expansion of more than 300 percent.[14]

In addition to low prices Henry's fortunes also suffered from a severe hail damage to his wheat crop in 1924 and 1925. When Christine wrote her sister of their difficult straits, Erma responded, "To think that your wheat should be lost again this year. Where is the justice in that? It is wrong to question but often we cannot but do that. Henry has such tenacity. . . . After losing all of the steer money, then to have courage to go back. I can't understand him."[15]

Erma was not the only one who admired Henry for having the tenacity and determination of a bull. Others who knew him noted that beneath his quiet, almost stoic, exterior lay an inner man of dogged determination who refused to be beaten. Ladd in later years once observed that his father "had the innate ability to voice pessimism and yet remain optimistic." If he commented on a bad turn of events, he often coupled it with humor. Once when a hailstorm ruined his wheat, he said that the moisture it brought was still good for the grass! If affairs looked hopeless, he kept his business to himself, rarely sharing with Christine more than the good news if he could help it.[16]

Henry Hitch was actually in worse financial shape than Stonebraker, whose liabilities were 74 percent of his assets in 1921. By 1925, Henry's liabilities constituted 87 percent of his assets. Unlike his fellow rancher, Hitch was not about to quit. When the Coldwater cattleman in his twilight years recalled this quandary, he stated flatly, "I never would have declared voluntary bankruptcy!" Even then Henry was optimistic about the future of the region. By early 1921 he had already offered to buy the Coldwater ranch from his father, but J. K. turned him down with the advice that because of the depression Henry would never be able to pay for the land.[17]

Tragedy followed adversity when J. K. Hitch became ill with heart disease in 1921. He and Josephine went to Kansas City to consult a specialist on May 16, 1921. After the examination, the physician gave him some medication, but prescribed nothing else except possibly some rest. The couple planned to catch a train for Guymon the next day. J. K. awoke just before seven the next morning. The sun was shining through their hotel window. J. K. arose from the bed, walked across the room, and pulled down the shade. He took only a step or two back toward Josephine before he suddenly clutched his chest in pain and fell across the bed. He died within minutes without regaining consciousness.[18]

His body was shipped back to Guymon where it lay in state at the house on Academy Street. Numerous friends and neighbors came to pay their respects. In the tradition of those times, photographs were taken of the body in the coffin. The arrangements were by Star Hardware, which handled everything from the coffin and hearse to opening the grave. The funeral was conducted at the Methodist Church, and interment was in the Guymon cemetery.[19]

J. K. had prepared his will in September 1918. He left one-half of his estate to be divided equally among the four children by his first wife (Henry, George, Della, and Josephine). The other half went to Josephine and her three children (Robert, Harry, and Kathryn). J. K. designated Josephine, Henry, and George as joint executors. The estate of the native Tennessean who had lived on the High Plains for more than forty years was extensive by any reckoning. His three ranches in Seward County, Texas County, and Hansford County totaled more than forty-seven square miles (30,223 acres). Value of all personal and real property was estimated at $410,330, with liabilities of $212,677.[20]

After the funeral Josephine and both groups of children met at the Coldwater headquarters to discuss the disposition of the land. Despite $212,000 in debts against the estate, Henry was opposed to selling any of the land to satisfy creditors. He believed that long-term credit arrangements could be worked out. His younger brother disagreed with him. George was not a plunger like Henry. He had never gone as deeply into debt as his older brother. He wanted to sell enough of the land to pay off all of the estate's indebtedness. After much discussion the family agreed to sell only the Texas land. They also decided to divide the land in the near future between the two groups of heirs in such a way that Josephine and her children would take the Kansas land, while Henry, George, and their sisters would retain the Coldwater ranch.[21]

After the sale of the Hansford County holdings the estate still carried an indebtedness of about one hundred thousand dollars. The heirs subsequently incorporated the estate temporarily as the Hitch Land and Cattle Company. Meanwhile, the Coldwater ranch was leased to Henry with an understanding that he would eventually buy out the other heirs.[22]

Henry Hitch cut his expenses to the bone. His family had never lived "high on the hog." Their clothing, buying habits, and automobiles did not distinguish them from many of their less-affluent neighbors. Now it was necessary to live more frugally. They drove old cars, in particular a faded red one that in earlier days had affectionately been named Patricia. Now in its old age with frequent breakdowns, it was referred to simply as "Old Pat." Much of the food for the family and hired hands was raised on the Coldwater and canned in gallon jars by Christine. The large garden was irrigated by windmill, and the orchard, the first that J. K. had planted on the ranch, usually yielded abundant fruit.

The only vacations were those annual occasions when Henry, Christine, and the children piled a few pieces of luggage into "Old Pat" and headed for Trinidad, Colorado, to visit Christine's mother, stepfather, and other members of her family. Henry loved the Rockies and usually took a day or so to drive into the mountains from Trinidad. The forests and snow-capped peaks refreshed and strengthened him. When Christine wrote her sister that they planned to drive to Colorado in the summer of 1926, Erma wrote back, "It will be lovely for you all to have the time in the mountains. They feed Henry like manna."[23]

Henry loved trees so much that he created his own miniature forest. When he had moved Christine into the stone house in 1910, he had begun planting more trees around headquarters. The annual tree plantings continued until the houses and outbuildings were almost hidden by a large grove of elms and cedars. A hired hand stated that his boss was more lenient with a worker who wrecked a piece of machinery than one who collided with one of his trees.[24]

In those difficult years Henry Hitch began instilling a fear of poverty and a mind for business in his children. He taught them to save their money and to buy only those things that were necessary. When young calves were orphaned, he usually turned them over to the children, who in turn fed them by bottle until they were weaned. When the calves were sold, the money was invested in cattle or stocks (securities) in their names. Henry owned no more than two or three suits at a time and usually wore those only to church, funerals, and weddings. When he needed a new suit, he agonized over buying what he regarded as a luxury.[25]

The children took their studies seriously. Their grades in school ranged from good to excellent. Ladd demonstrated an early tendency to write well. One of his themes, written at about age twelve, was entitled "The Dark Attic of A Deserted House." At the time he noted that "it took me 30 min. to write it." Although the novice used an excessive number of adjectives, as duly observed by his teacher, he showed imagination, organization, and forcefulness.[26]

Minor sibling conflicts are a normal part of family relationships, and the Hitch family was no exception. Christine's great capacity for showing love and patience exerted a softening influence on the children's occasional quarrels. In the spring of 1930, however, Christine went to Wichita, Kansas, for surgery and was away from home for a few weeks. The role of mediator then fell on Henry's shoulders. In any conflict between son and daughter, a father may feel the need to protect the daughter. Ladd wrote to his mother complaining of the "unequal" discipline he believed his father was meting out. According to Ladd's complaint, Henry scolded him more often than he did Joyce. Moreover, Joyce was allowed to stay in bed ten minutes longer than Ladd. On one occasion during a brother-sister spat, Ladd wrote: "Daddy was all over me in a second and he looked like a mad bull charging. He . . . gave me a licking while he was bawling me out. I'd a million times rather be up there with you with nothing to do than be down here dodging charging bulls, etc."[27]

The normal workload of the ranch usually sapped enough of the children's energy to prevent scuffling around the house. Marjorie helped her mother with cleaning, sewing, washing, ironing, and cooking. Joyce and Ladd were becoming cowhands and spent more and more time in the saddle. At age twelve Ladd was thin, weighing only about a hundred pounds. Henry gave him a spirited sorrel horse named Derby. When not working cattle with the horse, Ladd "rode pasture," keeping an eye out for sick or missing stock and new calves. He carried a .22 caliber pistol primarily for shooting at rattlesnakes and rabbits. In the early morning or late afternoon he occasionally jumped a coyote. Like Henry in his younger days, Ladd could not resist the chase. Horse and rider melted into a dead run across the prairie as the crafty animal darted ahead. Gradually

Derby would close the gap, and Ladd would begin firing. Usually the coyote escaped after the boy discharged the last shell in his revolver, but occasionally the proud hunter brought down his prey.

Ladd began working in the hay meadows when he was twelve for thirty-five cents a day. At four in the morning he wrangled the horses and mules from the horse pasture to the corral where they were fed their morning oats. His first job was driving the team that pulled the ropes for the big hay stacker. Those horses furnished the power for elevating each load deposited by the buck rake to the top of the stack by means of ropes and pulleys. At the top a worker, called the stacker, positioned each bunch of hay for balance. By the time Ladd reached fourteen he was driving the sulky rake that windrowed the hay. It was pulled by two small mare mules named Buck and Flossy, a bay and a buckskin, just behind the mower. Henry himself often drove the mower. He enjoyed seeing the alfalfa or grass drop behind the sickle bar and sniffing the aroma of new-mown hay.

Henry placed Ladd in charge of the haying crew when the boy was sixteen years old. Then Ladd began driving the big buck rake that gathered the hay and pulled it to the stacking machine. Haying season was the hardest work of the year. The crop matured in the summer. No matter how tightly a man buttoned his collar, sweat mingled with chaff always seemed to work down his shirt. Both men and animals rested during the noon hour. While Ladd and the hired hands took their meal in the field, shaded by the wagons, the horses and mules were fed another ration of oats. After eating, the men lay down under the hay wagon for a short nap. A good way to awaken everyone quickly was to shake the wagon by hand while yelling "Whoa!!"

Many a man, including Ladd, received a nasty bump on the head from time to time while attempting to get from under the wagon while still drowsy.[28]

A near tragedy, which could have destroyed lives as well as the historic stone house, occurred shortly before noon on December 26, 1928. Marjorie had brought a can of gasoline into the kitchen to clean a dress. While the volatile liquid was drying on the garment, ten-year-old Ladd walked into the kitchen intending to roast a marshmallow on the range. When he struck a match, the dress burst into flames. Christine heard the children's cries for help and ran into the kitchen. Flames had jumped to the oilcloth wallpaper but had not yet reached the gasoline can. She led the children outside and yelled toward the outbuildings in the hope that some hired hands were nearby. John Knight and another hand named Packer were working on a truck when they heard her voice. The men ran to the house. Knight saw that the fire was in the kitchen and asked Christine, "What's on fire?" When told it was gasoline, he sprinted into the bunkroom, pulled a spread from a bed and dipped it into a tank of water on the porch. Knight then draped the covering over his head and entered the smoke-filled room. Flames had not reached the can. Quickly he threw the wet spread over the container and rushed it from the house. He and Packer completed the task by dousing the walls of the kitchen with buckets of water. Within a few minutes the flames were extinguished. The children's burns, though painful, were not serious. The only casualties were Marjorie's dress and some wallpaper.[29]

Henry's finances began to improve in 1926, as prices for livestock began to move upward. In the period 1926–1928 prices advanced about $3.00 per hundredweight to a high of $10.59. Even more encouraging for Hitch was the fact that prices for his grass-fed cattle climbed at a faster pace than prices for grain-fed livestock. His indebtedness by the summer of 1925 stood at $229,000. In the spring of 1926 he had reduced that to $169,850. He estimated his net worth in 1927 to be $184,580, a significant gain over the previous year.[30]

During both low and high prices stockmen were using more registered breeding stock to raise heavier animals. Henry had been raising registered Herefords since about 1915. In the early 1920s he helped form the Texas County Breeders Association to promote the sale of registered cattle. The group held the first of several annual auction sales in 1922. That year the Coldwater rancher sold seven registered bulls and one registered heifer to local stockmen at prices ranging from sixty to one hundred dollars a head. Almost every year thereafter, he sold some animals at the sale. However, his herd was primarily for his own use in producing bulls for his commercial cattle. He did take pride in the beautiful white-faced animals, however, and usually showed some of them at the Texas County Fair. The Hitch herd of seventy-five to one hundred registered cows became one of the best-known purebred groups in the Panhandle.[31]

By the mid-1920s an important part of Hitch's operations involved a partnership with a cattleman named Frank Atkinson, whose Diamond Springs ranch was situated near Burdick, Kansas, in the lush bluestem grassland of the Flint Hills. The relationship between the Atkinsons and Hitches had existed for more than two decades. When J. K. Hitch was alive, Frank's father, William ("Uncle Billie") Atkinson, had visited the ranch often to buy steers for fattening in the Flint Hills before marketing them in Kansas City. The elder Atkinson said on many occasions that he "liked cattle better than people." When in

Texas County, he was always the house guest of Henry and Christine, and frequently he hunted ducks on the Coldwater or at Texas Lake. In 1919, Henry borrowed $15,000 from the Atkinsons, who carried the note during the depression of the early 1920s. In about 1925 Henry formed a partnership with Frank Atkinson whereby they bought steers, wintered them on the Coldwater, then shipped them to Daimond Springs for summer pasture. Hitch and Atkinson owned 1,542 two- and three-year old steers by 1927. Two years later that number had expanded to 1,935 head.[32]

It was not easy to finance the kind of operation in cattle, wheat, and land that Henry was running. The absence of long-term sources of credit for Panhandle cattlemen had long been a problem. To make matters worse, when livestock prices began to drop in 1920, the Federal Reserve Bank discouraged loans to stock growers by instituting the practice of rediscounting cattle paper at progressively higher rates than other kinds of loans, a policy that lasted about a year. In other words, larger livestock loans required higher interest rates than smaller loans. That practice made little sense to angry cattlemen who were losing money. They needed long-term, low-interest money to enable them to ride out the low-price cycle. Matters reached such a critical point for stockmen that the War Finance Corporation, created by the federal government during World War I, began loaning funds to cattlemen through various agencies outside the banking structure.[33]

Henry Hitch's sources of credit, like his father's, were primarily outside of commercial banking. He borrowed long-term money from friends, relatives, business associates, insurance companies, farm mortgage companies, and banks (when possible). Credit with acquaintances and mortgage companies had been used extensively by J. K.

Headquarters of Frank Atkinson's ranch at Diamond Springs, Kansas.

Hitch. For the most part, Henry used the same lines of credit employed by his father. From time to time his promissary notes were held by Guymon businessmen William Fletcher and I. E. Cameron, his cousin J. B. Langston, and the Atkinsons. Until 1928, Henry also borrowed a few thousand dollars from banks in Guymon and Liberal, Kansas, as well as from the Farmers State Bank in the Atkinsons' hometown of Burdick, Kansas. Federal Land Banks in Kansas and Texas and the Texas General Land Office were still other creditors that Henry used solely for the purchase of land in those respective states.[34]

The Coldwater rancher added another creditor in 1926. Frank Lindsay owned a ranch on Palo Duro Creek. He had settled in the Panhandle in 1902 after ranching in Mexico and southwestern Oklahoma. In the language of cattlemen, he ran a "steer operation." Lindsay bought lightweight yearlings, weighing three hundred pounds or so, from Mexico and pastured them for two or three years until they reached a thousand to twelve hundred pounds. After he sold his steers in 1926, he loaned Henry $15,000 and leased some grassland to him.[35]

Henry Hitch's most important financier was a Kansas City mortgage banker named Charles Baird, who had also been J. K.'s biggest creditor. Upon the elder Hitch's death in 1921, Baird held first mortgage notes totaling $90,600 on J. K.'s land. By the bottom of the depression in 1924, Henry owed Baird $100,000 but reduced that figure to $45,000 by 1926. When Christine in later years was asked about Baird, she remembered him as a kindly man. One time he sent her a sixty-pound can of honey as a gift. "Why," she recalled, "the Hitches borrowed so much money from Mr. Baird that we must have broken him." It is not known if Baird went broke, but by 1929, Henry's obligations to the mortgage banker for some reason had been shifted to the Liberty National Bank of Kansas City, Missouri, and the Commercial National Bank of Kansas City, Kansas.[36]

Despite his indebtedness business looked good to Henry Hitch in 1928. That year cattle prices topped $10.00 per hundredweight. Although wheat prices had plunged below $1.00 a bushel in 1921, the market was somewhat better in 1925 when the price rose to $1.46 at Oklahoma elevators. In 1928 it was $1.27 per bushel, still furnishing a fair margin to make a little money. Moreover, Frank Atkinson was holding $55,000 due Henry from profits on their Flint Hills steers.[37]

During these seemingly auspicious times, Hitch completed his purchase of the Coldwater ranch from the other heirs. Acquisition of the ranch added an indebtedness of $100,000, but increased his assets on paper to more than $650,000. On January 1, 1929, Hitch estimated his net worth to be $372,700, an apparently comfortable margin between liabilities and assets for any businessman.[38]

In the meantime Henry bought parcels of land bordering the ranch, as well as some nonadjacent tracts with good water and grass. When he encountered real estate agents Henry Wacker or E. E. McDaniels on the streets of Guymon, he told them to "see us" if certain desirable lands were placed on the market. McDaniels later recalled that he sold land to Henry as early as 1917 and continued to act as his agent in acquiring choice acreages over the next thirty years or so. By 1929 Hitch's Texas County holdings consisted of 15,400 acres of grassland, including the original ranch of his father, and 3,600 acres of farmland planted in wheat. In addition, he owned 800 cultivated acres in Seward County, Kansas, and 160 acres in Hansford County, Texas.[39]

The stone house continued to stand as the sentinel of

the Henry C. Hitch Ranch, but it underwent some changes. In 1920 Christine suggested to Henry that they put in a bathroom. At first Henry was lukewarm to the idea. The outhouse, about a block away and connected to the back porch by a long wooden plank walk, had been sufficient for him, nor did he complain about bathing in a washtub. But Christine felt strongly that the family needed an indoor facility. Consequently Henry hired a plumber and carpenter to install a bathroom just off the lower front hall. Within days after the project was completed, Henry had become so accustomed to the new world of indoor plumbing that he never would wish to go back to using the wooden plank walk.[40]

The house itself was enlarged about the same time the bathroom was added. The roof was raised six feet to make a large attic and an enclosed sleeping room above the front porch. The attic was reached by means of stairs that could be raised or lowered. For counterweights Henry used large blocks of salt normally deposited around the pastures for cattle to lick. In 1925 he began building an office on the east side of the house. Because it was difficult to find a good local stonemason at the time, the addition was not completed until 1929. The kitchen, on the north side of the house, was enlarged at the same time. Now sandwiched between the kitchen and the office, the old spring house was converted into a laundry with a half bath.[41]

The lighting system also underwent improvement. Henry installed an electrical generating plant to replace the kerosene lamps. The unit, powered by a one-cylinder gasoline engine, was housed in the basement. Every night Henry descended the stairs to crank the sometimes difficult-to-start contraption. A loud "POP-chug-chug-chug-chug-POP" indicated that the family would enjoy

The stone house after remodeling, ca. 1921.

the electric lights that night. But the "POPS" shook the house and the engine was a fire hazard. In a few years Henry replaced the generator with carbide lamps that provided as much light, but without the noise.[42]

Like the stone house, Guymon was also growing and changing. In 1921 the city installed an electrical generating plant and a water works complete with water tower. At about the same time Henry's cousin J. B. Langston branched out from hardware, automobiles, and farm implements to open the Church & Langston Electric Store, Guymon's first electrical appliance retail business. One of the new no-credit grocery stores, J. R. Paine's Cash and Carry Grocery, was opened for business. Ed T. Guymon divested himself of his last retail business in the town named after him. In February 1922 he sold his Star Hardware Company to three partners headed by Clarence T. Harryman, of Enid, Oklahoma, who changed the name to Guymon Mercantile Company.[43]

The new electric lights attracted farmers and ranchers to town on Saturday night like moths to a lantern. Saturday had long been the biggest day in town for merchants and farmers in rural communities. Now the electric lights on storefronts, movie marquees, and lampposts gave farm families who drove into town in the afternoon cause to remain until the late hour of nine or ten o'clock. Cars clogged the main street while drivers searched in vain for parking places. Men gathered on the sidewalks or sat on the curbstone in clusters of two to four to discuss the weather ("When's it gonna rain?" "How much did you get?"), the crops ("Do you have a good stand?" "How many bushels will your wheat cut?"), cattle ("Did you get a good price for your steers?"), and all the other topics most important to men who made their living from the combination of soil, weather, and market conditions.

Movies had become popular entertainment rather than an amusing curiosity. Ladd, Marjorie, and Joyce went to the Royal Theatre, which had replaced The Dime's one- and two-reel movies with longer feature films running from one to one and a half hours. Occasionally, Henry and Christine went to a movie. Christine especially enjoyed the frolicking exploits of Mary Pickford and Douglas Fairbanks on the silver screen. On the other hand, Henry liked "westerns" in which William S. Hart or Tom Mix championed the cause of justice against badmen with six-gun and Winchester.[44]

As the decade of the twenties neared its close, few men of J. K. Hitch's generation remained. One of the most colorful was Henry's beloved Uncle Charlie Hitch. In his late fifties, Charlie was not an old man by modern standards. In many ways, however, he was a world apart from Henry's generation. He believed that the new youth had little sense, and he mourned the passing of the old-time cattle industry. In an effort to keep the memory alive, Charlie held traditional Fourth of July celebrations similar to those earlier affairs at McDermott's Grove.

These Fourth of July barbecues and rodeos on his ranch were among the annual highlights of Texas County. Aside from the pens for livestock used in the rodeo, there were no other enclosures, such as chutes, or even an arena. Automobiles and wagons were parked to form a football-shaped enclosure. Much of the spectators' entertainment centered around the saddling of broncs in the open without benefit of chute. Ladd recalled that his Uncle Robert Hitch (J. K. and Josephine's son) mounted such a horse. When the men holding the bronc released him, rather than "bucking" immediately, the animal bolted across the enclosure at a dead run. Then the horse suddenly "swallowed his head," "broke in two," and sent Robert "above the tree tops."

On at least two occasions Charlie held an old-fashioned roundup in Cedar Canyon southeast of his ranch. Most of the participants were the old-timers who still had the strength to rope a steer, stretch him out, and brand him. Charlie brought up his ancient chuck wagon for the event and cooked dinner over a campfire. Years later people still remembered the sourdough biscuits served from his Dutch oven. Men often wore their oldest hats and clothes, while the women, in old-fashioned long calico dresses, converged on the scene to eat with their menfolk and reminisce.[45]

Although the Hitch business had become a large, complex operation, Henry's books for the most part were still kept in his khaki shirt pocket. Among the Henry C. Hitch

One of Charlie Hitch's "roundups," ca. 1920s. Courtesy of Mary Hitch Hall.

Papers is a small brown very-worn notebook measuring about three by five inches. In this Henry noted the wages of each hired hand (he had a page for each man) as well as those who did custom work. For example, he noted that one hand in haying season had worked forty days for $3.00 a day, five and one-half days at $2.00, and twelve days at $1.55 for a total of $149.60. After deducting $82.85, which the hand owed Hitch for groceries, supplies, and advances in wages, Henry noted that he owed the man $76.75. In another instance he jotted down John Knight's custom plowing of 520 acres at $0.90 an acre and 480 acres at $0.80 cents.

The rancher also used the notebook to record the wheat plantings and yields on his various parcels of land, the buying and selling of cattle, the number of cattle in each pasture, the number of railroad cattle cars ordered, and even nonbusiness memos to himself. He liked cowboy ballads, and on the back cover is the note: "Brunswick 131B. A Home on the Range. Vernon Dalhart." Vernon Dalhart was the show-business name of a professional singer from Texas named Marion Try Slaughter. He took his professional name from two northwest Texas towns, and in the late 1920s became one of the first solo country music singers in the nation just when records of such music were beginning to sell, mostly in rural areas and small towns in the South and Southwest. Brunswick was a record company. Henry obviously jotted down the record number with the intention of purchasing the "Home on the Range" recording. Another notation carried the name of a meat market in Gunnison, Colorado, and the words: "long steer horns with head horns 7 ft 11 in tip to tip straight across."[46]

A mounted longhorn steer's head, which he hung above his desk, remained one of Henry's prized possessions. Like

The "roundup crew" assembles around Charlie Hitch's 7̲ chuck wagon for a noon meal. Charlie is seventh from the̲ right. Courtesy of Mary Hitch Hall.

"Home on the Range," William S. Hart, and his growing collection of Indian arrowheads, it was a symbol of his heritage.

7. Hard Times and Black Dusters

As the crisp, cold dawn broke over the Coldwater on New Year's Day, 1929, there was no indication that another round of hard times was just around the corner. At that moment Guymon reflected a growing optimism of future prosperity. Advertisements in the local newspaper heralded the new Essex automobile with "76 improvements" at a price of only $695, and advised readers to "Get Your Atwater-Kent Radio Now" at Walden Battery and Electric Company. Only a couple of weeks before the New Year arrived, the editor boasted that on any Saturday from 9:00 A.M. to midnight, scarcely a parking place could be had on Guymon's newly paved Main Street. Indeed, many shoppers had to park a block away from the town's business district.

Between 1924 and 1929 a number of improvements had been made in the development of the town. The sewage system had been completed. The old municipally owned electrical generating plant had been replaced by a larger dynamo, owned by the franchised Inland Utilities Company, a subsidiary of the Fairbanks-Morse Company. Gas lines had been laid by the Texas County Gas Company. And the Guymon Telephone Company had announced plans to replace the old hand-crank phones with a central battery system (subscribers would need only to lift the phone from the hook to signal the operator). The civic improvement program, however, was not yet completed.

Most of Guymon's primary streets were still unpaved, but the *Panhandle Herald* had launched a crusade to remedy that problem. Its motto was "Let's Pull Guymon Out of the Mud in 1929."[1]

To Henry C. Hitch, the times appeared to be ripe for starting into the new business of townsite development. In 1926 the Rock Island Railway had begun to lay track from Liberal, Kansas, to Amarillo, Texas. The new steel ribbons would provide southwestern Kansas and the central Oklahoma Panhandle with a direct connection to Amarillo, primarily for shipping wheat to market. By 1927 Texas County produced more wheat than any other county in the state. In 1929 the county yielded more winter wheat than any other in the nation. The older Rock Island line ran southwest across the Panhandle to a junction with the Fort Worth and Denver City Railway at Dalhart. Thus freight and passengers not only were subjected to a dogleg route to Amarillo and points south but also had to change trains at Dalhart, Texas. The Rock Island planned to establish towns every ten miles along this new route. J. L. Williams, of Amarillo, probably representing a group of investors, platted a number of townsites along the line, including Hardesty, which first was named JoWilliams in honor of the promoter. However, local people did not like the cumbersome name, and it was renamed Hardesty after the old ghost town a few miles away.[2]

Ten miles south of Hardesty, barely on the Texas side of the line, the railroad cut through land owned by Henry and his brother George. Williams approached the Hitch brothers in early 1929. He offered to pay for platting and publicizing the town in exchange for sharing in the proceeds of lot sales and the right to use the Hitch name for the settlement. Thus the Hitch Brothers Townsite Company was chartered and Hitchland was born. A few lots

Henry Hitch in 1931.   Christine Hitch in 1931.

were sold and some houses sprang up in what recently
had been a wheatfield. Henry and his farm manager John
Knight established the Knight Oil Company, a wholesale
and retail business marketing gasoline, kerosene, and
petroleum products. Henry and George also formed the
Hitch Grain Company and invested more than $47,000 in
building an elevator.[3]

These ventures signaled the beginning of almost a decade of financial setbacks for Hitch. The stock market
began its nose dive toward a disastrous crash in October,

1929. By the middle of 1930 the Great Depression settled on the nation, and prices for everything from wheat and cattle to automobiles plunged. Hitchland was caught in the squeeze. During the second quarter of 1930 the Hitch Grain Company lost $2,746. This loss reflected more than $7,000 in credit extended by the company to its customers.[4]

By June, 1930, wheat had fallen to eighty-four cents a bushel. Two years later farmers were receiving only twenty-nine cents a bushel for the grain on Oklahoma markets, and the Chicago Board of Trade reported that wheat futures were at the lowest level since the commodity exchange had opened for business in 1848. Overproduction added to the depressed market when farmers harvested a bumper crop in 1931. In Pratt County, Kansas, one farmer simply decided to sell his 155 acres of wheat standing in the field at public auction because the price of harvesting and shipping it was below the cost of production. An angry man named Forrest Kennett refused to accept twenty-seven cents a bushel for a truckload of wheat in Bucklin, Kansas. He stuck a picture of a jackass to each side of his laden truck. One picture was labeled "wheat farmer" while the other bore the caption, "[federal] Farm Board" (an agency created by Congress in 1930). Kennett drove through town with the tailgate down, dumping his wheat on the streets.

Time magazine noted that the large wheat crop overflowing elevators throughout the Great Plains did not "deter the tycoons of southwestern wheat production."[5] In 1931 on the nearby Texas High Plains a former California businessman named Hickman Price was farming 23,000 acres with 50 tractors, 25 combines with his name painted on the sides, and 100 trucks. During harvest he employed 250 men who slept in mobile quarters pulled from field to field. Price even used 5 full-time messengers on motorcycles to coordinate his operations. The scale of his enterprise was gigantic—as was his accumulation of debts. By 1932 he was broke.

Henry Hitch's operations were not as large as those of his bankrupt Texas neighbor, but he and his brother George were the largest wheat farmers in Oklahoma, with some 4,500 acres in their partnership yielding 85,000 bushels in 1931. By the end of that season Henry was not bankrupt, but he was hurting. Moreover, his customers at the Knight Oil Company were unable to pay for the fuel, oil, and grease that they had used to plant and harvest the crop. In later years John Knight sadly recalled, "They was good honest men—the names on them books—but we didn't get no money from them because they couldn't pay it. Some of them died; some of them moved away. So there you are. You get into a hole once in a while." Knight and Hitch went out of business in 1931. At the time, the remaining inventory was debt-free, and the company had $1,200 in the bank. The men split the money and sold the business.[6]

Hitchland failed to develop primarily because of the depression. There were other obstacles, however. The state boundary on the northern edge of town was at issue, and a more accurate survey in late 1931 moved the line about 100 yards south, putting most of the town in Oklahoma. Those whose lands were now in Oklahoma had to pay a $1.25-per-acre preemption fee to the federal government. Finally, the number of farmers in the market area declined sharply in the next few years, casualties both of the depression and the Dust Bowl. Townsite promoter J. L. Williams wrote to Henry in early 1931: "I believe that Hitchland will make a good town, if the State Line question is ever worked out satisfactorily and the surrounding country settled up with farmers rather than big land owners, especially to the south and east, where the trade would naturally come from instead of going to Guymon." But that was only a hope. Williams was more realistic when he lamented, "Local as well as general conditions have been against us all the way through."[7]

If wheat farmers and townsite developers were beset by hard times, so were cattlemen. Between 1929 and 1931 the price for cattle fell 53 per cent. Henry sold a consignment of steers at Kansas City for $9.25 per hundredweight in April of 1931. In August that year another bunch of his steers sold for $7.75 per hundredweight. By the fall of 1931 prices were down to $5.50. In January, 1932, prices were slightly better when the Coldwater rancher sold a load of 1,200-pound steers at the Kansas City Stockyards for $7.50. By the end of 1932, however, prices had fallen to the unbelievable low of $4.94 per hundredweight.[8]

To make matters worse Henry's partner in Kansas, Frank Atkinson, owed him at least $65,000 and perhaps as much as $100,000, his share of their steer profits. Hitch had left the sum in Atkinson's possession for his use. The Kansas rancher, however, lost the money in the depression. Henry understood Frank's predicament all too well and did not press him for payment, but the partnership ended for the time being.[9]

Henry Hitch's finances then went from bad to worse. At the beginning of 1930 he estimated his net worth at $455,350. By the close of 1931 that figure stood at $191,450—with no ray of hope on the economic horizon. Hitch still owed several old debts to friends and relatives, including Frank Lindsay and William N. Fletcher. From time to time he was able to pay some of the interest on these notes. In addition, the indebtedness on his land stood at $163,000. His combined debts by late 1931 totaled $284,350. Balanced against his assets of $475,800, the debt

in ordinary times would have been manageable, but circumstances were far from ordinary. Prices for almost
everything, including land, continued to fall, gnawing
away at everyone's assets. Moreover, resources in agricultural lands could not be readily converted into cash
because the market for farm and ranch properties had all
but dried up.[10]

Most of Hitch's creditors did not press him. An exception was the Farmers State Bank in Burdick, Kansas,
which, like most financial institutions, was also hard
pressed for cash. When Henry sent the bank $500 to pay
the interest but none of the principal on his note in September, 1931, the assistant cashier wrote, "We do not want
to be mean about this note, but business is business and if
we can't meet the requirements of the banking department
[of the state of Kansas] it just means that much more
grief for us and we all have enough of it at this time."[11]

Despite his quiet inner strength and his optimism, Henry
Hitch had his back against the wall. When in 1932 he
bought a three-bottom plow from Guymon implement
dealer Orville Nash, he could only pay $65 down. His
friend Nash financed the remaining $200. In later years
Christine Hitch vividly recalled: "You could absolutely
make no money at anything. Anything you tried was a
loss and I even got to thinking, 'Are we rather dumb to
just stay here and plod on and on?' But everything we had
was here and you couldn't sell to anyone." Christine had
always bought groceries from a Guymon store on credit.
Once a year Henry paid the bill. By 1932 the grocery bill
was more than a year old. One Saturday when Christine
drove into Guymon to do her food shopping, the grocer
informed her that he could sell her no more supplies until the bill was paid. Shocked and hurt, she drove back to
the ranch. That evening when Henry came in, she quietly

told him of the bad turn of events: their grocery credit had been cut off.[12]

In a few days Henry walked into a Guymon bank where he already owed about $2,000. Of course, the note was past due. According to one source, he asked the banker for a $50 loan to put food on the table. Knowing of the rancher's massive indebtedness, the businessman replied that if it were not for Christine and the children he would not lend him a penny. Because the family needed groceries, however, he agreed to loan Henry $10, but said that he never expected to see the money again. About this same time Hitch became so discouraged that he informed the chief officer of one of the Kansas City financial institutions holding a large part of his mortgage that the bank might as well take over the ranch because he could not "make a go of it." The sympathetic banker responded that if Henry could not make a profit on the ranch, nobody else could! The offer was politely refused.[13]

One consoling factor for Henry and Christine was that their neighbors were in as bad, if not worse, financial shape. Ladd Hitch recalled that there were only two people in Guymon who drove new automobiles during the depression. One was Cousin J. B. Langston, a good businessman who was conservative with his money and always had some cash on hand. The other was a local bootlegger.[14]

The only alternative was to stick it out. Henry was no longer young. Approaching his fiftieth birthday, a time when many men of financial stature begin to anticipate at least semiretirement, he faced the most trying years of his life. The family adjusted to the hardships in several ways. Christine and Marjorie "made over" clothes for everyone to make do with their existing wardrobes. Ladd and Henry shot jackrabbits, and Christine once more made chili from the meat. The windmill-irrigated garden became more important. Ladd and Joyce commuted daily to Guymon High School in 1932 and 1933 in an ancient car suffering from mileage fatigue. Breakdowns were frequent. One door latch was worn out, but Henry fixed it by looping several strands of baling wire through the window and around the doorpost. Instead of using expensive alcohol as antifreeze for the radiator, Henry used the cheaper kerosene.[15]

During these difficult days, the Hitches and their Methodist brethren paused to celebrate the forty-fifth anniversary of their church. The Reverend R. L. Wells, with the help of the members, wrote and staged a pageant entitled "The March of the Kingdom in a Frontier Country." The first act began with the story of Mary Westmoreland Hitch, Henry's mother, pleading by letter to the Methodist conference for a preacher. Performed in June, 1933, the play featured many actors, among them Joyce Hitch and her cousin Elizabeth, George's daughter, who were descendants of charter members.[16]

As if the depression had not already taken enough of a toll, a drouth emerged to parch the land in 1931. By 1934 the southern Great Plains were enveloped in the Dust Bowl, a term first used by a newspaperman to describe conditions in the Oklahoma Panhandle.[17]

Blowing dust in the late winter or early spring was nothing new to the region. On February 19, 1910, at a Farmers' Institute conducted at Goodwell, Oklahoma, one James Weiser delivered an address on "The Blowing of Soils and How to Prevent It."[18] As early as 1889, when very little of the area was under cultivation, a severe dust storm had occured. The editor of a newspaper in Tascosa, Texas, reported the event in this way: "It . . . swept up the country all in one great big continuous sweep. In the latter half of the night it piled dust heaps everywhere, and sent it through and into the tightest of buildings. . . . It filled the river with sand till it went temporarily dry."[19]

Although such conditions were not unknown in the past, this drought, combined with high winds and millions of additional acres of land brought under cultivation since the beginning of World War I, produced more dust storms of greater severity than the region had previously experienced. In 1932 and 1933 as many as forty "dusters" peppered the Panhandle.[20]

The outlook was bleak in the fall of 1933, when Congressman (later Governor) E. W. Marland, of Oklahoma's Sixth District, asked Secretary of the Interior Harold Ickes about the status of proposed federal reclamation projects for the area. Ickes replied that the Oklahoma Panhandle "probably would have to be abandoned and the land turned back to public domain." According to the Secretary, the inhabitants could be resettled in the Imperial Valley of California. Ickes' statement set off a wave of indignation throughout all of Oklahoma. Governor William H. ("Alfalfa Bill") Murray angrily responded that, with the help of his National Guard, "they won't move one damned man out of this state." A newspaper editor in Buffalo, Oklahoma, stated that "a temporary drouth" did not require abandoning the Panhandle's otherwise productive farms. One farmer voiced the feelings of most residents when he proudly proclaimed, "This is as good as anybody's country and we are not going to leave."[21] Secretary Ickes extricated himself from the controversy within a few days by declaring that any exodus would have to be voluntary.

The drought continued to worsen over the next few years. Severe dusters continued for the next three years, but none were as bad as the one that rolled into the Pan-

handle on the afternoon of Palm Sunday, April 14, 1935.
A woman in Beaver recalled:

The day had been comparatively clear up to that time. Without warning, there loomed in the north, coming over the sand
dunes at a high rate of speed, a monstrous cloud of dust that
resembled huge rolls of black smoke, reaching from the ground
high into the air, and extending from east to west like a solid,
insurmountable wall.

As the storm approached the Coldwater, Ladd ran outside with his box camera and took three successive shots
of the phenomenon.[22]

Two Methodist ministers drove north out of Beaver that
afternoon in a new Ford coupe. Their destination was
Liberal, Kansas. About twelve miles north of town they ran
into the storm. The driver stopped the car and headed it
south to prevent the windshield from being sandblasted.
The men sat there for three hours. Dust penetrated the
cab so thickly that neither man could see the other. They
breathed through their handkerchiefs with difficulty. One
man feared they would smother. As the black "duster"
finally subsided, the driver started the car but could not
budge the vehicle. Drifts of sand had almost buried the
tires. One minister subsequently came down with an ail-
ment that local physicians had never seen before: dust
pneumonia.[23]

The worst of the Dust Bowl lasted from 1934 through
1936, although normal rainfall did not return to the Panhandle until 1938. Dust sifted into houses and drifted along
fencerows. On many farms sand reached the top of barbed-
wire fences. Fine dust even penetrated watch cases and
stopped the mechanisms. On the South Plains of Texas a
car engine suddenly stopped running in the midst of a
dust storm. The keen eye of a mechanic found that glass

had formed on the ignition points. In another freak occurrence a stack of grain-sorghum bundles caught fire when static electricity caused by a duster jumped from one to another parallel wire anchoring the stack. If such storms were hard on people and disastrous to crops, they were hell on livestock. Joyce's horse, the one Henry had given her when she was a child, died from ingesting dust. A rancher in eastern New Mexico commented, "Cattle are worse after one of these than . . . after a blizzard."[24]

The Hitch family awakened many mornings to find thick layers of dust on their blankets. Henry tried sealing the windows of the stone house with caulking to keep out the dirt, but it was impossible to prevent the fine dust from filtering through. During one storm the family ran to the cellar in an effort to escape the worst of the dust. One of the girls cried during the ordeal because she had dreamed the previous night that they had been smothered to death by such a storm.[25]

Black dusters were terrible experiences for those caught in them, but to the eye of an artist they were something more. As one storm rolled in slowly from the northwest during an otherwise calm spring day, Christine noted the "magnificent display of form and color." The mass consisted of "immense columns of different colors of soils—reds, browns, blacks—reaching high in the air and rolling in a majestic formation, but fearfully and steadily like doom descending on helpless humanity."[26]

In 1933, in response to the disastrous impact of the Dust Bowl, the federal government established the Soil Erosion Service (later renamed the Soil Conservation Service). The service selected H. H. Finnell, director of the Oklahoma Agricultural Experiment Station's branch on the campus of Panhandle A. and M. College at Goodwell, to supervise an experiment in soil conservation in nearby

A black duster rolls over the Coldwater, 1935. Note wagon in foreground.

Dallam County, Texas. Finnell used drought-resistant cover crops, terracing, contour plowing, and other means to halt the blowing soil and conserve the little moisture available. He was so successful that, when the federal government established a regional office at Amarillo, Texas, for the Soil Conservation Service in 1935, he was appointed director. In that position the soil scientist supervised conservation activities for most of the southern Great Plains.[27]

Henry Hitch was well acquainted with H. H. Finnell, the agricultural staff of Panhandle A. and M. College, and the work of the branch experiment station. In 1932, before Finnell began his work with the Soil Conservation Service, Hitch bought a three-row plow for the purpose of contour plowing to diminish soil erosion during high winds. He closely followed Finnell's work. One of the service's experiments was in the contour plowing of native grassland to prevent rainfall runoff. The area in Texas County selected for the study did not include the Hitch Ranch. Nevertheless, in the spring of 1935, without the benefit of a government subsidy, Henry contour-plowed two hundred acres on the north side of the Coldwater just above the valley itself. At first he spaced the twin furrows thirty feet apart, but when he added 1,800 acres more to his program in 1936 he narrowed the spacing to fifteen feet. Henry believed that, by conserving more rainfall, the furrowed land would yield more grass and carry more cattle.[28]

Before Hitch's pasture-conservation program, drought and low prices drastically reduced his ranching operations. Henry sold his entire herd of registered Herefords and most of his other cattle. By October, 1933, he had reduced the number of cattle on the Coldwater to a total of 721 head, including calves. The next year he sold most of his remaining stock, including 72 cows from his Seward County, Kansas, place. The cows were sold to the federal government for twenty dollars a head under the Emergency Cattle Purchase Program.[29]

That program was initiated in 1934 by the Agricultural Adjustment Administration (AAA) of Franklin D. Roosevelt's New Deal. Its objective was to decrease the supply of cattle in order to raise prices. Under the cattle-purchase plan the government paid stock growers prices ranging from four dollars per head for baby calves to twenty dollars for animals in good health and more than two years old. Sick, old, or badly starved cattle were shot to death by local men hired by the government. Livestock in good health were shipped to government feed lots or canning plants. The Federal Emergency Relief Administration then canned the finished beef and distributed it to the poor through relief programs. This "cattle kill" was not a source of pride for cattlemen. Many felt revulsion when they witnessed the shooting of young calves. Those who had long taken pride in their independence and individualism resented the idea of any kind of government aid. But, as John Knight put it, "You get into a hole once in a while." With all its drawbacks the program did reduce cattle numbers about 17 percent.[30]

Grass-roots administration of the federal program was in the hands of a local appraisal committee that worked closely with the county agent, an employee of the state agricultural extension service. Committeemen were nominated by the local AAA administrator and the county agent, and they were appointed by the secretary of agriculture. Henry Hitch was appointed to the Texas County appraisal committee. When a stock grower applied to the county agent to dispose of his cattle, two members of the committee and a veterinarian had to evaluate the livestock and set the price. The owner then moved the cattle to a designated area in the county on a certain date either for slaughter or for shipment. The average price paid for an animal was about fifteen dollars.

Henry was active as an appraiser. Occasionally he came across an emaciated cow that he believed was worth more than the government-designated ceiling price and bought the animal himself. One time he sent Ladd to the southwestern part of the county to pick up a half-starved Jersey milch cow. When the boy arrived, pulling a trailer, he found a crazed animal foraging only on green Russian thistles. The cow was not easy to load, but after a steady diet of hay for a few weeks she became the family's primary milch cow.[31]

Aside from rain, Hitch's greatest need was for emergency long-term credit. By 1932 the banking system throughout the nation was on the verge of collapse and could not help itself, much less a broke cowman. A small-town banker told a farmer at the time that banks were like cows: "If you don't feed 'em, they go 'dry.'" Dry banks had neither deposits nor money to lend. Neither did Henry's hard-pressed neighbors. The Coldwater rancher turned to the only alternative, a newly created agency of the federal government called the Reconstruction Finance Corporation (RFC), established under the administration of Herbert C. Hoover in 1932. The RFC primarily loaned money to business corporations and banks, but it also established twelve Regional Agricultural Credit Corporations (RACC). The RACCs borrowed money from the RFC to loan, in turn, to ranchers and farmers who still had some assets. Between 1932 and 1934 the RACCs loaned out $261 million.[32]

In the past Hitch had sealed grass-lease agreements with a simple handshake. In all his dealings with his old Kansas partner Frank Atkinson, he and Frank had never signed a written contract.[33] By contrast, the RACC required Henry to file written contracts in its office on all grazing or lease agreements. Moreover, the agency reserved the right to disapprove the contracts. Finally, the manager wanted Hitch to give him a written report from time to time on the condition of his livestock. To a man who had been in the cattle business all his life and who now owned one of the largest ranches in the Panhandle, such bureaucratic advice and paper work must have appeared less than useless.[34]

A more suitable solution to the credit problem was the creation of Production Credit Corporations (PCC) in 1933 to supercede the RACCs. The Farm Credit Act of 1933, which created PCCs, also provided for the gradual liquidation of the RACCs over the next few years. The primary difference between the two approaches to agricultural credit was that while the RACC had only its regional office in Wichita the PCC established local Production Credit Associations (PCA) in most counties. The PCAs elected their own boards of directors and staffed their offices with local people. Moreover, they were less bureaucratic. Initial capital, as with the RACC, was supplied by long-term, low-interest government loans.[35]

In October, 1932, Henry Hitch made application to the agency. The RACC of Wichita, Kansas, subsequently loaned him $41,000. The loan probably saved the Hitch Ranch, but at the cost to Henry of having to endure some government red tape. No creditor had ever before advised Henry Hitch on how to run his ranch. An old joke among ranchers told of a banker who once offered some advice to a cattleman. The old cowman curtly replied: "I s'pect that you don't know any more about the cattle business than I know about running a bank, so I'll make a deal with you. If you'll keep your nose out of my business, I'll stay out of yours."[36]

The RACC ignored this custom and freely dispensed advice through correspondence with Henry. On June 22, 1933, after a field inspector for the agency reported that the grass in Seward County was in poor condition, the manager of the Wichita RACC suggested that "you feed some cake" and offered to lend Hitch more money for that purpose. In another instance the assistant manager recommended that "you feed additional cake if necessary." When three steers died, the inspector suspected blackleg. The manager then chided the rancher: "I am wondering if you vaccinated these yearlings this spring. If you are not positive that they were vaccinated with good serum, it might be well for us to gather them up and give them another shot."

In 1935, Henry Hitch refinanced his RACC loan through the newly established Guymon Production Credit Association, which served much of the Panhandle. The officers included Frank Conner, of Keyes, president; A. E. Pittman, of Beaver, vice-president; and Elmer L. Fickel, of Guymon, secretary-treasurer. The directors were John Gardner, of Guymon; George Dysinger, of Hooker; and R. J. French, of Boise City. The cattle market improved slightly in 1935, and the Coldwater rancher began restocking his range. Although still in the midst of the drought, his pastures were somewhat improved as a result of liquidating the herd the previous year. Hitch sold enough livestock in the fall of 1935 to pay more than $18,000 of the RACC loan before refinancing the remainder through the PCA. The PCA loans over the next few years gave Henry the kind of flexible credit he needed to buy cattle and feedstuffs and greatly lessened the financial pressures that had plagued him throughout the depression. The relationship with the new credit agency proved so advantageous that from 1935 to the present members of the Hitch family not only have been major borrowers of the Production Credit Association but also have served on its board of directors.[37]

If the Production Credit Association provided Henry Hitch with the means to stave off bankruptcy, the discovery of natural gas in the Panhandle previewed a more prosperous future. As early as 1904 geologist Charles N. Gould, of the University of Oklahoma, had noted the existence of geological anticlines along the Canadian River in the Texas Panhandle. In 1918 the Amarillo Oil Company had employed Gould as field geologist and drilled the first gas well in that region. Excitement over the discovery well had spread into the Oklahoma Panhandle. In March, 1919, a group of Texhoma businessmen had formed the Home Development Oil and Gas Company. The editor of the *Texhoma Times* wrote: "Capital is running wild scouring the country for oil and the bringing in of the big gas well north of Amarillo stimulates our belief that we too [sic] can have oil and gas if we will go after it."[38]

The first test well in Texas County had been staked on the "Allison place" five miles north of Texhoma, and a wooden derrick was erected for a cable-tool rig in May, 1919. Drilling was hampered by lack of capital. Not until 1922 was the well finally completed. It yielded a little gas but no oil. The discovery failed to stimulate a boom in drilling activity.[39]

Meanwhile, oil fever struck southwestern Kansas. Henry Hitch had bought stock in several oil-exploration companies in Kansas. By January, 1920, a well was being drilled five miles west of Liberal. J. K. Hitch received a telegram informing him the five "prominent Liberal men" were leasing a block of land in Seward County. The men invited him to join them both in buying stock in the company and in leasing his land for drilling. In 1922 the rig of another company brought in the first gas well in the county, three miles west of Liberal.[40]

The businessmen who attempted to interest J. K. in their proposition owned the Beaver Oil and Gas Company, chartered in Kansas in 1919. A number of its investors were from Texas County and included Henry, George, and Charlie Hitch. The company drilled its Oklahoma test well thirteen miles southeast of Guymon, near the mouth of Coldwater Creek. The rig's steam engine and boiler arrived at Guymon in July, 1919. Workmen erected a wooden derrick in October. In January, 1920, the actual drilling began, but the well proved to be dry.[41]

In 1926 the first large-volume gas well was drilled in Texas County, and a vast new gas field was opened. The extent of the field was apparent when a similar high-production well was drilled into the same geological stratum near Hugoton, Kansas, in June, 1927. By the close of 1932 there were 115 wells in the Hugoton-Guymon field covering 250 square miles—and the region's gas resources had barely been tapped.[42]

Henry Hitch first leased some of his land to an oil-and-gas-exploration company on September 15, 1925, when Amerada Petroleum Company paid him fifty cents per acre for six quarter sections. The next year he leased land to the Amerada, Vickers, Papoose, and California companies, with most of the land going to the California Petroleum Company. The California lease yielded $10,800 at a time when Henry badly needed cash. In 1927, however, those companies dropped their leases. Over the next few years other petroleum concerns, including Texas, Argus, Shell, and Magnolia, leased various small acreages. The lease money dribbled in a few thousand dollars a year, the largest amounts being $4,770 from Skelly in 1930 and $7,120 from Magnolia in 1931.⁴³

The depression temporarily halted oil-and-gas exploration in the region. In 1936, however, petroleum companies once again began leasing land for drilling sites. Cities Service Company acquired 122 square miles of land north and west of Guymon, including much of the old Stonebraker-Zea Ranch. Perhaps as early as 1934 the Cabot Corporation offered Henry Hitch $2.50 per acre for a ten-year lease on most of the ranch. That was only $0.25 per acre annually, a low price for the gas potential. Henry may have realized it at the time. But it was the first opportunity since the late 1920s for him to acquire a sizable sum of cash.⁴⁴

The Coldwater rancher had long been interested in the securities market. As a young man he had bought stock issues in a number of risk ventures that proved worthless, including a marble quarry in Colorado, the Cannonball Motor Company of New Mexico, and several Kansas oil-exploration concerns. During the 1920s he took note of the meteoric rise of the stock market but invested only in those areas he knew best: land, cattle, and wheat. Steering clear of securities during that decade prevented him from becoming entangled in the stock-market crash of 1929. In the aftermath of the crash cautious souls refrained from buying stock issues on the bear market of the 1930s. It is a truism that in order to make money one must buy low and sell high. More than one would-be entrepreneur, however, has made the mistake of buying when the price was high only to be caught in a subsequent collapse of the market. As a friend of mine once put it: "When I could buy a cow and calf for $200, I didn't want 'em. But when the price went up to $500, I just had to buy a bunch of 'em."

Henry Hitch did not make that mistake. The low price

of blue-chip stocks encouraged him to enter the stock market as early as 1933, when he opened an account with the James E. Bennett brokerage firm of Chicago. Perhaps using money from oil and gas leases, he began making regular deposits of a few hundred dollars a month with his broker. He received information about the market from a number of sources, such as a two-page digest of stock tips from his brokerage company, a magazine entitled *Financial World,* and various other publications. It is anybody's guess how Henry used these data. Most of the information, like many of today's instant stock-market analyses, was ambivalent. Some sources also provided the beginning investor with needed information about corporate earnings, sales, and innovations.

Hitch began building stock portfolios for Christine and each of the children, as well as for himself. In retrospect we can see that he was buying stock in the bargain basement of the twentieth century. He purchased such issues as Cities Service for 2 1/4, Socony Vacuum (Magnolia Oil) for 11 1/2, Texas Corporation for 25 1/8, General Motors for 28 1/8, Studebaker for 3 7/8, North American Aviation for 6, Minneapolis Moline for 2 1/8, Curtis Wright for 3 1/8, ITT for 10 7/8, United Airlines for 3 7/8, Anaconda for 27 3/4, and RCA for 4 7/8. When Cities Service dropped to 1 1/2 in December, 1934, he promptly bought two hundred shares. Ladd occasionally asked his father why he bought this or that stock, hoping to learn some valuable knack for making money in the market, but Henry usually responded, "It just looks good" or "I just think we should buy it."[45]

Regardless of how he arrived at his decision about which issues to buy, he bought them low. Henry's entrance into the stock market was the beginning of financial diversification for the Hitch Ranch. Because twice in a decade he had been hurt by low prices for cattle and wheat, he was determined to extend his economic interests into the nation's industrial sector. The depressed stock market provided a means to that end.[46]

The children grew to maturity during the Depression. Marjorie was graduated from Guymon High School in 1929. She enrolled at Southwestern College at Winfield, Kansas, a Methodist institution, but transferred to Panhandle A. and M. College at Goodwell in 1931. She majored in home economics and commuted from Guymon by car, riding at first with fellow-student Bud Perkins. During the summer of 1931 she met a young man from Orlando, Florida, who was working with the wheat- and hay-harvesting crews on the Hitch Ranch. His name was W. K. Price, Jr. He had accompanied Carroll Langston, one of Marjorie's cousins living in Florida, to the seasonal harvest. Marjorie and W. K. were married the next summer, on August 12, 1932. When she graduated in the spring of 1933, the couple moved to Florida, where W. K. went into business.[47]

Joyce was graduated from Guymon High School in 1934 and entered Oklahoma College for Women (OCW) at Chickasha. She had many interests, including horses and music. She also became an accomplished pianist. At OCW she took up the English style of riding and was a polished equestrian when she left that institution. But the new field of radio broadcasting proved the most attractive. She moved to Washington, D.C. In 1938, while living there with her Aunt Erma Walker Monesmith, she took her bachelor's degree with a major in psychology from George Washington University. Joyce then got a job as a secretary on the staff of the Red and Blue Network (NBC) in New York City. There she lived with a sorority sister whose brother she began dating. He was John Gray, a young chemist from New York. They were married on September 4, 1941, and lived for the next few years in Stanford, Connecticut, where John worked for American Cyanamide.[48]

One of Ladd's early interests was airplanes. An aviation craze swept the nation in the late 1920s and reached Guymon about 1928. Charles A. Lindbergh's celebrated transatlantic flight and the beginnings of United States airmail service did much to publicize the romance and thrill of the skyways. One of Guymon's first pilots was a rural mail carrier named John Noonan, who hoped to log enough time to qualify as an airmail pilot. On a typical Sunday afternoon in the late summer of 1928, automobiles crowded around the "aviation field" south of town. Some came from as far away as Boise City. Noonan carried passengers aloft in his biplane for four dollars a couple. The editor of the Guymon newspaper noticed that "many more persons are showing greater confidence in the air and are beginning to enjoy one of the newest thrills which await them at their door." He also congratulated Noonan on "getting to the place where he makes those nice three-point landings, one right after another."[49]

Ladd Hitch followed the escapades of the new heroes of the air, such men as Lindbergh and Oklahoma's own Wiley Post. Henry was also fascinated by the possibilities of air travel. About 1930 a Ford Trimotor, the first commercial passenger plane produced in the United States, landed at the Texas County Fair. Henry took the children for their first airplane ride in the craft.

When the boy decided that he wanted to learn to fly, Henry did not discourage him. In 1934, Ladd began his flying lessons as a junior in high school. His teacher was Charlie Burt, the only other pilot in Guymon besides Noonan. Burt's plane was an Eagle Rock, one of the few biplanes with the lower wing longer than the upper one. The power was furnished by an OX-5, a ninety-horsepower V-8 engine first used in trainers in World War I. Burt paid for his plane primarily by barnstorming at county fairs in the region. When it was not in use, he tied the plane down on the leeward side of the aviation field's one hangar, which housed Noonan's aircraft.

Before each flight Burt had to adjust the rocker arms of the engine. Sometimes when taking off on the buffalo-grass runway, the plane barely cleared the barbed-wire fence enclosing the pasture. On many days dust storms forced the postponement of lessons. Burt taught the boy all he knew, but that did not include navigation or how to come out of a stall. Ladd, however, did learn the basics, and he acquired an unquenchable desire to learn more about flying.[50]

In the spring of 1934 the Guymon school district's revenues dried up, the result of delinquent property taxes during the Depression. The school closed its doors for the 1934–35 year. Many who finished their junior year simply never returned to school. Young Hitch commuted to Goodwell High School in order to graduate in 1935.

Ladd wanted to go to college, but was uncertain about where to go or what his major subject should be. Of one thing he was certain. He had no talent as an artisan. He later recalled with some exaggeration that at Goodwell he had worked most of an entire semester in Leon Fields' woodworking class trying to square a block of wood—unsuccessfully. Henry discussed the matter with his attorney and friend Ross Rizley, of Guymon. They decided that the young man should attend Oklahoma A. and M. College (later Oklahoma State University) and major in some area of agriculture. One reason for picking A. and M. was that a professor of animal husbandry named Oliver Willham, whom Henry knew and admired, had recently left Panhandle A. and M. to accept a similar position on the Stillwater campus. The final decision, of course, was Ladd's.

In September, 1935, Henry and Christine drove their son halfway across the state to the campus of Oklahoma A. and M. They helped him unload his luggage, took a short tour of the college, and left Ladd standing on the steps of his dormitory. As he watched his parents drive away, his eyes began to burn and tears rolled down his cheeks. Young Hitch had never been away from home for more than a few days at a time.

His formal education now began. Education in the broadest sense involves more than what can be learned from books. In later years Ladd recalled that he "lacked the social graces" when he first arrived on the campus. Henry and Christine had attempted to instill their frontier Methodist values in their children, not in a dictatorial manner but rather by example. Consequently Ladd had never learned to dance, play cards, or partake of other forms of recreation that once were widely considered sinful but now were accepted by much of Protestantism, including the Methodist Church. Ladd endured a painful readjustment in which he began to learn the ways of contemporary society. He joined Sigma Epsilon because that fraternity took in country boys who felt the same kind of initial social alienation when moving from a rural to an urban society.

In his courses Ladd worked hard and did well. When he turned in his first theme in English composition, the professor voiced her bias when she told him that he had written an excellent essay for an agricultural student. By the conclusion of that semester the young man from the Coldwater was on the dean's honor roll. He also decided that

The Henry C. Hitch family, 1937. Left to right: Joyce, Christine, Henry, Marjorie, and Ladd.

he was not quite ready to leave home, so he transferred to Panhandle A. and M. for the spring semester of 1936. He commuted to the Goodwell campus for the next three semesters, where Professor M. C. Hamilton, of the history department, broadened Ladd's horizons and made a lasting impression on him.

Ladd returned to Oklahoma A. and M. at the beginning of his junior year, and was graduated with a B.S. degree in animal husbandry in 1939. The best-known person in that field at A. and M. was W. L. ("Bliz") Blizzard, a nationally famous judge of beef-cattle shows. Ladd, however, had no association with that expert on registered cattle. He once reminisced that "Bliz" was much like Jesus Christ. "I had faith that he existed, but rarely saw him." The instructor who made the most important impact on the young man's thinking about cattle was his father's old friend Oliver P. Willham (who would later become president of the institution). Ladd took Willham's course in animal genetics and found that the professor was "not overly carried away with registered cattle." Instead, the animal scientist emphasized the genetic ability to produce maximum beef-carcass weights rather than pedigree. Ladd liked that practical approach, and when he returned to the Coldwater, the views of Willham remained a dominant influence in his approach to beef-cattle production.[51]

By the end of the 1930s the Dust Bowl had faded into memory. The drought began to taper off in 1937. Abundant rainfall returned on the heels of the last duster of the decade, the black blizzard of March 11, 1939. Heavy rains washed much of the loose topsoil, residue of the "dirty thirties," into the streams. The Coldwater, once a narrow creek with a number of deep pools, changed into a shallow, sandy-bottomed brook.[52]

Another significant change was that the wall of isolation that had divided the Panhandle from the remainder of the state since the creation of Oklahoma Territory began to crumble. Since its earliest settlement the Panhandle had been more closely connected to neighboring states than to Oklahoma. Hitch cattle had always been marketed in Kansas City thanks to the Rock Island Railway, which reached Tyrone in 1888 and Guymon in 1901. The nearest city by both rail and highway was Amarillo, Texas. Moreover, it was no more difficult to travel to the state capitols of Kansas and Colorado than to reach Oklahoma City, because no railroad offered a direct line of transportation to central Oklahoma. Aside from the lack of rail communication, the fact that the narrow strip of land jutted like a peninsula onto the boundaries of four other states was enough to produce some alienation from the Sooner State.

The result was a feeling of resentment by Panhandle citizens, who believed that the state political establishment, dominated by "easterners," did little to satisfy their needs. The editor of the *Cimarron News* in Boise City expressed this attitude in 1929, when he objected to an official map of Oklahoma that put "the three counties . . . clipped off and shunted down into a corner like an afterthought." He further noted that, because no rail line connected the region to Oklahoma City, Kansas received "99 percent" of the Panhandle's trade. Another regional editor wrote in 1913, "We want a [direct] railroad to Oklahoma City worse than any other thing I can think of."[53]

In 1912 the Wichita Falls and Northwestern Railway was completed to Forgan, seven miles north of Beaver City. That line was later absorbed by the Missouri-Kansas-Texas (M-K-T) Railway. One could then get to Oklahoma City by driving to Forgan by wagon or car, taking the M-K-T to Elk Ciy in the southwestern part of the state, and transferring to the Rock Island line. A traveler who desired to see much of the state could transfer from the M-K-T to the Santa Fe at Woodward, from the Santa Fe to the Frisco at Avard in Woods County, from the Frisco back to the Santa Fe at Enid and complete his ride into Oklahoma City on that line. Neither of these alternatives, however, constituted the kind of fast, direct service needed by the Panhandle.[54]

A direct route from Guymon to Oklahoma City was finally built, not as a railroad but as a highway. On October

13, 1932, the *Panhandle Herald* carried the banner head-line "Go Direct to Oklahoma City Soon." Grading for the new state highway, which would ultimately be designated SH3, was not completed until 1937. Paving came much later. As late as the early 1930s only about eight miles of paved roads existed in the entire Panhandle, including one stretch between Guymon and Hooker. The final link of hard surfacing on SH3, the seventeen miles from Balko to Elmwood, was not completed until August, 1952.[55]

The landscape, as well as the inhabitants, was further modified by a decrease in population, a result of the Dust Bowl migration to the West Coast. Between 1930 and 1940 the number of people in Texas County decreased from 14,100 to 9,896, about 30 percent. In 1937 a woman who had driven from Eva to Guymon noted that in that thirty-mile stretch of highway she had counted only six-teen occupied houses. Empty three- and four-room farm-houses dotted the wheat fields of the plains. Families who had worked the land, milked their Jersey cows, sold their cream and eggs at the local cream station, and gathered in town on Saturday night were gone, swept away like the dust. The experience left some inhabitants pessimistic about the future. One banker confessed privately to a journalist:

> I've lived here for half a century. This is my country, not only because of the farm and ranch lands I have owned and handled for so long, not only because of this bank which I established and to which I have given the best years of my life, but because this is the country where I have lived my life and made my home and had hoped to make a place for my son. But . . . but I have had to tell my son that my advice is to look somewhere else for his future. I am not sure that there is a future here.[56]

That was not the feeling of Henry Hitch. He was opti-mistic. Thousands of others in the region also voiced the same view. A county agent at Boise City believed that "this country will come back if improved practices as recommended by the government and the farmers' own experience are followed." Ed Morrison, the president of Panhandle A. and M. College, stressed that the people must remain on the land to carry out soil-conservation techniques. He believed that, if the region were abandoned, wind erosion would spread to neighboring areas like an advancing desert. "To abandon the dust bowl would be to abandon America," he emphasized. Most agriculturists who dug in their heels and refused to leave probably felt as strongly about the Panhandle as did the leather-faced man wearing khaki clothes and a rolled brim, grease-stained hat who pointed to the same journalist and exclaimed:

Listen! If this country could produce the trainloads of products that it did before we knew anything about how to farm this land, before we had put this great [soil conservation] program into effect, what will it be capable of in the future?

Its future is just opening up. It is just being tamed. There will be as much difference between this country in the past, productive as it was, and what it will be in the future as there is between a wild flea-bitten longhorn and a modern purebred whiteface steer. Then we will really go places. Our future is all before us.[57]

That articulate spokesman, nameless, in an article appearing in the *Oklahoma Farmer-Stockman* of 1937, could well have been Henry Hitch. Hitch never looked back. Before the dust had settled and the rains had returned, he had remained the supreme optimist.

8.   A New Generation

The Panhandle's biggest annual event was the Pioneer Days celebration initiated at Guymon in 1933. It was an offshoot of Charlie Hitch's roundups of the 1920s and the McDermott Grove Fourth of July celebrations of the 1890s. The festivities centered around May 2. That date was picked to commemorate the passage into law of the Organic Act of May 2, 1890, which had authorized the establishment of Oklahoma Territory and attached the Panhandle to that territorial government. In other words, May 2 was the anniversary of the first legally constituted government for the region.

In 1940 the program began with a rodeo on the night of May 1, followed by a parade the next morning. The "Pioneer Queen" that year, chosen by a local committee, was Della Hitch Keating, Henry Hitch's older sister. Her float led the entourage. Other floats included one entitled "Hard Times," another labeled "Family Picture," and one called "Bone Picker." The entry that attracted the most attention was "Saturday Night," a depiction of a grandmother rocking a baby and reading her Bible while a mother bathed the older children in a wash tub. Seventeen high school bands from across the Panhandle, joined by a few from neighboring Texas and Kansas, marched between the floats playing the rousing brass "runs" of John Philip Sousa's music.

The parade of both old-timers and youngsters provided

"Uncle Charlie" and "Aunt Josie" Hitch dressed for Pioneer Days, ca. late 1930s. Courtesy of Mary Hitch Hall.

a contrast between a bygone era and a new generation. Uncle Charlie Hitch proudly drove his old chuck wagon down the paved streets of Guymon. He could not help but recall the days a half century ago when no buildings, not even the old Senate Saloon, had yet been built on those buffalo-grass plains. Behind the chuck wagon rode twenty-two-year-old Ladd Hitch, his fiancée, Lala Moores, and his sister Joyce, all mounted on golden palomino horses.

George Hitch and a favorite roping horse, ca. 1940s. Courtesy of Willa Nethery Hitch (Mrs. George Hitch).

After the parade, an old-timers' dinner was held at the Methodist Church. Nostalgic conversations replaced the usual talk of weather, cattle, and crops. At the dinner of 1940, Christine Hitch met an elderly woman who vividly recalled that Mary Westmoreland Hitch and her children had spent the night at her house in Seward County when moving to the sod house on Coldwater Creek more than half a century before. To Christine's delight, this woman "told me more of how she looked than any one else had before."[1]

The afternoon of May 2 another rodeo performance entertained the crowd. Those pioneers who had lived in the county for at least fifty years were admitted free of charge. In the late afternoon a "Coronado Pageant," performed by local students to commemorate the passage of the Spanish explorer through the Panhandle, was staged in the downtown area. After the day's festivities, the Hitch family drove home for a little rest and then returned to Guymon that night to see a western movie, "Virginia City," starring Errol Flynn.[2]

Ladd had returned home to the Coldwater after his graduation from Oklahoma A. and M. College in 1939. Henry started him out at fifty dollars a month plus room and board as comanager of the ranch. The elder Hitch also cosigned his son's note at a local bank to provide him with money to buy calves in partnership with a friend named Ed Love. The partners wintered their calves on wheat before sending them to market.[3]

Henry added more land to his holdings in the 1940s. The ranch now consisted of about fifteen thousand acres, but Hitch rented thousands of other acres, most of them sown to wheat. He also leased a few thousand additional acres of grassland at prices ranging from twenty to twenty-five cents per acre per year. Most of the plowing, disking, sowing, and harvesting of wheat was done by neighboring small farmers using their own equipment. Henry paid them by the day. This arrangement not only saved Hitch money, which otherwise would have been tied up in more farm implements, but also it supplemented the income of several neighbors.[4]

Soon after Ladd returned, he persuaded his father that a daily planning session was needed in their operations. Consequently in 1940 the family began assembling immediately after breakfast, which usually consisted of chicken-fried steak, biscuits, and gravy prepared by Henry. The group met in the office or kitchen over a last cup of breakfast coffee. For about thirty minutes, Ladd and Henry discussed the day's work with their foremen.

The informal early-morning sessions grew out of the need for a more efficient daily work pattern in an agricultural empire still owned and operated exclusively by a single family. Subjects at the meetings varied from where to get the highest price for a thousand head of steers to the need to give a few head of thin cows an extra helping of cottonseed cake. In the winter, decisions had to be made not only about feeding operations, but also about moving cattle from pastures to wheat fields and back. How many livestock could be grazed on a certain pasture or wheat field? How good was the grass or wheat? How many cowhands would be required to make the move?

During the spring and summer, farming had to be correlated with all cattle operations. Haying, pulling a sucker rod out of a water well to replace the leathers, riding pasture, building fence, treating sick cows, and harvesting wheat were all happening at the same time. A rancher could easily "meet himself coming and going." The morning meetings attempted to prevent wasted time resulting from having no clear lines of authority or forethought about possible problems of the day. The meetings were so successful that they became a permanent part of the Hitch Ranch.[5]

Joyce Hitch continued to help with the cattle until she married. In March, 1940, when Ladd and a hired hand planned to drive about a hundred head of livestock from one corner of the ranch to Uncle Charlie Hitch's wheat pasture, a distance of about ten miles, Christine wrote in her journal that Joyce would probably not go with the men because she "would get too tired and dusty." In the margin she later added: "Joyce went."[6]

If Ladd introduced some significant changes, the advent of World War II created new circumstances that also affected the ranch. Prices for agricultural commodities, despite government price ceilings and rationing, rose to prosperous levels. The average price for beef on the hoof in 1940 was $7.95 per hundredweight. By 1943 the price had risen to $12.22. In January 1940 wheat brought an average price of $0.83 a bushel at Oklahoma elevators, but rose to $1.45 by January 1944.[7]

Because the United States created the largest military force in its history, the agricultural industry suffered a manpower shortage. Whereas the Hitches usually had hired young single men in the past, they now were forced to begin hiring older family men above the draft age. Henry subsequently moved a number of small houses for those families onto the area around his headquarters. Moreover, the new hired hands were not willing to rise before dawn and be at work by 6 A.M. Thus 7:30 or 8:00 A.M. became the standard time for starting the workday, right after the thirty-minute planning session, which began at 7:00 or 7:30 A. M. The Hitches also began sleeping later, all except Henry who found it next to impossible to break a lifetime habit of rising by 5:00 A.M. Of course, the eight-hour workday did not exist on the ranch. Its length varied with the seasons. Summer haying always involved long days with the crew often working until dark. On the other hand, winter workdays were usually short and consisted primarily of feeding cattle.[8]

The overall quality of the labor force improved with the hiring of married men. They were more likely to remain longer, were more conscientious in their work, and demonstrated a more responsible attitude. Many of the new workers lived in Guymon. A bus owned by the ranch drove them out from town each morning. The children of hired hands living on the ranch rode the same bus into Guymon to attend school. When the bus carried the workers back to town at the end of the day, the children rode back home by return trip. The hired hands from town took their meals at a kitchen on the ranch manned by a full-time cook. Henry paid top wages, with periodic increases for those who remained as permanent hands. It was said that Hitch never turned down anyone who asked him for a job. As in all agriculture, however, the work was hard and much of it was drudgery. Consequently, the ranch always had a high turnover of workers. Neighbors frequently commented on the quality of Hitch's hired hands. A friend once told Henry that he was very impressed with the intelligence and hard work of the cowhands and farm laborers. Henry responded with his usual wit: "They ought to be good. We had to sift through several thousand to find these few good ones."[9]

Wheat continued to be the primary farm crop through most of the 1940s. Henry bought three Gleaner-Baldwin twelve-foot combines in 1940 at a total cost of $4,000 plus the trade-in of two old combines. The implement manufacturer financed the machines over a two-year period. In 1942 and 1944, Hitch harvested bumper crops of wheat on

Overflow at the Hitch Grain Company elevator at Hitchland in the wake of a bumper crop, ca. 1944.

10,000 acres. The yield averaged an incredible forty bushels to the acre in 1944 for a total of 400,000 bushels.[10]

After harvesting the crop of 1944, which grossed about $332,000, Henry settled some old debts he had accumulated in the 1920s, most of which were unsecured notes in the hands of friends and relatives. During the hard times of the 1920s and 1930s, he had been able to pay only part of the interest on the notes every few years or so. Occasionally the remittance was in something other than cash. For example, Henry on one occasion paid Frank Lindsay in seed wheat. In 1942 he remitted to Lindsay a registered palomino stallion named "Sonny Boy." Lindsay's son-in-law, Guymon automobile dealer Clarence Alexander, traded the prize horse to a St. Louis automobile dealer for a new Chrysler.[11]

One day in the late summer of 1944 Alexander received a telephone call from Henry Hitch's attorney, Ross Rizley. The prominent Panhandle lawyer asked Alexander if Lindsay would discount the interest on the $12,000 note upon full payment of the principal. The note with accumulated interest amounted to about $36,000, but Lindsay agreed that for $12,500 he would consider the debt closed. Hitch met Lindsay at the Alexander Motor Company. Bud Perkins, who at that time worked as a salesman for the automobile agency, greeted several men who walked through the showroom door one by one and headed straight for Clarence's office. The tinge of excitement, occasional laughter from the office, and good humor from almost all concerned finally led Perkins to ask Alexander, "What is all the excitement about?" Alexander replied, "Henry Hitch is paying off some old debts today."[12]

At the end of 1944, Henry's financial condition was better than it had been for a quarter of a century. His land was almost debt-free. Most of his remaining debts were in short-term notes for funds used to purchase cattle and put in crops. For those needs, he continued to use the Production Credit Association of Guymon. He had been buying blue-chip stocks since the early 1930s, and the stock market continued to rise, a trend which would last until the late 1960s. Henry continued to purchase stock, putting together a portfolio that would have done credit to the most sophisticated urban investor.

Hitch further diversified his holdings when he became interested in orange groves. This occurred as a result of his and Christine's periodic visits to the home of their older daughter, Marjorie Hitch Price, and her husband, W. K. Price, Jr., at Orlando, Florida. In 1947 the Hitches and Prices in partnership began buying raw land at Leesburg and Fort Pierce, Florida. Price became the developer and manager of the groves as the land was cleared and planted. The initial investment for putting in citrus trees was large. Because of the dangers of frost and hurricanes, the business was risky. As a hedge, Henry and W. K. decided to put part of the groves at the relatively frost-free area near Fort Pierce and the remainder at the hurricane-proof land at Leesburg, northwest of Orlando. Eventually the families developed twenty-one hundred acres of profitable orange groves.[13]

Henry conducted much of his business from the office that had been added to the house in the 1920s. The room was filled with mementos he treasured: scores of arrowheads mounted in glass-covered frames, a mounted longhorn steer's head, his stamp collection, Christine's paintings, and other memorabilia. A visitor in 1958, after noticing the fields clear of weeds, the fat livestock, and the general orderliness of the ranch, ribbed Hitch about the disorderly appearance of his desk. She noticed that it was "heaped a foot high or more with miscellaneous papers and no one but Henry is allowed to touch it. . . . Left alone, undisturbed by alien hands, Henry knows just how deep to burrow for anything demanded."[14]

Hitch finances were further enhanced when Cities Service and Phillips Petroleum companies drilled gas wells on the ranch in the 1940s. Some of the land had been leased for oil and gas exploration as early as the 1920s, and virtually all the ranch was leased in the early 1930s, but no wells were drilled until the war years.[15]

The Coldwater rancher, who had almost been bankrupt twice in the previous two decades, was a wealthy man by any measure at the end of the war. However, his standard of living remained about the same. He still had only

two or three suits at most. Although generous in his phil-
anthropies, he still did not enjoy spending money on himself. He did, however, add some improvements to the
family's personal comforts. In 1940, Henry bought a wind-
generated electrical plant. Commonly called "wind
chargers," such devices had been used on a few American
farms since the early 1920s. The most popular make—and
the one purchased for the ranch—was the Wincharger,
manufactured by Zenith. It consisted of a six-volt generator, slightly larger than a common automobile generator,
with a propeller mounted on its shaft and a streamlined
metal tail to keep the device headed into the wind. The
Wincharger was usually housed at the top of a wooden
tower twenty to forty feet high.

Generating only half a kilowatt or less, the plant was
primarily used to power the lights and radio. The six-volt
bulbs were usually only twenty-five watts at the most, but
they were improvements over kerosene lamps. One important obstacle to wind power on the plains was that it
could be undependable. In the heat of summer, there often
were days of absolutely no wind to turn windmills. During
such extended periods cattlemen either had to drive their
livestock to the nearest stream or pond for water or bolt
a "pump-jack" onto the mill's sucker rod. A tractor or
small gasoline engine then supplied the power for the
"pump-jack."

If the wind failed on some days, it was completely undependable at night. Although high winds might blow during
daylight hours, they usually subsided or even ceased at
night. Consequently, when one needed a stiff breeze most
to turn the Wincharger, it could not be depended upon. Of
course several storage batteries were used, but their capacity was often not sufficient for both lighting the house and
running the radio.[16]

In the latter part of April, 1940, a local dealer began installing a Wincharger at the Hitch house and wiring it for electricity. The task took two weeks and interfered with normal household chores. At times Christine had her doubts that the workmen would ever finish. One Friday she noted in her journal that the men that day were "to put up the tower I think."[17]

Wind-generated electricity was used until 1950 when the local Rural Electrification Administration cooperative extended its lines to the ranch. For the first time in forty years of marriage, Henry and Christine were able to read by the light of honest-to-goodness 100-watt light bulbs.

In addition to reading, the most popular home entertainment for the family centered around the radio. Their favorite radio shows featured such comedians as Jack Benny, Fibber McGee and Molly, Edgar Bergen and Charlie McCarthy, George Burns and Gracie Allen, and the incomparable Fred Allen, not to mention scores of plays, detective and mystery stories, and musical programs. Of one night of entertainment Christine wrote in her journal, "We had a restful evening with radio."[18]

Henry Hitch remained the consummate trader, not only in cattle and horses but also in most other things. Clarence Alexander recalled that on those occasions when Henry bought a car from him, he was a "tough trader." When the family wanted to trade its Plymouth for a Buick in 1940, Cousin Jim Langston who owned the Guymon agency drove out to the Coldwater, ate dinner with the family, and talked cars. The Buick retailed for $1,250 with options including a radio, which Henry justified having because he needed to listen to the daily stock market quotations. After much haggling over the trade-in difference, Langston and Hitch got to within five dollars of an agreed price. Christine noted, "It rests there awhile but [we] will likely take it." The next day, Henry went into town and paid Langston's price, but "he will give us seat covers if he gets more than $425 out of the Plymouth," Christine wrote in her journal.[19]

The family expanded with the addition of a new daughter-in-law. Lala Moores was a native of Vian, Oklahoma. Her grandfather had been a cotton farmer, and her father was a cattleman and proprietor of a livestock auction business. Lala was graduated from Oklahoma A. and M. with a major in mathematics education. Proficient at tap dancing and ballet, she had been one of a group of student entertainers on campus. President Ed Morrison of Panhandle A. and M. hired her ostensibly to be the campus supervisor of the National Youth Administration (NYA), a New Deal program that provided on-campus jobs for students. Actually her primary job was to teach dancing. A friend of Ladd Hitch, Ted Voiles, of Hooker, first told him about the attractive dark-haired dancing instructor. Ladd took the opportunity to meet her when he brought his mother to Goodwell for a tea given by the No Man's Land Historical Society. He and Ted Voiles, who already had met Lala, walked into her office as she was trying to do the paper work for her first NYA payroll. According to Ladd's recollections, she "was more concerned with the job at hand than meeting a new person."

Young Hitch, however, overcame that obstacle during the next few days and began dating Lala. They were married on November 4, 1940. Two years later the couple built a two-story home just west of the stone house erected by Ladd's grandfather and only a few yards south of his grandmother's grave. Their first child, Paul, was born on May 25, 1943. Their second baby, born January 17, 1946,

Ladd and Lala Moores Hitch, 1941.

was a girl. She was named Jane. And Jim, born February 21, 1953, was the youngest child.[20]

Like his father and grandfather, Ladd acquired land. In the 1940s he began buying land in western Texas County and eastern Cimarron County, some for as little as fifteen dollars an acre, but much of it for thirty-five to forty dollars an acre. He bought the properties on long-term credit.

In some instances Henry cosigned his notes or became a partner in the purchases. Like his father, Ladd recalled that he was "extremely aggressive" in acquiring land. In other words, he was eager and willing to plunge into debt in order to buy any good land appearing on the market.[21]

The younger Hitch resumed his interest in flying after the outbreak of the war. In 1942 he entered a civilian pilot training school sponsored by the federal government at Texhoma. The objective of the program was to give young men who wanted to become military pilots a headstart. On completion of the course Ladd was granted a pilot's license. He and two other men from Guymon then bought a two-place Taylorcraft.

In February, 1943, while Henry and Christine were in Florida visiting Marjorie and W. K. Price, Ladd took a cross-country flight. That day he first began to understand how a private aircraft could be used to save time in the family business. He afterwards wrote to his parents:

Bob Conklin and I took off for Liberal. We flew along, both over and under scattered clouds at about 2000 ft. and arrived at the ranch in about thirty-five minutes. We circled the whole outfit several times, looked at all the wheat and cattle . . ., landed twice, talked to Claud awhile, and then went on to Liberal, landing there about 1:15. . . . We took off from Liberal and went to Perryton [Texas] in forty minutes, landed there . . . . Then we . . . took off straight west from Perryton, and were soon over the Palo Duro breaks, and circled over the [Frank] Lindsay outfit a couple of times. We then went on to look over all our cattle and [flew] back into Guymon about 1 hour out of Perryton. . . . I had never before realized how far and fast you can travel in these little "slow" planes.[22]

Not long after Ladd acquired the Taylorcraft, the government requisitioned it for training purposes and took it to New Mexico. A few months after he lost the plane,

Ladd accompanied a load of cattle to Kansas City. There he stumbled onto a Luscombe 8A for sale, and he and his Guymon partners bought it. Because he had never flown long distances across unfamiliar terrain, the young rancher hired a pilot to fly him and the Luscombe to Wichita, Kansas. Ladd soloed off the Wichita runway, located the railroad tracks running westward on that clear day, and followed the steel ribbons into Guymon. After the war the "flying club" bought back the Taylorcraft from the government and sold the Luscombe to Clarence Alexander. By 1948 the "club" had broken up and sold its plane. That year the young Coldwater rancher and his brother-in-law John Gray purchased an aircraft, and in 1950 Ladd bought the first Cessna for the ranch.[23]

The airplane became an integral part of Hitch operations. Because of the remoteness of Guymon from urban business and financial centers, Ladd used the plane extensively to conduct one-day business in Kansas City, Wichita, Denver, or Oklahoma City. On one occasion he remarked that without the airplane "it would take forever to go anywhere." Other Guymon business leaders followed Hitch's lead. By the late 1940s automobile dealers Clarence Alexander and Orville Nash were flying their own planes, and within a decade a modern Guymon airport served more than a score of locally owned aircraft.

Although Ladd wanted to enter the navy as a pilot in the early part of the war, he was needed on the ranch. The Selective Service extended a draft exemption from military service to Ladd and other such young men who served in management positions on farms and ranches. But in 1944 the government began to revoke those exemptions. Young Hitch entered the Navy that year and was sent to the Great Lakes Naval Training Center near Chicago. He became a naval officer, but could not qualify for

The Henry C. Hitch family in 1945. Left to right: W. K. Price, Jr., Marjorie Hitch Price, John Gray, Joyce Hitch Gray, Lala Moores Hitch, and Ladd Hitch. Christine and Henry are at the right. Grandchildren in front are (left

A view of the family's houses at ranch headquarters in the 1960s. Stone house is on the right. Ladd's house is to the left. The Gray's home is beyond Ladd's house, but is hidden from view by trees.

pilot's training because his vision was not a consistent 20/20.[24]

While Hitch was in the Navy, Marjorie and W. K. Price moved from their home in Florida into Ladd's house on the Coldwater in order to help Henry with the ranching operations. In 1945, however, the Prices were able to move back to Orlando, Florida, at which time Joyce and John Gray decided to leave Connecticut and settle permanently on the ranch. Soon after the war the Grays built their own spacious home just west of Ladd's house. After the young rancher's return, he and John Gray became business associates in several endeavors, including land development at Guymon. Gray also moved into broadcasting, buying and managing radio stations at Guymon and Liberal.[25]

When Ladd Hitch returned from the service, he began to take an active role in Panhandle politics. The Republican Party elected him Texas County chairman. The Hitches had long been Republicans. J. K. Hitch originally had migrated westward from East Tennessee, a strong Republican Party enclave since the days of the Civil War, and remained a member of the GOP throughout his life. Although the Panhandle had long been a strong Republican region, especially Texas County, a party organization was practically nonexistent there until a leading Guymon attorney and Hitch family friend, Ross Rizley, ran for Congress in 1940. The county and regional party organization grew out of that successful effort, and "Judge" Rizley became the leader of the GOP in northwestern Oklahoma.[26]

Rizley was a native of the Panhandle. Born in 1892 in a dugout on a fresh homestead in old Beaver County, the attorney had labored as a cowboy and rural schoolteacher before working his way through the Kansas City School

of Law. He came to Guymon in 1920 to practice law with
H. E. G. Putnam, and was elected for one term to the
Oklahoma Senate in 1930. He emerged as a statewide political figure when the party nominated him to run for
governor in an unsuccessful race in 1938.[27]

Ladd and Henry remained close friends of the Congressman, who subsequently was appointed to a federal judge-
ship. In later years Ladd became a state committeeman
but never ran for any political office. When Richard Nixon
was elected President in 1968, Hitch was mentioned as a
strong possibility for the position of Secretary of Agriculture, but that was as close as he came to holding a government position. Neither Ladd nor his father ever desired
political office. Henry believed that politics usually "ruined a man." He often said that he had never seen a man
elected sheriff who was "worth a damn afterward." Although both father and son were Republicans of strong
conviction, neither man was "carried away" with politics.
As Ladd once put it, his first allegiance was to the Oklahoma Panhandle and Texas County. Consequently, the
Hitch family's primary concern had been the economic
and civic development of the region, Texas County in
particular.[28]

That regional loyalty motivated the Hitches to become
involved in a number of endeavors through the years, including the formation of Oklahoma's first permanent
statewide cattlemen's organization. The state cattle industry had long been handicapped by the absence of organization. Livestock producers through the years had formed
a number of county and regional organizations, most of
which were short-lived. J. K. Hitch probably had belonged
to the Beaver River Cattlemen's Association, formed as
early as the late 1880s. When that organization held a
meeting at Hardesty May 7–8, 1901, R. B. "Dick" Quinn,

editor of the *Hardesty Herald,* was serving as secretary, but within a few years the group was disbanded. Other such organizations included the Cattlemen's Association of the Indian Territory, the Northeastern Oklahoma Cattlemen's Association, and the Osage County Cattlemen's Association.[29]

Ranchers in northwestern Oklahoma early became interested in putting together a statewide group. As early as 1903, an Oklahoma Live Stock Association existed. Much of that organization's leadership appears to have come from northwestern Oklahoma. When a meeting was held at Wichita, Kansas, February 11–13, 1903, speakers for the group included the Kansas Populist Congressman "Sockless" Jerry Simpson, the governor of Kansas; O. C. French, of the Oklahoma Live Stock Sanitary Commission; and John Fields, the director of the Oklahoma Agricultural Experiment Station. The most popular address at the meeting was delivered by Oklahoma State Senator D. P. Marum, of Woodward, who suggested that the most pressing need for cattlemen was to build stockyard markets and packing houses in Oklahoma and southwestern Kansas. "Packing can be done here as well as any place else. You have access to cheap feed," he told his audience.[30]

The Oklahoma Live Stock Association faded out of existence, but some former members who were perplexed by falling cattle prices attempted unsuccessfully to form a similar organization in 1919. That year, on October 7, stock growers from northwestern Oklahoma and the northeastern Texas Panhandle met at Woodward. An older D. P. Marum was elected president. The angry participants blamed low prices on the policies of the meatpacking industry. They probably took their cause too far in a resolution stating "that America's characteristics of bravery and wholeheartedness are due to the fact that we are a meat-eating nation."[31]

In the absence of a statewide organization, in 1928 an estimated 25 percent of all Oklahoma stockmen belonged to the large Texas and Southwestern Cattlemen's Association (TSCA) with headquarters in Fort Worth. J. K. Hitch had been a member of this organization in the 1890s when it was still called the Cattle Raisers Association of Texas. As early as 1916, the TSCA had 1,000 Oklahomans as members. That year the "brand detective" for the TSCA in Oklahoma, C. H. Bailey, reportedly broke up several cattle rustling gangs.[32]

In November 1938 cattlemen formed the Oklahoma Livestock Growers' Association. This group in 1941 began to publish the first magazine devoted to the cattle industry. Dubbed the *Ranchman,* the publication outlived the organization, which lapsed into inactivity during the war years. Some stockmen tried to revive the association in 1948, but to no avail.[33]

The origins of a permanent statewide organization may be found in a regional group that Henry Hitch helped found in 1945 while Ladd was still in the Navy. It was named the Northwest Oklahoma Cattlemen's Association (NOCA), and resulted from a meeting of Panhandle and northwestern Oklahoma livestock producers at Woodward in June that year. J. O. Selman, of Woodward, was elected the first president, and Henry was chosen the Texas County representative on the board of directors. Housed at first in the offices of the Production Credit Association of Woodward, the group began publishing the *Northwest Oklahoma Cattleman* in late 1945. During the next decade both Henry and Ladd served as presidents of the organization.[34]

Since the days of the early range-cattle industry on the Great Plains, one of the primary reasons for the formation of stock growers' associations was to combat cattle rustling. In 1895, Temple Houston, son of the famous hero of Texas and a practicing attorney at Woodward, represented the cattle interests of northwestern Oklahoma when he traveled to the territorial captial of Guthrie to lobby for a strong anti-rustling bill in the Oklahoma legislature. Rustlers made off with Hitch Ranch stock from time to time. In the early 1920s, Henry began missing one or two head of stock at a time from one part of the ranch. That led him to believe that the thief was a neighbor. His suspicions were confirmed one day when he stumbled onto a cache of hides on the neighbor's property, all bearing his Lazy 8 brand. Hitch took the evidence to the sheriff and swore out a warrant for the man's arrest. The rustler, who had been supplying his father's local butcher shop with beef from the Coldwater herd, was tried and convicted for the crime. By the time the trial ended, however, Henry had become convinced that the fellow had learned his lesson. Before sentencing, the rancher circulated a petition requesting judicial clemency among Texas County's leading citizens. The result was that the judge gave the rustler a suspended sentence.[35]

Local cow thieves were a nuisance, but most of the thievery in later years appeared in the form of criminals who quietly drove trucks into pastures on moonlit nights, loaded twenty or so head at a time, and drove them to distant markets. In the spring of 1950, rustlers stole twelve head from a northwestern Oklahoma ranch during a dust storm. One outfit in Woodward County was losing an average of thirty head of cattle a year to such thieves by 1950.[36]

The old cattlemen's associations created that detective

of the range, called a "brand inspector," to cope with rustling. Brand inspectors usually concentrated their efforts at livestock marketing areas and stockyards, searching cattle pens, railroad cars, and bills of sale for evidence of stolen livestock. A seasoned inspector retained in his memory thousands of brands, only occasionally resorting to brand books for identification of a mark.

Before hiring brand inspectors, the NOCA had to get approval as a law enforcement agency from the Packers and Stockyards Division of the United States Department of Agriculture. Under this act the stockyards frequented by the inspectors had to provide them with pertinent records. Salaries of the inspectors, under the law, were partly offset by levying a fee of five cents per head on all cattle coming through the yards. In July 1948 the NOCA made application to the USDA. The agency granted its approval on January 3, 1949. Only three livestock markets—the cattle auctions at Woodward, Seiling, and Beaver—were affected by the order. Seiling and Beaver readily complied with the order.

The Woodward Livestock Commission Company formally protested to the United States Department of Agriculture, however, and a public hearing was held November 1–3, 1949, at Woodward. The attitude of the association toward this defiance was voiced by the secretary of the NOCA when he wrote: "The time is at hand when the Northwest Oklahoma Cattlemen's Association has been challenged, and we are not going to stand idly by. We might have to mandamus the county attorneys to get the job done, but its [sic] a coming reality . . .."[37] Will Rogers, Jr., former Oklahoma congressmen-at-large, officiated at the proceedings. Each side had its attorneys on hand. Among the witnesses called by the association were the Brand Commissioner of Kansas, the president of the

Oklahoma State Board of Agriculture, a representative of the Brand Registry Department of the Oklahoma Department of Agriculture, a member of the Oklahoma Highway Patrol, sheriffs from several northwestern Oklahoma counties, and a number of prominent state cattlemen. Within a matter of weeks after the hearing the federal government gave final approval to the NOCA, and its brand inspectors went to work.[38]

One of the most important accomplishments of the NOCA was a new state brand law that greatly aided the work of the inspectors. As early as 1899 a bill was introduced in the territorial legislature "to provide for the registration of brands and marks." The law allowed stockmen to register individual brands in their respective counties. The basic weakness in the statute was that the state had no central agency for registration. Texas had a similar law, but the old and powerful Texas and Southwestern Cattle Raisers Association served as a kind of unofficial brand registration agency for the state. Oklahoma had no powerful statewide association at this time. In 1947 the NOCA attempted to correct that deficiency in the law by getting its legislative friends to sponsor a new brand-registration bill. The legislature failed to pass the bill primarily because it would have made the branding of all cattle compulsory. Another distasteful provision for many was that no duplicate brands were allowed.

When the legislature convened in 1949, the NOCA once again lobbied for brand reform. Sen. Dwight Leonard, of Beaver, introduced a bill to establish a Division of Brand Registry within the State Department of Agriculture. His bill further proposed that: (1) all brands within the state had to be registered with the new agency, but branding would not be compulsory; (2) county clerks could no longer act as local brand registers; (3) all county brand records were to be turned over to the new agency; and (4) the director of the Division of Brand Registry was directed to publish a State Brand Book every fifth year beginning in 1950. Although duplicate brands were to be allowed, NOCA leaders believed that dissemination of the Brand Book would gradually eliminate duplication through voluntary brand changes.[39]

The act was signed into law by Gov. Roy. J. Turner, a cattleman himself, in the spring of 1949. The new law required two distinct symbols per brand. Consequently, those stock growers using only a single letter or number had either to change or add to their brands. J. K. Hitch had eventually dropped the LV brand of the Westmorelands and was burning only his Circle onto the hides of his cattle when he died in 1921. Henry Hitch had added another adjacent circle to his father's brand to make his own Lazy 8 (∞) which was also only one figure. To comply with the new law, Ladd and Henry changed their brand to the Quarter Circle Circle (⊙) on October 4, 1949. In a few years the brand became known as the "Cap O."[40]

In 1952, during a period reminiscent of the drouth and low prices of the 1930s, the NOCA combined with other smaller state stock growers' groups to forge the first permanent statewide organization: the Oklahoma Cattlemen's Association (OCA). The NOCA became "affiliated" with the new group and eventually dissolved altogether when the new OCA became firmly established. Ladd Hitch was elected first vice-president of the OCA in 1965 and served as president during 1966 and 1967. Under his leadership funds were raised for constructing a permanent ranch-style headquarters building at the Oklahoma City Stock Yards. Moreover, Ladd also spurred the association into raising about $50,000 for building a bull-testing center at Oklahoma State University (formerly Oklahoma A. and M.).[41]

With Ladd assuming much of the responsibility for running the ranch, Henry and Christine were able to devote more of their time to their philanthropic endeavors. One of their favorite charities was the Methodist Church. Henry's mother had been responsible for organizing the first Methodist Church in Texas County. The Hitch family remained staunch members of that faith. Christine served for a number of years as a Sunday school teacher of teenage girls. In her later years she taught a women's class despite the fact that since the late 1930s she had been painfully afflicted with rheumatoid arthritis. By 1940, Henry had to help her up the steps of the church. She never complained. Indeed her cheerful disposition, sense of humor, and willingness to help in all worthwhile activities were sources of strength for the Guymon church. In addition, Christine remained an active member of the state PEO sisterhood, and regularly entertained the Methodist minister and his family with a Sunday dinner at the Coldwater headquarters.[42]

Henry's church work was as unpretentious and quiet as the man himself. Serving on the church's various financial and business committees, he became known both as a liberal contributor and a staunch supporter of worthy projects regardless of cost. Hitch was a member of the building committee that launched a drive to raise $50,000 for constructing a new church on November 1, 1942. As the money came in, the committee put the funds in War Bonds and a large thermometer-style poster registered the progress of the drive from month to month. By the end of the war, the goal had been expanded to $100,000. An architect prepared plans for the proposed structure. When

Henry and Christine in front of the stone house, ca. 1960.

the building committee met with the finance committee on February 4, 1948, Henry Hitch was among those who voiced the opinion that the structure would be inadequate. Some members of the finance committee, while wanting a larger, more expensive building, balked at the idea of spending more money. Could the church really afford it, they asked. After listening to much discussion on the subject, Henry told the group, "We can do it." That settled the matter. The committee revised the goal upward to $300,000 and sent the architect back to his drawing board. In April 1951 the large, new structure was completed. Victory Memorial Methodist Church was dedicated on Sunday, January 11, 1953, by Bishop W. Angie Smith in memory of those young men and women from Guymon who had served in World War II.[43]

Henry and Christine also were active in the No Man's Land Historical Society formed on October 3, 1934, to support the new No Man's Land Historical Museum on the campus of Panhandle A. and M. College. The Hitch family had long been interested in the college, which was founded in 1909. Both Marjorie and Ladd had attended the institution. Henry had known several agricultural scientists connected with the institution at one time or another, including Oliver Wilham, later president of Oklahoma State University, and H. H. Finnell of the Soil Conservation Service. Hitch also was a close friend of Ed Morrison, the president of the college. By 1940 the family often drove the ten miles to Goodwell after church services on Sunday to eat with President Morrison, faculty members, and friends in the college cafeteria.

When the No Man's Land Historical Society was organized, Henry and Uncle Charlie Hitch were appointed to the board of directors. The first president was Boss Neff, who had settled in the region shortly after J. K. Hitch arrived. On April 8, 1940, Ed Morrison presented plans to the society for building a $40,000 structure to house the museum. The job of raising money for the building was halted by the war, but within weeks after the surrender of Japan the board organized a finance committee to solicit the needed funds. Henry served on this committee and played an active role in getting others to serve in a similar capacity and to contribute money. It was not his nature to serve as chief spokesman for any cause. He preferred to work quietly in the background. Thus while Judge F. Hiner Dale served as chairman of the drive for Texas County, Henry worked as vice-chairman under Dale. During a meeting of the finance committee it was Henry who suggested that letters asking for donations be sent out over the popular Boss Neff's signature in order "to give it [the appeal] a large circulation."[44]

When the committee met in June, 1949, almost $20,000 had been raised. On that occasion Marvin McKee, now president of Panhandle A. and M., announced that the Oklahoma Legislature had appropriated $30,000 for the building if that amount could be matched by local contributions. The committee then set out to raise an additional $10,000 that year. The effort was successful.

The new $60,000 No Man's Land Museum was completed and dedicated in 1951. It was as much a monument to the philanthropic work of Henry Hitch as it was to the pioneers of the old Neutral Strip, few of whom were still alive. Boss Neff did not live to see the new building. Both he and Charlie Hitch died in 1947. Josie Westmoreland Hitch, who had been married to Charlie for more than fifty-six years, followed him in death only a few weeks later. In spite of his reluctance, the society elected Henry Hitch as Neff's successor, a position Henry held until his death twenty years later.[45] It was fitting that Henry serve in that capacity, for he was more than simply a part of the past that the society commemorated. His roots were deep in that heritage of the High Plains. He was one of the last living links between an earlier, more difficult, less complex age and a period of complex technology, commonplace luxuries, and hard decisions.

9. The Making of a Feedlot Empire

Twentieth-century technological advancements have affected virtually every aspect of American life in ways that are more often quantum jumps than evolutionary changes. American agriculture has certainly been no exception. Power sources have shifted from horses and mules to two-row gasoline tractors to massive diesel-engine machines capable of plowing 160 acres a day. Hybrid grains have increased crop production several times beyond what once was considered a normal yield. Whereas irrigation farmers once determined when to set their siphon tubes by scraping the soil with their boot toes, computerized sensors now provide more accurate information resulting in a more efficient use of water. Beef-cattle production on the Great Plains has changed from simple cow-calf or steer grass-finishing operations to feedlots stocked with 20,000 head or more gorging themselves on rations balanced by computers.

The Hitch family had always remained sensitive to innovations in agriculture. J. K. and Henry had been among the first in the Panhandle to plant alfalfa for hay, to raise registered Herefords to provide bulls for their commercial herd, and to use tractors and combines in their vast wheat-farming efforts. Later Ladd Hitch's early morning meetings demonstrated his organizational skills and his insistence on experimenting with new approaches to cut costs and to make the ranch operation more efficient.

THE HENRY C. HITCH RANCH : 1967

SEWARD

MORTON   KANSAS   STEVENS

T 6 S   R 9 E   R 12 E   R 13 E   R 14 E   R 15 E   R 16 E   R 17 E   R 18 E

T 5 N

Tyrone
Baker
Adams
Hooker
Straight
Optima
Hardesty
Hitchland
Guymon
Goodwell
Texhoma

Master Feedlot No. 1
Texas Co. Feedlot
Hitch Ranch Feedlot
Texas Lake

OKLAHOMA

SHERMAN   TEXAS

HANSFORD   OCHILTREE

R 19 E

Pony Cr.
Cow Cr.
Goff Cr.
Coldwater Cr.
Beaver River
Rock Cr.
Palo Duro Cr.
Kiowa Cr.
Mackaber Cr.
Chicago Cr.
N. Frisco Cr.
Frisco Cr.
Tepee Cr.
Sand Cr.
Beaver River

64   54   64   3   136   207   136   95   54   3   64

HOLDINGS IN KANSAS

R 35 W   R 33 W

T 32 S   T 33 S

Cimarron River
83
270
270
SEWARD COUNTY
13 mi. N. to Sublet -
5 mi. S. to Liberal
11 mi. W. to Hugoton

TEXAS

CIMARRON   TEXAS

T 4 N   Eva   Burton
T 3 N
T 2 N   Griggs
T 1 N

R 8 E   R 9 E   R 10 E   R 11 E

95   64   3

DALLAM

Each Township contains 36 (1 square mile) sections

6	5	4	3	2	1
7	8	9	10	11	12
18	17	16	15	14	13
19	20	21	22	23	24
30	29	28	27	26	25
31	32	33	34	35	36

0   5   10
miles

3   Highways
+++ Railroads
–   State Boundaries
- - - County Boundaries

■   Henry C. Hitch Ranch Holdings
Feedlots
○   Towns

J. L. Rogers

The Henry C. Hitch Ranch in 1967.

Soon after he was elected president of the Oklahoma Cattlemen's Association in 1965, Ladd implied that although livestock producers had been fairly successful in increasing production and keeping costs pared to the bone, they had not done well in marketing their product. "Marketing," he wrote, "is our biggest problem today. . . . It remains for us as cattlemen to become more solidly organized in presenting an honest and pleasing picture to our prospective buyers, our bankers, and to the housewives buying beef in every grocery store throughout the land."[1] Under Ladd's leadership, and with his father's support, the Henry C. Hitch Ranch between 1950 and 1970 changed from one of the largest ranches in the region into a large-scale beef factory.

The transformation began with the drilling of irrigation wells after World War II. The idea of irrigating the fertile flatlands of the Oklahoma High Plains was not new at the time. In 1895 the Optima Irrigation and Improvement Company was organized at Optima. Dyke Ballinger, Henry's early teacher and later an official of Beaver County, was probably a member of this organization. Although the company doubtless hoped to build a canal to water crops from the Beaver River, the canal failed to materialize.[2]

Interest in irrigation was revived in 1910 because of a drouth on the southern Great Plains. A few large irrigation wells delivering a thousand or more gallons a minute were sunk into the Ogallala aquifer on the High Plains of Texas, Kansas, and New Mexico in 1909–10. On March 1 and 2, 1910, a Northwestern Oklahoma Irrigation Congress met at Guymon. Among the leaders of the congress were John L. Gleason, D. C. Quinlan, M. W. Pugh, W. L. Roberts, and R. B. "Dick" Quinn, the pioneer Hardesty newspaperman. Speakers for the gathering included the former governor of Oklahoma Territory Thompson B. Ferguson, of Watonga, and the Oklahoma commissioner of charities, Kate Barnard, who was referred to in the local newspaper as "a go getter, to use the slang phrase of this section." Other addresses were delivered by gubernatorial candidates J. B. A. Robertson, Lee Cruce, and Joe McNeal. M. W. Pugh, of Cimarron County, introduced a resolution for the federal government to establish "experiment pumping stations . . . in the several counties within the area covered by said congress for the purpose of demonstrating the practicability and cost of irrigation." Another resolution insisted that the National Reclamation Service immediately survey possible reservoir sites in the region.[3]

The same week of this irrigation meeting, Stonebraker's Anchor-D Ranch sold four thousand acres to Edward F. Shellanburger, a steel manufacturer from DeKalb, Illinois. Shellanburger reportedly planned to plat his land into irrigation farms complete with wells and small reservoirs, and to put the properties on the market.

Irrigation enthusiasts abounded in the Panhandle in 1910. Doc Hover, manager of the Farmers' Union Milling Company of Guymon, installed a huge 14-foot wheel on his windmill and proudly announced that he was building a cement storage reservoir 60 feet long, 25 feet wide, and 5 feet deep, from which he hoped to irrigate two acres of truck garden and fruit trees. In October that year a group left Guymon one Sunday morning in an automobile caravan. The citizens drove 65 miles northwest to Richfield, Kansas, in Morton County, in order to view the marvels of a flowing artesian well some 580 feet deep. On the following Tuesday night, October 11, artesian well boosters held a mass meeting in Guymon. Developers of the new "university addition" to the town proposed to raise money for test drilling an artesian well on their plat by increasing

An unsuccessful effort to find artesian water in Texas County, 1911.

the price of each lot by twenty-five dollars. If successful, the lot owners would use the water as a domestic water source, not for irrigation. But such a well would demonstrate the existence of the artesian water for potential irrigation purposes. Seventy-five lots were sold at the meeting and the owners agreed to drill a well to a maximum depth of 2,000 feet if enough money could be raised.[4]

These early schemes never matured. No artesian water was discovered, and the drouth was over by 1913. In addition, the nonartesian ground water in many places was three hundred or more feet deep, making it expensive to tap. In the 1930s, however, Panhandle A. and M. College drilled a well to irrigate its farm. Henry and Ladd visited that well occasionally and watched it churn hundreds of gallons per minute to the surface. In the early 1940s, Ladd convinced Henry to drill a well, but the war intervened, creating an acute shortage of irrigation hardware.

When the young rancher got out of the navy in 1945, he inspected a number of irrigation wells on the Texas High Plains, a region that had been steadily expanding its irrigated acreage from relatively shallow wells since 1934. He looked at wells to the north at Hugoton, Kansas, which, like the Panhandle, drew its water from three hundred feet or more below the surface. After viewing the Hugoton pumping units, Hitch concluded that the irrigation of grain sorghums and wheat could be profitable in Texas County. In 1947 he and Henry drilled their first irrigation well, staking it on the north side of the ranch. At the time there were only two other wells in the county aside from Panhandle A. and M. College's pumping plant. Both, however, were small, drawing from shallow water formations near creeks and irrigating only a few acres of truck gardens.[5]

Nothing seemed to come easy for the tenacious Hitches. Irrigation was no exception. It took time to find a rotary rig, the kind used in drilling wells of larger diameter than that required by windmills. Ladd finally brought in one from outside the Panhandle. The first well was not adequately cased and it caved in. The driller bored a second well, but it "sanded in" around the casing perforations. Finally a third well was drilled and gravel-packed to prevent sand from shutting off the water. That one was a good well, producing eight to nine hundred gallons a minute.[6] When another of the region's cyclical drouths began in 1951, Ladd Hitch drilled several more wells, all gravel-packed. By 1958 some four thousand acres of grain sorghums, alfalfa, and wheat were being watered by nineteen wells on the ranch.[7]

To fuel his pumping plants, Ladd turned to the cheapest energy then available—natural gas. The Cities Service Company, one of the gas-well operators on the ranch,

An early irrigation well on the Hitch Ranch, ca. late 1940s.

allowed the Hitches to tap their own wells and thus obtain the gas at a wholesale price. But the Phillips Petroleum Company, the other major gas producer on the ranch, refused to allow irrigators to tie into their own wells. In 1955, Ladd Hitch organized the High Plains Natural Gas for Irrigation Association. That same year this group successfully lobbied in the Oklahoma legislature for a bill that required the operating companies to furnish irrigators with gas from wells situated on their own land. The bill was signed by Governor Raymond Gary.

Phillips announced plans to fight the law to the United States Supreme Court if necessary. On August 26, Hitch and other interested agriculturists and local businessmen met in an auditorium on the campus of Panhandle A. and M. College to denounce the Phillips action and to pledge financial support to litigate the case through the courts. The oil company won the case when the Oklahoma Supreme Court declared the law unconstitutional. Other companies, however, tended to follow the lead of Cities Service rather than Phillips, which thereby lost the general good will of irrigation farmers in the region. In later years Ladd remarked, "I have always resented the fact that Phillips would not allow the gas from under our own land to power our own irrigation wells."[8]

Young Hitch's plunge into irrigation illustrated a significant aspect of his relationship with his father. Although Henry was not overly enthusiastic about irrigation on so broad a scale, he allowed his son complete independence in his work. Ladd recalled, "Father many times thought I was too adventurous in expanding irrigation and in other areas, but he always supported me in my endeavors and took pride in the results, which were usually but not always good."[9]

Irrigation opened the gate for yet another experiment: a feedlot enterprise. It is ironic that the southern Great Plains, long a producer of both cattle and feedstuffs, had failed to develop a major feedlot industry before the 1960s. A few cattlemen and stock farmers had always "finished out" their yearlings in the region with home-grown feed, primarily grain sorghums.[10]

Most feeder cattle produced in the region were shipped to the corn belt of the Midwest or to the irrigated region of southern Arizona or California's Imperial Valley. For example, the David Rankin farms of Tarkio, Missouri, had 1,900 cattle in its feedlots at the turn of the century. Most of them bore the XIT brand of the Texas Panhandle ranch. In the 1930s the Ernie Nefstead farm of central Illinois finished out steers bought from the King Ranch of Texas.

In 1952 the Hitch Ranch sent some of its own cattle into a feedlot near Phoenix for custom finishing. The Arizona feedlots not only used feeder stock produced in the Oklahoma Panhandle and West Texas, but also purchased threshed grain sorghum grown in the same region to feed the animals. As Ladd put it, "They bought our cattle and bought our grain and the only asset they had was a little better weather for feeding cattle." The cattle market dropped sharply the next year. In the first significant break in the livestock market since the Great Depression, average prices dropped from $25.71 to $17.66 per hundredweight in the early 1950s. The Hitches took what cattlemen called a "severe beating" on their Arizona cattle when they sent them to market in 1953.[11]

The Arizona lesson was not lost on Ladd. Because of the cost-price squeeze, he decided that if Arizonans could make money importing both Oklahoma cattle and grain, a Panhandle cowman should be able to make a go of it by feeding his grain to his cattle. Actually the Hitches had already been feeding out a few hundred head of their cattle each year. As early as 1950, hired hands erected some wooden feed bunks on the north side of the ranch between the irrigated cropland and the grassland near one of the breaks (or gullies) leading to the Coldwater. According to long-time employee Kenneth Frantz, troughs had been used to feed cottonseed cake to a group of steers.[12]

In 1953 the Hitches began building a modern feedlot at that site to utilize their own home-grown feedstuffs. At first only four pens were constructed. The only other feedlot in Texas County at the time, and perhaps in the entire Oklahoma Panhandle, was one owned by a cattleman named Morris Freeman at Texhoma. Ladd fed ensilage cut from tall grain sorghums and grain threshed from the heads of milo maize. The ensilage was stored in trench silos cut into the banks of the breaks and in an elevator at the site.[13]

Ladd encountered a number of problems at first. For example, in order to forgo the construction of an expensive feed mill, he bought a mixer box from a Kansas City firm and mounted it on a truck. When the first load of ensilage was dumped into the box with a tractor-mounted scoop, the machinery locked down. It obviously was not designed to handle coarsely ground grain sorghum. Hitch sold the machine back to the manufacturing firm at a considerable loss and began looking at other boxes. Mixer boxes that were sufficiently powerful to mix the ensilage required much larger, more expensive trucks. Finally he found the kind of box that suited the job. Manufactured by a small machine shop in Garden City, Kansas, the machine had a pair of large augers in the bottom rotating in opposite directions rather than the single auger of most boxes. The mixer box was also mounted on scales, with a stamping device located in the cab of the truck so that the feed could be accurately weighed before being augered into feed bunks as the vehicle moved slowly down each "alley."

Nontechnological problems were more difficult to

solve. Guymon did not have a single professional veterinarian at the time. There were no packing houses in the
Panhandle to furnish a convenient market. Moreover,
meat processors repeatedly demonstrated a bias against
grain sorghum-fed beef. On a number of occasions when
Ladd contacted packing firms, the first question asked by
the prospective buyer was, "Are your cattle corn-fed?"
When Hitch replied that they were fattened on milo, the
usual response was, "Oh well, we might try a load," as
though the packer were offering an extraordinary act of
charity. Worse, the steers fed on milo brought lower prices
than their cornfed cousins in many cases, although the
consumer could not taste the difference in tenderness or
texture.[14]

Hitch hired an experienced feeder named Cecil Reedy
to manage his feedlot and gave him a relatively free hand
in its day-by-day operation. Under Reedy's supervision the
facility was gradually enlarged "like a patch quilt" during
the next several years, according to Reedy's wife, Juanita,
who kept the records detailing feeding rations for each pen.
Within a couple of years the feedlot had a one-time capacity of 1,000 head, but Ladd continued to enlarge the operation. At first Reedy's rations ratio was usually determined
by the quantity of ensilage harvested. The more ensilage
available, the less grain in the rations, and vice versa. The
feedlot manager subsequently experimented with various
grain–ensilage-roughage mixtures, feeding at one time up
to 50 percent grain. He used a large chalkboard in the
office to keep a daily account of ratios and quantities for
each pen. Juanita Reedy then transferred the figures to
legal pads for permanent records.[15] The operation of a
large feedlot was indeed complex. When someone asked
Ladd if he really believed that the Panhandle was a cattle-
feeding country, he replied with his characteristic grin,

"Yes, this is a cattle-feeding country, but there aren't many cattle feeding people [here]."[16]

The biggest obstacle to feeding was the low price of cattle throughout the middle 1950s. Ladd recalled that the operation lost money from 1952 until 1957. Although Henry at first was not enthusiastic about the feed yard, he became convinced, after watching it grow, that the enterprise would have a profitable future when livestock prices moved upward once more. The wisdom of Henry Hitch's movement toward diversifying his financial interests now paid off. In 1958 his gross dividends from the stock that he had been buying since 1933 amounted to more than $114,000. That, coupled with natural gas royalties, helped to cushion the losses in cattle. Henry simply dipped into those earnings to offset the feedlot losses.[17]

In striving to cut costs and improve the efficiency of their operations, the Hitches retained the nationally prestigious Doane's Agricultural Service to do a "linear program analysis" in the late 1950s. Doane's reported that for the most profit the Hitches should continue to market their feedstuffs through their cattle and in addition eliminate their cow-calf herd and utilize the grass exclusively for feeder-cattle conditioning before putting them into the lot.

The ranch always had pastured some steers, but the heart of the operation had been its cow-calf commercial herd. After the depression of the thirties Henry had even restocked the headquarters pasture with a registered Hereford herd. Ladd was convinced that Doane's analysis was correct. Doing away with the cows would clear the way for a much greater turnover in numbers of cattle pastured on grass and hay. Theoretically, the greater the turnover in numbers, the bigger the profit—if the market price did not slip. Ladd put it this way: "From that time

Part of the Hitch Ranch feedlot, ca. 1960.

forward we have set as a goal the raising of mass forage on our property and converting that forage into grain-fed beef. . . . Father was always a little nervous about going forward in the full finishing of cattle to the U. S. Choice grade [achieved only through feedlot finishing], but he always supported me in my efforts and we continued to grow."[18] Subsequently the Hitch Ranch began culling its herd of commercial cows. Finally, on May 2, 1960, Henry and Ladd conducted a dispersal sale at Guymon at which they auctioned off not only the remaining cream of their herd, but also their entire group of registered Herefords, consisting of 117 cows and 31 bulls.[19]

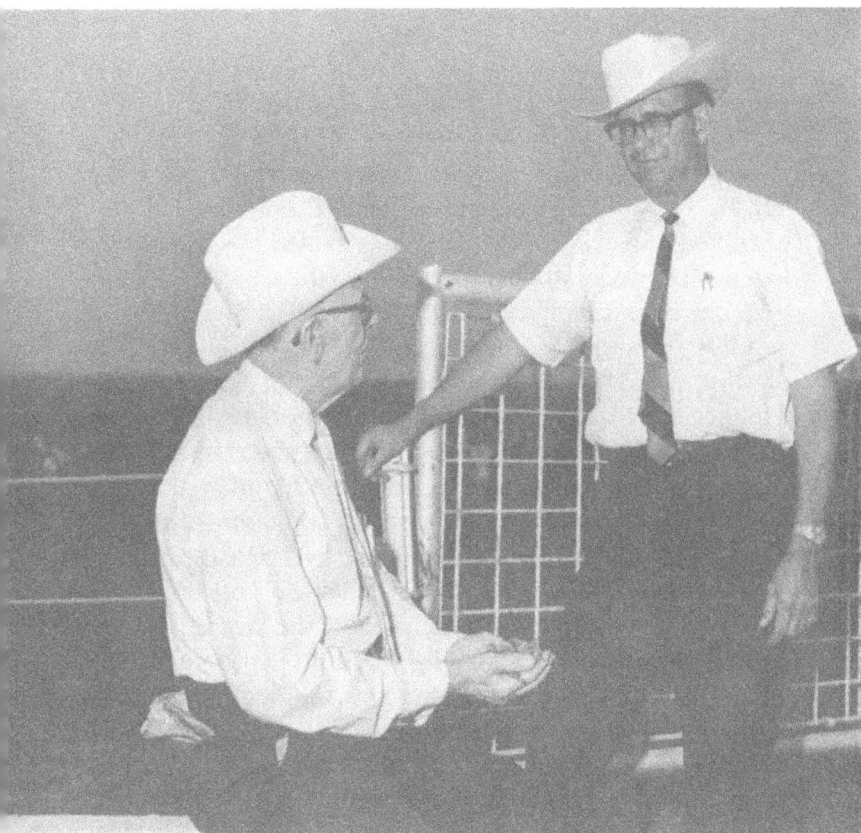

Henry and Ladd at the feedlot, ca. 1962.

The Henry C. Hitch Ranch became a modern beef factory. Steers were purchased every few weeks, put on grass, wheat pasture, or hay for a few weeks, then transferred to the feedlot. After approximately ninety days in the lot the animals were sold to packing-house agents. By 1958 the feedlot contained 5,000 head. Seven trench silos held 3,500 tons each of ensilage cut from 1,200 irrigated acres.

That fall, seventeen ensilage cutters harvested the crop and a steady stream of trailers was pulled from field to silo where the forage was dumped. Crawler tractors then leveled the ensilage in the trenches before the feed was covered with large plastic sheets. Combines cut and threshed redheaded milo and trucks hauled the grain to the tall steel cylindrical bins surrounding the elevator. One to five carloads of finished cattle a week were shipped to market, primarily to Oklahoma City.[20]

On the southern Great Plains south of Colorado the Hitches were among the earliest operators of large feedlots. W. L. Stangel, a prominent animal scientist at Texas Tech, had advocated turning the High Plains region into one big feedlot since he first arrived at Lubbock in 1925. Of the few lots in the entire region by 1960, the custom feed yard of D. W. Lewter near Lubbock, with its thirty-thousand-head capacity, was probably the largest (custom lots finish out cattle belonging to others on some kind of commission basis). In 1959, Stangel and Sam Thomas, of the Southwestern Public Service Company (a regional electrical utility concern) in Amarillo, organized the first of several tours of feedlots in the Midwest, California, and Arizona for cattlemen from Texas, Oklahoma, and New Mexico. The purpose of the two men was to arouse the cattlemen's interest in constructing similar lots.[21]

About the time those tours began, the Hitch Ranch feedlot had a modern grinder-mixer plant installed, and its storage bins were enlarged to hold 200,000 bushels of feed grain. Cecil Reedy now had his blackboard in a glass-enclosed cubicle beside stationary scales. Feed trucks drove onto the scales, and Reedy pushed a button or two that released premixed feed in any ratio into the truck's hopper. With four hired hands Reedy handled the entire feeding operation of several thousand head with more ease than he had once fed fewer than a thousand cattle.[22]

By the middle 1960s, aided by a steady rise in cattle prices, a boom in feedlot construction had hit the plains. In 1967 there were 274 yards in the Oklahoma, Texas, and New Mexico region of the High Plains, feeding almost 1 1/2 million head of cattle a year. Two years later there were 29 feedlots in the Oklahoma Panhandle alone with a one-time total capacity of 358,000 head. Two-thirds of the lots in the region had been established after 1960. Some had capacities of 50,000 head.[23]

Riding the trend, Ladd Hitch not only enlarged the ranch feedlot to 20,000 head, making it into probably the largest noncustom yard in the nation, but also he began building custom lots. In 1965 he formed a company to construct the Texas County Feed Lot with a 50,000-head-per-year capacity northeast of Guymon. Ladd retained 27 1/2 percent of the stock in the company, and Henry owned an additional large block of the shares. Stock was also owned by Ralph Grounds, his son R. G. Grounds, and Ray Kimsey, all of Guymon. The remaining shares were divided among Leo Winters, of Hooker, the Oklahoma state treasurer, and three men who owned a packing plant at Dodge City. Two years later the Hitches formed another company with Ralph and R. G. Grounds and Leo Winters to build a 22,000-head, one-time capacity feedlot southwest of Hooker. They named it Master Feeders. In 1969 the company built Master Feeders II south of Garden City, Kansas, in the midst of an irrigated corn region. That lot finished cattle exclusively on high-moisture ensilage corn produced by local farmers and marketed at the facility. Later the Groundses and Winters sold their interest in Master Feeders to Ladd's son Paul and son-in-law, Clark Willingham. Another significant change occurred in the 1960s when Ladd began to replace grain sorghum

Henry C. Hitch driving through the pastures on the ranch, ca. 1960. Here he stops to talk with Joe Fitzgerald, the farm and irrigation manager. Courtesy of Joe Fitzgerald.

production on the ranch's cropland with irrigated corn, which produced more ensilage per acre. And milo was replaced with shelled corn grown under sprinkler irrigation on the 2,000 acres of Seward County, Kansas, land that centered around Henry Hitch's original homestead.[24]

Hitch enterprises outgrew the office-den that Henry had added to the stone house in the 1920s. In 1951 Henry and Ladd moved two desks into an office in the newly completed Dale Hotel in Guymon. The office was shared with E. E. McDaniel, an old friend and real estate agent through whom Henry had been buying land for more than

Henry in the early 1960s, dressed to ride in the annual Pioneer Days celebration at Guymon.

three decades. The new location was appropriate. The hotel had been built by an eminent Texas County jurist, F. Hiner Dale, with liberal financial support from Guymon businessmen who desired to provide the Panhandle with a "first-class" hostelry and small convention center. Embedded in the marble tile floor of the lobby were most of the historic brands of the central Panhandle, including the Anchor-D (⊕), the OX, Boss Neff's ℕℲ, Henry Westmoreland's LV, J. K. Hitch's simple Circle, Charlie Hitch's 7, George Hitch's Circle-Cross L (♀), and the Henry C. Hitch Ranch's Lazy Eight (∞).

E. E. McDaniel eventually bought the hotel, and the ranch leased two offices on the mezzanine in 1965. Henry and Ladd shared one room. The bookkeeper, Joe McGrew, and a secretary shared the adjoining office. In the next few years Hitch enterprises expanded until the ranch leased the entire mezzanine and two additional rooms in the hotel for storage purposes. The most striking feature of the Hitches' office was the longhorn steer's head, acquired by Henry in the 1920s, that was mounted on the wall behind his desk.[25]

Henry remained physically strong as he moved into his twilight years. He gave no indication of retiring as he continued to deal in cattle and the stock market. Only in his 70s did his full head of hair begin to gray. He posed for a photograph on his eightieth birthday. When he saw the picture, he noted with a grin that he looked somewhat "mature." Yet he could easily have passed for a man fifteen years younger. Always in good health and rarely suffering even a head cold, he was in a hospital bed only once in his life. That was for a hernia operation in his later years. He resented giving those few days to a convalescent bed.

Hitch resumed his old partnership with Frank Atkinson

Henry C. Hitch at age eighty.

of Kansas in the 1950s. They had been partners in a steer operation during the 1920s. Henry wintered the animals and Atkinson finished them out on the bluestem grass of his ranch at Diamond Springs, Kansas. Just before the Great Depression, Atkinson owed Henry a great deal of money, his share of partnership earnings. The Depression wiped out that money. Atkinson approached Hitch in 1952. He told Henry that there was no way he could pay off the debt using his resources only. On the other hand, if Henry would extend him his (Hitch's) line of credit and form another partnership, Atkinson would buy the steers, pasture the animals, and market them. Henry agreed to the proposal. Low cattle prices caused the partners to lose money at first, but when the market began to recover by 1955, they began to make a profit. By 1958 Frank Atkinson had paid Hitch the $100,000 he owed him, and they had another $250,000 in the partnership. But the decline in the cattle market in 1963–64 hit them hard. They lost the $250,000 and another $100,000 as well. Henry had gone full circle. He and Atkinson decided to end the partnership for good.[26]

Henry enjoyed leaving his office in the Dale Hotel in the middle of the afternoon to drive through the feedlots and the ranch on his way home. When it was time for the late afternoon stock market quotations to be broadcast, he would turn on his car radio while cruising slowly through the pastures. He not only enjoyed looking at beautiful sleek cattle, but also he took special note of any sick livestock he chanced upon. Farm manager O. C. "Cotton" Furnish said that Henry could "smell" a case of screwworms (maggots that feed on even the slightest wounds of livestock). He occasionally paused to speak with a hired hand about his work. Sometimes in the summer the Coldwater rancher would get Bud Perkins, who was now an

Guymon residents on a fishing excursion to Canada in the early 1950s. Henry and Ladd are second and third from left. Orville Nash is fourth from the left.

oil company jobber in Guymon, to drive with him to the Colorado Rockies for a two-to three-day jaunt. Christine's sister Erma Walker Monesmith once noted that those mountains were like "manna" to Henry. On those short drives Henry and Bud would often reminisce about the old days. Bud very much enjoyed those insights into the past.[27]

For recreation Henry also enjoyed more extensive travel. In 1952 and 1953 he joined Ladd and several other Guymon men who flew their private planes to Canada for fishing vacations. Of course, he and Christine traveled to Orlando, Florida, almost every year to visit the Price family and to inspect their orange groves. In 1956, Henry was invited to visit the Soviet Union on an agricultural tour sponsored by the Oklahoma Publishing Company and

Henry inspects a collective dairy farm during the tour to Russia, 1956.

conducted by journalist Roy P. Stewart. He enthusiastically joined the group for the gruelling twenty-day tour that stretched from Leningrad to the Caucasus Mountains. He never seemed to tire and even chose an optional side trip through western Europe and Great Britain before returning.[28]

As Henry Hitch approached his eighty-first birthday in 1965, he drove to Alaska with his son-in-law John Gray, who owned radio stations in Guymon and Liberal. The elderly rancher's only regret in traveling was that Christine was unable to join him most of the time because her arthritis was getting worse. She required a cane, but she bore the pain and encouraged Henry in all his activities as she always had done. Moreover, she rarely allowed her

Henry on a side tour of Herefordshire, England, during his return from Russia, 1956. He stands at the far left.

illness to stand in the way of her religious, social, and family obligations. She was not above poking gentle fun at her condition. When she wrote to her sister in 1971 she noted, "I am feeling very well. Even my dreadful feet responded to the podiatrist when I told him to make me comfortable enough to go to the many weddings. I give

Henry and Christine celebrating their fifty-fifth wedding anniversary in 1965. Behind them are (left to right) Joyce, Ladd, and Marjorie.

them constant care . . . and different shoes. My closet looks like I might be a centipede."[29]

Despite her arthritis, Christine, who once had observed beauty even in a dust storm, continued to marvel at the aesthetic nature of agriculture. Once she wrote to Erma of their wheat: "We are in harvest. It is not too good this year—but it is beautiful—the waving golden fields—I love it at every stage—from the fresh turned earth—the heavy green with cattle contentedly grazing on it—to the cut stubble."[30]

Although she was heavily involved in a number of civic and philanthropic activities, Christine continued to take an active interest in the welfare of the hired hands' children. Long after most of their neighbors had gotten rid of their milch cows, the Hitches kept a few because Christine insisted that the ranch provide the children with milk at no cost to the workers. When the wife of one hired hand deserted her family, the Chicano father put his three children in an Oklahoma City orphanage. The children wanted to remain with their father and demonstrated their displeasure by fleeing the orphanage. Hearing of their plight, Christine brought the children back to the ranch and hired a woman specifically to care and cook for them.[31]

Christine Hitch's later years were filled with honors. In 1962 she was one of ten finalists for Oklahoma's Mother of the Year Award. Two years later she rode in the Pioneer Days parade in Guymon as that year's "Pioneer Queen," clothed in a long Victorian-style gingham dress complete with bonnet. In 1972 she became the first citizen of the Panhandle to be inducted into the Oklahoma Hall of Fame, and Oklahoma City University conferred on her an honorary Doctor of Humane Letters degree in recognition of her philanthropy.[32]

After World War II, with the building of a more extensive network of hard-surface roads in rural areas and the development of faster automobiles and pickup trucks, farmers and ranchers of the region began moving to town in greater numbers. They became commuters, driving

Christine as Pioneer Queen of the Pioneer Days celebration at
Guymon in 1964.

President Dolph Whitten of Oklahoma City University awards Christine an honorary Doctor of Humane Letters degree, 1974. Courtesy of Oklahoma City University.

each day to their farms and back, while their families enjoyed the material and social advantages of small-town living. That trend continued until the crumbling silhouettes of vacant houses dotted the countryside. The Hitch family, however, bucked the mainstream. Most of them remained on the Coldwater and built or enlarged their homes until the headquarters resembled a small town, lacking only a general store and a post office.

The family at this time consisted of a number of grandchildren who were as near to each other in their relationships as the family houses. The children of Ladd and Joyce were more like brothers and sisters than cousins. When Joyce's daughter, Christina ("Tina") attended Oklahoma State University, she roomed with Ladd's daughter Jane. When she was graduated from the university with a B. A. degree in music education, she married Edward Herron, who received his bachelor's degree in business administration from Oklahoma State. The couple moved to the Coldwater in 1971 and built a house just west of her parents' home. Ladd's oldest son, Paul, like his father, was graduated from Oklahoma State University. He then took his master's in business administration from Stanford University and returned to the Coldwater to work with Ladd in the feedlot business in 1967. That same year he married Linda Surguy, a teacher and graduate of Oklahoma State.

Two of the children settled elsewhere. Ladd's daughter Jane, who was chosen Miss Oklahoma in 1964, was graduated from Oklahoma State and married attorney Clark Willingham, a graduate of Texas Tech and Southern Methodist University's School of Law, in 1969. The couple moved to Dallas, but remained associated with Hitch enterprises. Joyce's son Bradford was attracted to scholarly pursuits. He was graduated from Oklahoma State, took his M. A. degree in sociology from the same institution, and was awarded the Ph. D. degree from Yale University. He joined the faculty of the University of North Carolina, then went to Columbia University on a Ford Foundation grant before joining the National Commission for the Protection of Human Subjects of Bio-Medical and

The stone house today, home of Paul and Linda Hitch.

Behavioral Research in Washington, D. C. There he completed a book entitled *Human Subjects in Medical Experimentation.*[33]

Marjorie Price's children, W. K., Jr. ("Dub") and Karick, were reared in Florida. "Dub" entered a seminary and became a minister, while Karick moved into the business world. The Prices continued to visit regularly with the Hitches; Henry, Christine, and their children and grandchildren periodically traveled to Florida or the Prices trekked to the Coldwater.

The family, however, was not immune to tragedy. In 1964 W. K. Price was suddenly seized by a fatal heart attack while he and Marjorie were playing golf with another couple at Orlando. Karick, only 26 years old at the time of his father's death, assumed the management of the orange groves, became successful at it, and was eventually appointed an officer in the Florida Citrus Commission. An even greater shock was the death of Ladd's youngest child, Jim. The blond handsome youth was seventeen years old, a gifted athlete, an A student, and one of the most popular boys in Guymon High School. He played golf until sunset on March 3, 1970, returned home, and spent several hours studying that night before retiring. The next morning when Lala went to his room at about six o'clock, she could not awaken him. The cause of death was fulminating viremia, an extremely rare and often fatal disorder.[34]

Financial success never changed Henry Hitch. His philanthropic and civic responsibilities increased as he was named a director of the new Cowboy Hall of Fame in Oklahoma City and of the Oklahoma State Fair. He also served as a trustee of the Guymon Memorial Foundation (which built a nonprofit convalescent home for the elderly), of Oklahoma City University, and of the IOA Boys Ranch at Perkins, Oklahoma. A number of honors came his way, but probably none produced a greater feeling of pride than when his late father was inducted into the Cowboy Hall of Fame. After Henry's death he, too, would be inducted into the Hall. Despite wealth and honor, he remained a man of the Panhandle soil who felt at home only on the Coldwater. The Longhorn steer's head and a fresh painting of J. K. Hitch's original sod-house claim by the well-known western Oklahoma artist Augusta Metcalf, both of which hung in his offices at the Dale Hotel, revealed more about Henry Hitch than his financial statement. I have been told by a number of Guymon and Texas County folks that Henry "never acted like a rich man," perhaps the greatest compliment that could be uttered about a wealthy person by people from the short-grass country.

He continued to rise at 4:30 or 5:00 A.M. Much of the time he cooked his favorite breakfast of steak, biscuits, and gravy for the family. On Saturday, December 30, 1967, Henry rose early as usual and cooked breakfast. At 7:30 the family gathered around the big round dining table for the morning meeting and another cup of coffee. They talked of many things, including the progress of their new Masters Feedlot under construction near Hooker. Toward the end of the meeting, Ladd handed his father some business papers about a tax matter. Suddenly a painful seizure gripped Henry, and he fell forward from his chair. He was already unconscious. Within a matter of seconds Henry Hitch was dead of a heart attack.[35]

The funeral was held on January 1, 1968, in the Victory Memorial Methodist Church that Henry's mother had been instrumental in starting at old Roy in 1888. No one had been more responsible for the present spacious sanctuary than Henry himself. W. Angie Smith, the Methodist bishop for the Oklahoma and New Mexico district, delivered the funeral sermon. The Masonic Lodge, of which Henry had been a member for half a century, conducted the burial services at the Guymon cemetery.[36]

At the time of his death Henry was eighty-three years old. Only a couple of weeks before, he had climbed to the top row of the bleachers at the livestock auction in Guymon to sit beside an old friend and fellow cattleman named Tom Pugh. Pugh had asked him about the citrus farm in Florida. Henry had delighted Tom with details of its operation and beauty. They probably also had reminisced about many things—the tough days of the depression and dust bowl, changes in the cattle business, and things about cattle and horses that only another old cowman could fully appreciate. During the course of that conversation Pugh remarked that Hitch had certainly "cut a wide swath" and acquired a vast estate in the process. Henry candidly told his friend that the only difference between him and many other hard-working ranchers was that he had never been afraid of going deeply into debt to invest in land. He said that during his lifetime he had borrowed every dollar he could for that purpose.[37]

Henry Hitch had loaned money as readily to neighbors in need as he borrowed it, usually without mentioning it to any member of the family. After his funeral a number of friends told family members that Henry at one time or another had loaned them money without so much as a promissory note.[38] Perhaps the greatest tribute to Henry Hitch was that made by State Treasurer Leo Winters, of Hooker, who remarked: "He's the only rich man I've ever known I have never heard anyone say a bad word about. But then again, on second thought, I never heard Mr. Henry say anything bad about anyone else."[39]

Epilogue

The contemporary Henry C. Hitch Ranch has continued to expand its interests. In addition to 17,000 acres of grassland, the cropland in Texas County and Seward County by 1968 consisted of 8,000 acres watered by forty-five irrigation wells. Ensilage from hybrid corn was produced in Texas County while the Seward County land furnished shelled corn. Virtually every acre of crop production was marketed through the ranch's feedlots. In 1973, Ladd Hitch installed thirteen center pivot sprinkler systems, each capable of watering about 120 acres, along the Coldwater Valley to increase hay production. The land remained in the hands of various members of the family. Henry put much of it into a trust before his death; consequently, most of the land is owned by this trust or jointly by Christine and the trust. The family manages its interests within several corporate umbrellas, such as the Henry C. Hitch Ranch, the Henry C. Hitch Farm, and the Henry C. Hitch Feed Lot. Those concerns, wholly owned by the family, lease their lands from the family and the trust because of an Oklahoma law that prohibits corporate ownership of agricultural acreage.

Family corporations also control other operations. Feeders Grain and Fertilizer, Inc., was organized to buy additional grain for the feedlots. Ladd put together Master Cattle Company to buy large numbers of feeder cattle for feedlot customers and the ranch, as well as to market

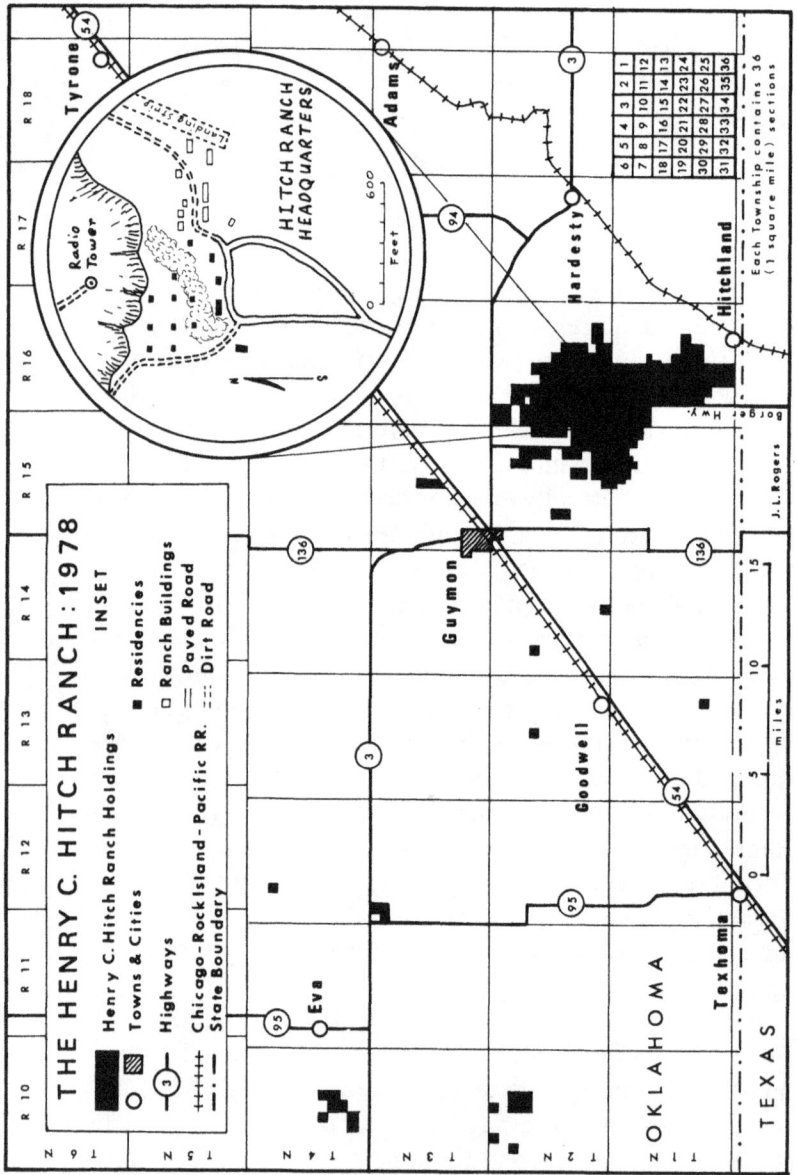

The Henry C. Hitch Ranch in 1978.

the finished beef. By 1968 that company was buying and selling more than 150,000 head per year. An article in the *Oklahoma Cowman* stated that Ladd Hitch "is the largest handler of cattle in the state, and one of the most progressive men in the industry today . . ., and is in large measure responsible for the dramatic growth in feeding in Texas County, Oklahoma's largest feeding area."[1]

Master Cattle Company also secured a seat on the Chicago Board of Trade and opened a brokerage firm named Master Commodities on the mezzanine of the Dale Hotel specializing in live cattle futures. In the rooms of Master Commodities, a large board continually flashes daily market and futures prices across one wall. To lessen his risks, Ladd and his staff use the facility to "hedge" in live cattle futures.[2]

The growth of the feedlot industry under Hitch leadership has been an economic "lightning rod" attracting related industries to the Guymon area. For example, Swift and Company in 1967 opened a packing plant at Guymon with an annual slaughtering capacity of 145,600 head. Two years later Ladd and Paul Hitch organized Diversified Data, Inc., to bring the first computer to the Panhandle. The firm opened its offices in Guymon with a small staff. At first its only customers were Hitch enterprises, but gradually Diversified Data began to attract other Guymon businessmen to use its services. In the early 1970s the family bought a packing house in Booker, Texas, near Perryton. And in 1977 Ladd organized a company to establish daily air transportation of freight and passengers between Guymon and Oklahoma City.

Today the Hitch family has interests in sixteen different corporations, ten family partnerships, and a number of trusts. Hitch enterprises probably meets the largest single payroll in the Panhandle, with about 325 employees rang-

O. C. ("Cotton") Furnish, (center) manager of the Henry C. Hitch Ranch, with Paul Hitch (left) and Ladd Hitch (H. C., Jr.).

ing from computer technicians and veterinarians to cow hands.[3] The economic significance of the Henry C. Hitch Ranch for Texas County is perhaps best summarized by longtime family friend Orville Nash, one of Guymon's most prominent businessmen. Nash put it this way: "I always liked to see the Hitches succeed because when they did, they reinvested their earnings in Guymon."[4] The fact the inhabitants refer to Guymon today as the "Hub City" of the Panhandle in no small measure is due to Hitch entrepreneurship.

Dr. Don Williams, center, manager of the Hitch Ranch Feedlot.

In recognition of Ladd Hitch's accomplishments, *Feedlot Magazine* chose him as the nation's National Beef Feeder for 1965. *Progressive Farmer* named him its Man of the Year in Oklahoma Agriculture for 1970. In 1973 the *Record Stockman,* a weekly newspaper published in Denver, Colorado, polled its readers for a list of persons considered the most significant leaders of the industry. Among those final twenty-nine "Stockmen of the Century" was Ladd Hitch.[5]

Although Hitch serves as president, the family's corporations are not one-man operations. In addition to Ladd, Paul, and Clark Willingham, the enterprises have a number of capable associates and managers. Ladd believes, "Two heads are better than one, and good ideas usually come out of any discussion of a particular problem when two interested people sit down and talk it over." Because the Hitches want to attract a capable managerial staff, their salary scale compares favorably with other businesses of comparable size. The quality of the field managers, each of whom has been with the Hitch Ranch for more than twenty-five years, leaves Ladd and Paul free to concentrate on policies rather than on day-to-day operations. The ranch manager, O. C. ("Cotton") Furnish, is responsible for processing shipments of cattle into the ranch. Before turning the animals into grass pastures he supervises the branding, vaccination, and ear-marking operations. Sick cattle are treated. In winter he oversees the haying of cattle in the pastures. After a few weeks or months on grass or hay, Furnish moves the livestock to the ranch feedlot where Dr. Don Williams, a veterinarian and animal nutritionist, serves as manager.

Joe Fitzgerald, the farm and irrigation manager, directs the cutting of ensilage and harvesting of wheat by "custom" operators. During the summer he flies over the fields almost

Ladd and Paul Hitch beside the ranch's Cessna Skymaster. Courtesy of Donald A. Brown, Farm Credit Banks of Wichita, Kansas.

every day in one of the ranch's Cessna airplanes to check the thousands of acres of watering systems in Oklahoma and Kansas. In less than two hours Fitzgerald can do the work of several men working the better part of a day on the ground. When he discovers a problem, he simply radios the information to one of the hands in a pickup who, in turn, makes the correction or repair. Consequently, farm hands are able to make better use of their time with other tasks in the fields. Communications are almost instantaneous by means of a two-way radio network linking the Hitch offices with managers and hands in twenty-eight vehicles owned by the ranch. The automobiles of Master

Henry Hitch, Ladd (H. C., Jr.), and Ladd's son Jim pose with their first airplane.

Cattle Company's order buyers are equipped with mobile telephones.[6]

The Hitch family obviously has come a long way since that day almost a century ago when James K. Hitch first viewed the lush bottomland of the Coldwater Valley. When Donald Brown, an agricultural journalist from Wichita, Kansas, visited the ranch's offices to gather materials for an article in 1977, Ladd told him, "I'm not going to climb on a horse to have my picture taken. That's not how I spend my day." Instead, Hitch's day begins soon after the morning meeting when he drives from the ranch into Guymon. He spends most of the morning in the rooms of Master Commodities and in his office just down the corridor where he has a small TV monitor spliced into the Chicago futures markets. The most crucial decisions of the day are made in those hours. Much of the time he is on the phone or in conference like any other business executive.

Some days he takes a short drive to the airport west of town to board his Cessna Skymaster, a high-wing plane powered by twin-engines—one in the nose and the other at the rear of the fuselage—which gives him an unobstructed view of the terrain. If he has paper work or reading to do, he turns on the auto pilot. After flying to Wichita, Oklahoma City, or some other city on business, he can be back in the office late that same afternoon or early the next morning.[7] Indeed Ladd Hitch's average day is a far cry from the early workdays of his grandfather or his father when they rode long hours in the saddle or transported the pieces of a combine to the ranch by horse-drawn wagon. The two eras are as different as a pair of spurs and a computer.

Yet on the Coldwater one is never really far from the past. Paul Hitch, his wife, Linda, and their children live in the stone house built by his great-grandfather (after Henry's death Christine moved next door into Ladd's and Lala's house). The ruins of other early stone houses stand here and there along the valley of the Coldwater. Flying over the area, one can see an occasional pockmark left by some early settler's long-vanished dugout and the traces of wagon ruts winding across the Hitch Ranch as part of a road that once connected Guymon to Hansford, Texas.

Driving up the Coldwater from the ranch headquarters

Ladd Hitch, agri-businessman, today. Courtesy of Donald A. Brown, Farm Credit Banks of Wichita, Kansas.

where J. K. Hitch first erected a sod house more than ninety years ago, the visitor follows a pasture road that was first laid out by the Hitches and Westmorelands. All the land in the valley to the Texas line is still retained by descendants of those families. Charlie Hitch's sole surviving daughter and her husband, Mary "Lit" and Leo Hall, live in the family ranch house at the south end of the valley. The Roy cemetery can be seen east of the old Westmoreland ranch. A few weathered headstones of flat native rock and an ancient barbed-wire fence mark the small enclosure. However, the oldest grave in the

Ruins of the George Westmoreland house today.

Ruins of the Tom Murphy homestead on the Hitch Ranch in 1965.

The Roy cemetery today.

Stone barn on the Charlie Hitch Ranch today.

valley is not in that cemetery. It is in the back yard of Ladd Hitch's home under a large elm tree. There lies the ivy-covered grave of Mary Westmoreland Hitch, symbolizing the historic link between the generations that have molded the Henry C. Hitch Ranch.

Notes

CHAPTER 1

1. The author draws solely upon his early background in ranching, a personal inspection of the Hitch Ranch and an attempt at "historical imagination" for this completely plausible scene.

2. Carl Coke Rister, *No Man's Land,* pp. 31–33.

3. Harry E. Chrisman, *Lost Trails of the Cimarron,* pp. 75–76.

4. Ibid., pp. 169–70.

5. Rister, *No Man's Land,* p. 34; Chrisman, *Lost Trails of the Cimarron,* pp. 78–80.

6. Chrisman, *Lost Trails of the Cimarron,* p. 83.

7. Rister, *No Man's Land,* pp. 31–45.

8. Personal interview with Henry C. Hitch by John Gray, ca. 1967, Guymon, Okla., in Living Legend Library, Oklahoma Christian College, Oklahoma City (hereafter cited as personal interview with Henry C. Hitch, LLL).

9. J. R. Spears, "No Man's Land," *New York Sun,* January 20, 1889, quoted in Rister, *No Man's Land,* pp. 3–4.

10. *Guymon Herald,* February 24, 1910; Jimmie L. Franklin, *Born Sober: Prohibition in Oklahoma,* p. 3.

11. Rister, *No Man's Land,* pp. 31–33; Chrisman, *Lost Trails of the Cimarron,* pp. 48–57.

12. Chrisman, *Lost Trails of the Cimarron,* pp. 109–10.

13. Ibid., pp. 145–46.

14. Harry E. Chrisman, *Fifty Years on the Owl Hoot Trail,* pp. 41–42.

15. Chrisman, *Lost Trails of the Cimarron,* pp. 255–62.

16. Ibid., quoted on p. 86.

17. Quoted in Rister, *No Man's Land,* p. 44.

18. Personal interview with Henry C. Hitch, LLL.

19. Rister, *No Man's Land,* pp. 58–61; Oliver Nelson, *The Cowman's Southwest: Being the Reminiscences of Oliver Nelson,* p. 231.

20. Quoted in Rister, *No Man's Land,* p. 3; J. R. Spears, "Story of No Man's Land," *Chautauquan,* vol. 10 (October–March, 1889–90), pp.

176–78, in American Periodical Series, Series 3, microfilm reel no. 175.

21. Rister, *No Man's Land,* pp. 63–64; Oscar Kinchen, "The Squatters in No Man's Land," *Chronicles of Oklahoma,* vol. 26 (Winter, 1948–49), pp. 389–90.

22. George Rainey, *No Man's Land,* pp. 123–24.

23. Kinchen, "The Squatters in No Man's Land," p. 387.

24. Ibid., pp. 390–93.

25. Ibid., p. 387; Rainey, *No Man's Land,* pp. 50–55.

26. Kinchen, "The Squatters in No Man's Land," p. 394.

27. Ibid.

28. Allan G. Bogue, *From Prairie to Cornbelt: Farming on the Illinois and Iowa Prairies in the Nineteenth Century,* pp. 31–39.

29. Ibid., pp. 33–35.

30. Rister, *No Man's Land,* pp. 100–101.

31. Nelson, *The Cowman's Southwest,* p. 306.

32. Rister, *No Man's Land,* p. 108.

33. Carl Coke Rister and Harry E. Chrisman have different interpretations of this vigilante action. These differences appear to stem from the fact that Rister's sources consisted of reminiscences of Beaver City citizens who helped form the Respective Claims Committee and Cimarron Territory while Chrisman rests his account on the recollections of Oliver Nelson and other nontownsmen who were involved in the cattle industry. I have leaned toward Chrisman's interpretation because it rests heavily on Nelson's remarkably clear memory and because Nelson who was himself first a cowboy and then a squatter appears to be the most objective witness of those events available to the historian. See Rister, *No Man's Land,* pp. 96–128; Chrisman, *Lost Trails of the Cimarron,* pp. 111–43; Nelson, *The Cowman's Southwest,* pp. 306–12.

34. Kinchen, "The Squatters in No Man's Land," p. 396; Rister, *No Man's Land,* pp. 120–28.

35. Chrisman, *Fifty Years on the Owl Hoot Trail,* pp. 37–39.

36. Elmer E. Brown, Oklahoma City, July 28, 1904, to Governor Thompson B. Ferguson, T. B. Ferguson Collection, Box 6, Western History Collections, University of Oklahoma, Norman.

37. Rister, *No Man's Land,* pp. 140–52.

38. Ibid., pp. 158–59.

39. Quoted in ibid., p. 163.

40. Quoted in ibid., p. 162.

41. Ibid., pp. 157–65. This analysis is based on a comparison of the members' names with data found in Vicki Sullivan and Mac R. Harris, comps., *Index to the 1890 Oklahoma Territorial Census for the Counties of Kingfisher, Payne and Beaver.*

CHAPTER 2

1. Jennie Small Owen, comp., and Kirke Mechem, ed., *The Annals of Kansas,* vol. 1, p. 4; William W. Savage, Jr., *Cowboy Life: Reconstructing an American Myth,* pp. 7–8.

2. Genealogy file, Henry C. Hitch Papers, Oklahoma Heritage Association, Oklahoma City (hereafter cited as HCHP).

3. Charles A. ("Charlie") Hitch, "Memoirs," typewritten copy, ca. 1946–47, pp. 1–2, HCHP (hereafter cited as Hitch, "Memoirs").

4. Ibid., pp. 2–3, 46, 53; U.S. Census Bureau, *Census of 1870,* Greene County, Mo., p. 170; *Census of 1850,* Bradley County, Tenn., p. 342, National Archives, Washington, D.C.

5. Hitch, "Memoirs," pp. 2–3.

6. Ibid., p. 3; Undated newspaper clippings, genealogy file, HCHP; Ray Allen Billington, *Westward Expansion,* pp. 675–87.

7. Joseph G. McCoy, *Historic Sketches of the Cattle Trade of the West and Southwest.*

8. Ibid., pp. 345–50; Odie B. Faulk, *Dodge City: The Most Western Town of All,* pp. 58–61.

9. Hitch, "Memoirs," p. 4.

10. U.S. Bureau of Land Management, *Kansas Tract Books,* certificate no. 4994, sec. 5, Twnp. 31, R. 34W, Kansas State Historical Society, Topeka, Kans.; Hitch, "Memoirs," pp. 3–5; personal interview with John Knight by author, August 4, 1976, Stratford, Texas, HCHP. A personalized envelope, ca. 1918, of J. K. Hitch, in HCHP, shows Hereford cattle with LV on the left hip and a circle on the right hip.

11. Hitch, "Memoirs," pp. 6–10.

12. Chrisman, *Fifty Years on the Owl Hoot Trail,* pp. 25–28.

13. Quoted in William L. Brush, "The Early History of Seward County" (M.A. thesis, University of Wichita, 1954), pp. 3–4.

14. *Kansas Tract Books,* certificate no. 4994; Hitch, "Memoirs," p. 5; personal interview with Henry C. Hitch. LLL; J. K. Hitch Homestead Application no. 103, final certificate No. 64, Beaver City Land Office, Record Group no. 49, National Archives, Washington, D.C.

15. Hitch, "Memoirs," pp. 10–11; Chrisman, *Fifty Years on the Owl Hoot Trail,* p.98.

16. Hitch, "Memoirs," pp. 4–5, 11; Rister, *No Man's Land,* p. 53.

17. Hitch, "Memoirs," p. 4; Agnes Langston Becton, Orlando, Fla., October 8, 1977, to author, HCHP.

18. Della Hitch Wright Homestead Application no. 102, final certificate no. 65, Beaver Land Office, Record Group No. 49, National Archives, Washington, D.C.

19. J. K. Hitch Homestead Application no. 103, final certificate no.

64, Beaver Land Office, Record Group no. 49, National Archives, Washington, D.C.; Roy P. Stewart, "Henry C. Hitch and His Times," *Chronicles of Oklahoma,* vol. 50 (Spring, 1972), p. 46.

20. Undated letter from Henry C. Hitch to Harry Chrisman, in Chrisman, *Lost Trails of the Cimarron,* p. 296; personal interview with Henry C. Hitch by Jane Hensley, ca. 1965, Guymon, Okla., copy in HCHP.

21. *Guymon Daily Herald,* April 28, 1964; George M. Shirk, *Oklahoma Place Names,* pp. 75, 183. Roy Westmoreland later moved to the Imperial Valley, California, where he became a prominent citizen. Westmoreland, California, is also named for him.

22. Quoted in Hitch, "Memoirs," pp. 60–61.

23. Ibid., pp. 61–65; Mrs. R. A. Gruebbel, *A History of Victory Memorial United Methodist Church,* pp. 4–5, 10, copy in HCHP.

24. Personal interview with Henry C. Hitch, LLL. Laura B. Hamner, "Light 'n Hitch," radio broadcast over KGNC, Amarillo, Texas, October 12, 1958. Miss Hamner's weekly narrative of regional history was based on her own personal experiences as an early pioneer and on interviews with her subjects. Transcript in Panhandle-Plains Museum, Canyon, Texas.

25. Personal interview with Henry C. Hitch, LLL.

26. Brush, "The Early History of Seward County," pp. 12–34.

27. Personal interview with Henry C. Hitch, LLL.

CHAPTER 3

1. Personal interview with Henry C. Hitch, LLL.

2. J. K. Hitch Homestead Application no. 103, final certificate no. 64; Della Hitch Wright Homestead Application no. 102, final certificate no. 65, Beaver Land Office, Record Group no. 49, National Archives, Washington, D.C.; personal interview with Henry C. Hitch, LLL; Genealogy file, HCHP.

3. Zellner Glenn, "Rock or Sod Made Early Homes," *Guymon Daily Herald,* April 28, 1964, sec. D, p. 1.

4. Personal interview with Henry C. Hitch, LLL.

5. Hitch, "Memoirs," pp. 11–13, 16–17; photograph of bunk house in HCHP.

6. Hitch, "Memoirs," pp. 12, 15.

7. Moita D. Davis, "Boss Neff," *Chronicles of Oklahoma,* vol. 26 (Summer, 1948), pp. 163–68.

8. Pauline Bond and Gladys Egan, eds., *A History of Beaver County,* vol. 1, pp. 30–31.

9. Hitch, "Memoirs," pp. 24–29.

10. Ibid., pp. 39–41; personal interview with Henry C. Hitch by Jane Hensley.

11. Chrisman, *Fifty Years on the Owl Hoot Trail,* pp. 90–93; Boss Neff, "Memoirs," *Old Timers News Year Book* (Keyes, Okla.: Old Timers Publishing Co., 1976), p. 99.

12. *Guymon Herald,* August 11, 1904; July 16, 1908; David B. Gracy II, "A Preliminary Survey of Land Colonization in the Panhandle-Plains of Texas," *Museum Journal* (Texas Tech University), vol. 11 (1969), pp. 50–79; Donald E. Green, *Land of the Underground Rain: Irrigation on the Texas High Plains, 1910–1970,* pp. 62–69.

13. J. K. Hitch Homestead Application no. 103, final certificate no. 64; Della Hitch Wright Homestead Application no. 102, final certificate no. 65, Beaver Land Office, Record Group no. 49, National Archives, Washington, D.C.

14. Walter Prescott Webb, *The Great Plains,* pp. 416–17, 419, 431; Gilbert C. Fite, *The Farmers' Frontier, 1865–1900,* pp. 21–23.

15. Paul W. Gates, "Homesteading in the High Plains," *Agricultural History,* vol. 51 (January, 1977), pp. 109–33; J. K. Hitch land and financial transactions file, HCHP.

16. See map of J. K. Hitch Ranch holdings; J. K. Hitch Homestead Application no. 103, final certificate no. 64; Della Hitch Wright Homestead Application no. 102, final certificate no. 65, Beaver Land Office, Record Group no. 49, National Archives, Washington, D.C.; J. K. Hitch land- and financial-transaction file, HCHP.

17. Rupert N. Richardson, *Texas: The Lone Star State,* pp. 300–301.

18. Personal interview with Henry C. Hitch, LLL; personal interview with Henry C. Hitch by Jane Hensley; Texas General Land Office, *Abstract of all Original Land Titles Comprising Grants and Locations to August 31, 1942,* vol. 5, pp. 380–93.

19. Stewart, "Henry C. Hitch and His Times," pp. 48–49.

20. J. K. Hitch land and financial transactions file, HCHP. Last Will and Testament of James K. Hitch, no. 653, Texas County District Court Clerk's Office, Guymon, Okla.

CHAPTER 4

1. Personal interview with Christine Hitch, January 4, 1977, Guymon, Okla., HCHP.

2. Personal interview with Henry C. Hitch, LLL. Stewart, "Henry C. Hitch and His Times," p. 52.

3. Personal interview with Henry C. Hitch, LLL.

4. Stewart, "Henry C. Hitch and His Times," p. 53. Edward Everett Dale, *The Range Cattle Industry: Ranching on the Great Plains from 1865 to 1925,* p. 92; Faulk, *Dodge City: The Most Western Town of All,* pp. 180–86.

5. Chrisman, *Lost Trails of the Cimarron,* pp. 247–54; Hitch,

"Memoirs," p. 15; personal interview with Henry C. Hitch, LLL.

6. Hitch, "Memoirs," pp. 15–16; Chrisman, *Lost Trails of the Cimarron,* pp. 250–51.

7. Personal interview with Henry C. Hitch, LLL; personal interview with Henry C. Hitch by Jane Hensley.

8. Genealogy file, HCHP.

9. *Guymon Daily Herald,* April 25, 1974.

10. Stewart, "Henry C. Hitch and His Times," p. 55.

11. Chris Emmett, *Shanghai Pierce: A Fair Likeness,* p. 10.

12. Personal interview with John Knight by author; personal experiences of the author.

13. Stewart, "Henry C. Hitch and His Times," pp. 54–55.

14. Ibid., p. 57. The version that Henry Hitch recited to Roy Stewart varies slightly from the one he had copied on some Amarillo hotel stationery years before. I have used the longhand version in HCHP.

15. Joseph J. Duncan, Antelope, Okla., February 26, 1902, to Dennis T. Flynn; G. W. Staub, Woodward, Okla., March 1, 1902, to Dennis T. Flynn, Thompson B. Ferguson Collection, box 4, Western History Collections, University of Oklahoma, Norman (hereafter cited as Thompson B. Ferguson Collection).

16. Governor Thompson B. Ferguson, Guthrie, Okla., April 7, 1905, to Ethan Allen Hitchcock, secretary of the interior, Oklahoma Territorial Papers, Record Group no. 828, microfilm roll no. 3, National Archives, Washington, D.C. (hereafter cited as Oklahoma Territorial Papers).

17. C. W. Stewart, Beaver, Okla., March 25, 1905, to President Theodore Roosevelt, Oklahoma Territorial Papers; George H. Healy, Beaver, Okla., to Governor Thompson B. Ferguson, April 28, 1904, box 6; Thompson B. Ferguson, Guthrie, Okla., May 3, 1904, to George Healy, Letterpress Book no. 6, Thompson B. Ferguson Collection.

18. *Guymon Herald,* February 9, 1911.

19. Ibid., January 13, 1910, January 19, 1911.

20. Ibid., February 9, 1911.

21. Christine Hitch, Guymon, Okla., August 10, 1976, to author, HCHP.

22. Personal interview with Christine Hitch by author, August 3, 1976, Guymon, Okla., HCHP; *Guymon Herald,* January 27, 1910; February 24, 1910. Edward Everett Dale, "The Frontier Literary Society," *Frontier Historian: The Life and Work of Edward Everett Dale,* ed. Arrell M. Gibson, pp. 152–66.

23. Personal interview with Christine Hitch by author, August 3, 1976; Christine Hitch, Guymon, Okla., February 20, 1978, to author, HCHP; Stewart, "Henry C. Hitch and His Times," p. 58.

24. Hattie Cline Bickle, "A Word Picture of the Cline Family"

(mimeographed, ca. 1955); copy of birth records in Walker family Bible; obituary of Judith Walker in genealogy file, HCHP; personal interview with Christine Hitch by author, August 3, 1976.

25. Personal interview with Christine Hitch by author, August 3, 1976.

26. Personal interview with Christine Hitch by author August 5, 1976, Guymon, Okla., HCHP; personal interview with Ladd Hitch by author, August 4, 1976, Guymon, Okla., HCHP.

27. Hattie Cline Bickle, "A Word Picture of the Cline Family," genealogy file, HCHP.

28. Marjorie Hitch Price, Orlando, Fla., March 1, 1977, to author, HCHP; author's conversations with Christine Hitch on various occasions in 1976 and 1977.

29. Christine Hitch, Guymon, Okla., February 20, 1978, HCHP.

30. Stewart, "Henry C. Hitch and His Times," p. 58; personal interview with Christine Hitch by author, August 3, 1976, Guymon, Okla.; copy of marriage license, HCHP; personal interview with Henry C. Hitch, LLL.

31. Personal interview with Christine Hitch by author, January 7, 1977, Guymon, Okla.; personal interview with Christine Hitch by author, August 3, 1976, Guymon, Okla., HCHP.

CHAPTER 5

1. Personal interview with Henry C. Hitch, LLL.

2. *Beaver Herald,* April 29, 1909; *Guymon Herald,* February 24, 1910.

3. *Guymon Herald,* February 3, 1910, April 16, 1908.

4. *Guymon Herald,* January 6, 1910, January 27, 1910, February 24, 1910.

5. Ibid., January 6, 1910, January 13, 1910, January 20, 1910, February 17, 1910.

6. Ibid., October 6, 1910, October 13, 1910, January 5, 1911.

7. Ibid., February 24, 1910.

8. Personal interview with Christine Hitch, August 3, 1976.

9. Personal interview with Christine Hitch, January 3, 1977.

10. Personal interview with Christine Hitch, August 3, 1976; Stewart, "Henry C. Hitch and His Times," pp. 58–59.

11. George Hitch, April 29, 1907, Guymon, Okla., to Henry C. Hitch, HCHP.

12. Telephone conversation with Christine Hitch by author, June 18, 1977, HCHP.

13. Author's observations of library of Henry C. Hitch and conversations with members of the Hitch family.

14. Quitclaim deed for mining claim on Little Eldorado Creek from George Mulligan to Lyman Savage, June 19, 1905, HCHP.

15. Author's observations of library of Henry C. Hitch.

16. Quoted in Stewart, "Henry C. Hitch and His Times," p. 60.

17. *Guymon Herald,* November 10, 1910, January 19, 1911.

18. Personal interview with Christine Hitch, August 3, 1976.

19. Ibid.; Marjorie Hitch Price, March 1, 1977, Orlando, Florida, to author, HCHP; Stewart, "Henry C. Hitch and His Times," p. 61.

20. Personal interview with Christine Hitch, August 3, 1976; Joyce Hitch Gray, Guymon, Okla., February 21, 1977, to author, HCHP.

21. Joyce Hitch Gray, Guymon, Oklahoma, February 21, 1977, to author; Marjorie Hitch Price, Orlando, Fla., March 1, 1977, to author, HCHP; personal interview with Christine Hitch, January 7, 1977.

22. Joyce Hitch Gray, Guymon, Okla., February 21, 1977, to author; Marjorie Hitch Price, Orlando, Fla., March 1, 1977, to author, HCHP.

23. Marjorie Hitch Price, Orlando, Fla., March 1, 1977, to author, HCHP.

24. Ibid.; Christine Hitch, Guymon, Okla., April 20, 1977, to author, HCHP.

25. Personal interview with Christine Hitch, August 3, 1976; Agnes Langston Becton, Orlando, Fla., October 8, 1977, to author, HCHP.

26. Gruebbel, *A History of Victory Memorial United Methodist Church,* pp. 4–6.

27. Personal interview with Christine Hitch, August 3, 1976.

28. Financial statement of Henry C. Hitch for 1914, HCHP.

29. Personal interview with Henry C. Hitch, LLL; stock certificates in the Crystal River Marble Company, HCHP.

30. Various stock certificates in HCHP.

31. James D. Hamlin, *The Flamboyant Judge,* pp. 222–25.

32. Cashier of the Northwest Oil and Development Company, Denver, Colo., September 6, 1916, to Henry C. Hitch; warranty deed to Wyoming land, September 6, 1916; various stock issues in HCHP.

33. Samuel W. Tait, Jr., *The Wildcatters: An Informal History of Oil Hunting in America,* pp. 116–49; information supplied the author by Paul Bonnifield, Yampa, Colo., from his research on the history of oil-and-gas development in the Panhandle, author's personal files, Edmond, Okla.; *Guymon Herald,* October 2, 1919; *Texhoma Times,* May 30, 1919.

34. Stewart, "Henry C. Hitch and His Times," pp. 61–62; personal observations and experiences of the author.

35. John T. Schlebecker, *Cattle Raising on the Plains, 1900–1961,* pp. 59–60.

36. Financial statements of Henry C. Hitch for 1914, 1915, and 1920, HCHP.

37. Ibid.; Bond and Egan, *A History of Beaver County,* vol. 2, pp. 470–71.

38. Financial statment of Henry C. Hitch for 1915, HCHP.

39. Personal interview with John Knight by author, August 4, 1976, Stratford, Texas, HCHP.

40. Ibid.; typewritten statement of Christine Hitch, March 30, 1971, HCHP. Lee Tucker, "The Big Snow of 1918–19," *Second Annual Old Timers News Year Book,* ed. Lee Tucker, pp. 15–16.

41. Christine Hitch, Guymon, Okla., February 16, 1977, HCHP.

42. Ibid.

43. Donald E. Green, "Beginnings of Wheat Culture in Oklahoma," in *Rural Oklahoma,* ed. Donald E. Green, p. 67.

44. U.S. Census Bureau, *United States Census Report, 1900,* vol. 6, pt. 2, p. 179; *United States Census Report, 1910,* vol. 7, pp. 386–87; *United States Census Report, 1920,* vol. 6, p. 642.

45. Financial statement of Henry C. Hitch for 1916, HCHP; personal interview with Bill Bratton by author, August 7, 1976, Spearman, Texas; personal interview with Clarence Alexander by author, January 6, 1977, Guymon, Okla.; personal interview with Tom Pugh by author, January 6, 1977, Texhoma, Okla., HCHP.

CHAPTER 6

1. Personal interview with Ladd Hitch by author, August 1, 1976, Guymon, Okla., HCHP; personal interview with Bud Perkins, January 5, 1977, Guymon, Okla., HCHP.

2. Schlebecker, *Cattle Raising on the Plains, 1900–1961,* pp. 72–74.

3. Form letter from George A. Dixon, Kansas City, Mo., October 31, 1919, to Henry C. Hitch; J. C. Brewer, Kansas City, Mo., May 10, 1920, to Henry C. Hitch, HCHP.

4. Quoted in Gilbert C. Fite, *George N. Peek and the Fight for Farm Parity,* p. 4; *Guymon Herald,* October 5, 1922.

5. Schlebecker, *Cattle Raising on the Plains, 1900–1961,* pp. 93–94; Green, *Land of the Underground Rain,* p. 121; *Guymon Herald,* June 23, 1921.

6. *Guymon Herald,* January 26, 1922, August 17, 1922, July 14, 1921.

7. Personal interview with Henry C. Hitch by Jane Hensley; personal recollections of author.

8. Personal interview with Ladd Hitch by author, August 3, 1976, HCHP.

9. Financial statements of Henry C. Hitch for 1915, 1920, 1921 and 1925, HCHP.

10. Green, "Beginnings of Wheat Culture in Oklahoma," pp. 67–68;

Jesse Harder, "Wheat Production in Northwestern Oklahoma, 1893–1932" (M.A. thesis, University of Oklahoma, 1952), pp. 47–48.

11. Green, "Beginnings of Wheat Culture in Oklahoma," pp. 70–71. Personal interview with John Knight.

12. Personal interview with John Knight.

13. Financial statements of Henry C. Hitch for 1928 and 1929, HCHP.

14. *United States Census Report,* 1920, vol. 6, p. 642; U.S. Department of Agriculture, *United States Census of Agriculture, 1935,* vol. 1, p. 737.

15. Erma Walker, Denver, Colo., May 4, 1925, to Christine Hitch, HCHP.

16. Personal interview with Ladd Hitch by author, August 4, 1976, Guymon, Okla., in author's notebook, HCHP; personal interview with O. C. ("Cotton") Furnish by author, August 5, 1976, Henry C. Hitch Ranch, Texas County, Okla., HCHP.

17. Personal interview with Christine Hitch, August 3, 1976; personal interview with Henry C. Hitch by Jane Hensley.

18. Personal interview with Christine Hitch, January 4, 1977.

19. Last Will and Testament of J. K. Hitch, creditor claims against estate, no. 653, Texas County District Court Clerk's Office, Guymon, Okla.; personal interview with Joyce Hitch Gray, August 5, 1976, Guymon, Okla., HCHP.

20. Last Will and Testament of J. K. Hitch.

21. Personal interview with Christine Hitch, August 3, 1976.

22. Financial statements of Hitch Land and Cattle Company for 1927 and of Henry C. Hitch for 1923–29, HCHP.

23. Erma Walker, Denver, Colo., August 9, 1926, to Christine Hitch, HCHP; personal interview with Christine Hitch, August 3, 1976; personal interview with Ladd Hitch, August 1, 1976.

24. Personal interview with O. C. ("Cotton") Furnish.

25. Personal interview with Christine Hitch, August 3, 1976; personal interview with Ladd Hitch, August 3, 1976, August 4, 1976; Marjorie Hitch Price, Orlando, Fla., March 1, 1977, to author, HCHP.

26. Undated paper by Ladd Hitch, ca. 1930, HCHP.

27. Ladd Hitch, Guymon, Okla., June 10, 1930, to Christine Hitch, HCHP.

28. Personal interview with Christine Hitch, August 4, 1976; Joyce Hitch Gray, Guymon, Okla., February 21, 1977, to author; personal interview with Ladd Hitch, August 1, 1976; Ladd Hitch, "Recollections of the Dirty Thirties" (manuscript, 1977), HCHP.

29. Personal interview with John Knight; *Panhandle Herald,* December 27, 1928.

30. Financial statements of Henry C. Hitch for 1925, 1926, and 1927, HCHP.

31. *Guymon Herald,* March 30, 1922; personal interview with Ladd Hitch, August 3, 1976.

32. Personal interview with Ladd Hitch, August 1, 1976; Christine Hitch, Guymon, Okla., March 2, 1977, to author; financial statements of Henry C. Hitch for 1919, 1925, and 1927, HCHP.

33. Schlebecker, *Cattle Raising on the Plains, 1900–1961,* p. 75.

34. Financial statements of Henry C. Hitch for 1920s, HCHP.

35. Personal interview with Clarence Alexander, son-in-law of Frank Lindsay, by author, January 6, 1977, Guymon, Okla., HCHP.

36. Last Will and Testament of J. K. Hitch, creditor claims against estate, no. 653, Texas County District Court Clerk's Office, Guymon, Okla. Personal interview with Christine Hitch, January 6, 1977. Financial statements of Henry C. Hitch for 1924, 1926, and 1929, HCHP.

37. G. P. Collins and W. G. Hill, *Prices Received by Oklahoma Farmers, 1910–1957,* Oklahoma Agricultural Experiment Station Bulletin no. P-297 (June, 1958), p. 17; Schlebecker, *Cattle Raising on the Plains, 1900–1961,* p. 75; financial statement of Henry C. Hitch for 1928, HCHP.

38. Financial statement of Henry C. Hitch for 1929, HCHP.

39. Ibid.; personal interview with E. E. McDaniels by author, August 6, 1976, Guymon, Okla.; personal interview with Tom Pugh, January 6, 1977, Texhoma, Oklahoma, author's notebooks, HCHP.

40. Personal interview with Ladd Hitch by author, January 3, 1977.

41. Ladd Hitch, Guymon, Okla., February 20, 1978, to author, HCHP.

42. Ibid.; personal interview with Ladd Hitch by author, January 3, 1977.

43. *Guymon Herald,* February 2, 1922, July 14, 1921, July 21, 1921.

44. Personal interview with Christine Hitch, August 3, 1976; author's recollections of Saturday nights in a rural Texas Panhandle town.

45. Personal interview with Ladd Hitch, January 3, 1977.

46. Notebook of Henry C. Hitch for 1920s, HCHP; Bill C. Malone, *Country Music, U.S.A.,* pp. 55–58.

CHAPTER 7

1. *Panhandle Herald,* December 13, 1928, January 3, 1921, January 24, 1929.

2. Donovan L. Hofsommer, *Katy Northwest: The Story of a Branch Line Railroad,* p. 82; "A Trip over the New Line, Liberal to Amarillo," *Rock Island Magazine* (July, 1929), p. 6. Green, "Beginnings of Wheat Culture in Oklahoma," p. 67.

3. Personal interview with Ladd Hitch, January 3, 1977; personal

interview with John Knight; J. L. Williams, Amarillo, Texas, January 14, 1931, to Henry C. Hitch; audit report of the Hitch Grain Company, Hitchland, Texas, June 26, 1930, by the Sunflower State Accounting Company, Hutchinson, Kans., HCHP.

4. Audit report of the Hitch Grain Company, Hitchland, Texas, June 26, 1930, by the Sunflower State Accounting Company, Hutchinson, Kans., HCHP.

5. *Time,* vol. 18 (July 27, 1931), p. 10. For a more detailed account of Price's operations the previous year see Gary L. Nell, "Agricultural History of the Texas Panhandle, 1880–1965" (Ph.D. diss., University of Oklahoma, 1972), p. 153; G. P. Collins and W. G. Hill, *Prices Received by Oklahoma Farmers, 1910–1957,* Oklahoma Agricultural Experiment Station Bulletin P-197 (Stillwater, Okla.: Oklahoma Agricultural Experiment Station, 1958), p. 17.

6. Personal interview with John Knight; *Time,* vol. 18 (July 27, 1931), p. 10.

7. J. L. Williams, Amarillo, Texas, January 14, 1931, to Henry C. Hitch, HCHP; *Panhandle Herald,* October 27, 1932.

8. Schlebecker, *Cattle Raising on the Plains, 1900–1951,* p. 199; T. J. Sinnard, of Yancey, Sinnard, and Roberts, Livestock Commision Merchants, Kansas City, Mo., April 1, 1931, to Henry C. Hitch; O. M. Hoover, of Austin-Hamill-Hoover Live Stock Commission Company, South St. Joseph, Mo., August 24, 1931, to H. C. Hitch; T. J. Sinnard, Kansas City, Mo., February 8, 1932, to Henry Hitch; livestock-sale receipt of National Live Stock Commission Company, Kansas City, Mo., January 13, 1932, to Pogue Brothers Feed Lot, Frank Atkinson, and H. C. Hitch, HCHP.

9. Personal interview with Christine Hitch by author, August 3, 1976; financial statements of Henry C. Hitch for 1930 and 1931, HCHP.

10. Financial statements of Henry C. Hitch for 1930 and 1931, HCHP.

11. Albert R. Wallace, Burdick, Kans., September 15, 1931, to Henry C. Hitch, HCHP.

12. Personal interview with Orville Nash by author, January 5, 1977, Guymon, Okla., HCHP; personal interview with Christine Hitch, August 3, 1976, January 5, 1977.

13. Personal interview with Bud Perkins by author, January 5, 1977, Guymon, Okla., HCHP.

14. Hitch, "Recollections of the Dirty Thirties."

15. Personal interviews with Christine Hitch, August 3, 1976, January 4, 1977.

16. Gruebbel, *A History of Victory Memorial United Methodist Church,* pp. 6–7.

17. Guy Logsdon, "The Dust Bowl and the Migrant," *American Scene,* vol. 12, no. 1 (1971).

18. *Guymon Herald,* February 3, 1910.

19. John L. McCarty, *Maverick Town: The Story of Old Tascosa,* p. 241.

20. Vance Johnson, *Heaven's Tableland: The Dust Bowl Story,* p. 144.

21. Jeff Holladay, "The Great Panhandle 'Exodus' Furor," *Orbit Magazine* (Oklahoma City), June 19, 1977, pp. 6–8.

22. *Tulsa Daily World,* May 5, 1935; Hitch, "Recollections of the Dirty Thirties."

23. "A Dust Bowl Experience" (anonymous typewritten MS, n.d.), HCHP.

24. Hitch, "Recollections of the Dirty Thirties"; William G. DeLoach Diary, March 22, 26, 1936, Southwest Collection, Texas Tech University; Donald E. Green, *Fifty Years of Service to West Texas Agriculture: A History of Texas Tech University's College of Agricultural Sciences, 1925–1975,* p. 75.

25. Christine Hitch, "I Remember" (typewritten copy, 1971) in HCHP. Hitch, "Recollections of the Dirty Thirties."

26. Christine Hitch, "I Remember."

27. Nall, "Agricultural History of the Texas Panhandle, 1880–1965," pp. 177–178.

28. Personal interview with Orville Nash; Quentin Williams, Guymon, Okla., November 12, 1936, to D. A. Dobkins; U.S. Department of Agriculture, Soil Conservation Service Region 6, Amarillo, Texas, radio broadcast release on "Contour Plowing in the Oklahoma Panhandle, n.d., Information Division, Segregated Correspondence, Amarillo Office of Soil Conservation Service, National Archives, Washington, D.C.

29. Hitch, "Recollections of the Dirty Thirties"; personal interview with Ladd Hitch, January 3, 1977; memorandum "cattle count Coldwater Ranch" October 2, 1933, HCHP; copies of Public Voucher and Emergency Cattle Agreement, July 26, August 15, 1934, Liberal, Kans., HCHP.

30. *Panhandle Herald,* November 10, 1932. Irvin May, Jr., "Welfare and Ranchers: The Emergency Cattle Purchase Program and Emergency Work Relief Program in Texas, 1934–1935," *West Texas Historical Association Year Book,* vol. 47 (1971), pp. 3–19, provides an insight into the program in a neighboring state. See also C. Roger Lambert, "The Drought Cattle Purchase, 1934–1935: Problems and Complaints," *Agricultural History,* vol. 45 (April, 1971), pp. 85–94; Schlebecker, *Cattle Raising on the Plains, 1900–1961,* pp. 140–42; "Do You Have Cattle to Sell?" *Oklahoma Farmer-Stockman,* vol. 47 (September 1, 1934), p. 4; author's conversations with father, Lewis Green, Wellington, Texas, who sold cattle to the government program and observed the "cattle-kill."

31. "Do You Have Cattle to Sell?" p. 4; Hitch, "Recollections of the

Dirty Thirties."

32. Schlebecker, *Cattle Raising on the Plains, 1900–1961,* p. 126; W. Gifford Hoag, *The Farm Credit System: A History of Financial Self-Help,* p. 241; personal interview with Artemus ("Artie") Baker by author, June 3, 1968, Pecos, Texas, Southwest Collection, Texas Tech University.

33. C. W. Floyd, Wichita, Kans., May 18, 1933, June 22, 1933, to Henry C. Hitch; R. W. Phillips, Wichita, Kans., April 22, 1935, to Henry C. Hitch, HCHP.

34. E. J. Dignan, Wichita, Kans., February 15, 1935, to Henry C. Hitch, HCHP.

35. Hoag, *The Farm Credit System,* pp. 237–38.

36. H. D. Ewers, Treasurer of RACC, Wichita, Kans., January 24, 1933, to Henry C. Hitch; financial statement of Henry C. Hitch rendered to Reconstruction Finance Corporation, October 26, 1932, HCHP.

37. E. J. Dignan, Wichita, Kans., October 14, 1935, to Henry C. Hitch; E. L. Fickel, Guymon, Oklahoma, December 31, 1935, to Henry C. Hitch; account statement for Henry C. Hitch by Regional Agricultural Credit Corporation of Wichita, Kans., November 4, 1935, HCHP; personal interview with Ladd Hitch, August 4, 1976.

38. I am indebted to Paul Bonnifield, of Yampa, Colorado, for information and research items on the early history of natural-gas exploration in the region. See also *Texhoma Times,* March 21, 1919, October 3, 1919; Charles N. Gould, "The Beginnings of the Panhandle Oil and Gas Field," *Panhandle-Plains Historical Review,* vol. 8 (1935), pp. 24–35.

39. *Texhoma Times,* May 30, 1919, November 25, 1921, November 24, 1922.

40. Telegram, L. V. Gardner, Liberal, Kans., July 6, 1920, to J. K. Hitch, HCHP; *Guymon Herald,* January 29, 1920.

41. *Guymon Herald,* September 11, 1919, October 2, 1919, January 1, 1920, January 15, 1920; stock certificates in the Beaver Oil and Gas Company, August 2, 1920, January 15, 1920, HCHP.

42. *Panhandle Herald* (Guymon), December 1, 1932.

43. Hitch Ledger Book, pp. 54–55, HCHP.

44. Information supplied by Paul Bonnifield; Hitch, "Recollections of the Dirty Thirties."

45. Brokerage account sheets, receipts, and stock-market analyses in stock market file, HCHP; personal interview with Ladd Hitch, August 3, 1976.

46. Personal interview with Ladd Hitch, August 3, 1976.

47. Marjorie H. Price, Orlando, Fla., March 1, 1977, to author; personal interview with Bud Perkins; personal interview with Christine

Hitch, January 7, 1977; Hitch, "Recollections of the Dirty Thirties."

48. Personal interview with Joyce Hitch Gray.

49. *Panhandle Herald* (Guymon), September 6, 1928.

50. Personal interview with Ladd Hitch, January 3, 1977.

51. Ibid.; Philip Reed Rulon, *Oklahoma State University—Since 1890,* p. 282.

52. Christine Hitch, "I Remember" (typewritten MS. n.d.), HCHP; Rister, *No Man's Land,* p. 185.

53. *Cimarron News* (Boise City), July 19, 1929; *Beaver Herald,* January 30, 1913; quoted in Fred Floyd, "The Struggle for Railroads in the Oklahoma Panhandle," *Chronicles of Oklahoma,* vol. 54 (Winter, 1976–77), pp. 497, 498.

54. For a history of this branch of the M-K-T, see Hofsommer, *Katy Northwest.* Floyd, "The Struggle for Railroads in the Oklahoma Panhandle," p. 501.

55. *Panhandle Herald* (Guymon), October 13, 1932; Robert A. Woodrom, "Road Building in the Panhandle," *Second Annual Old Timers News Year Book,* Keyes, Okla. Old Timers Publishing Co., 1977, pp. 9–10; telephone conversation with Jerry Cannedy, Oklahoma State Department of Highways, Oklahoma City, December 27, 1977.

56. Francis A. Flood, "The Dust Bowl Is Being Tamed," *Oklahoma Farmer-Stockman,* vol. 50 (July 1, 1937), p. 3; U.S. Bureau of the Census, *United States Census Report, 1940,* vol. 2, pt. 5, p. 828; U.S. Bureau of the Census, *United States Census Report, 1930,* vol. 3, pt. 2, p. 602; Rister, *No Man's Land,* p. 186.

57. Flood, "The Dust Bowl Is Being Tamed," p. 23.

CHAPTER 8

1. Journal of Christine Hitch, May 2, 1940, HCHP.

2. Ibid.

3. Hitch, "Recollections of the Dirty Thirties."

4. Ibid.; Journal of Christine Hitch, March 26, 1940.

5. Personal interview with Christine Hitch, August 4, 1976.

6. Journal of Christine Hitch, March 26, 1940.

7. John T. Schlebecker, *Cattle Raising on the Plains,* p. 172. Collins and Hill, *Prices Received by Oklahoma Farmers, 1910–1957,* p. 17.

8. Personal interview with Ladd Hitch, August 3, 1976.

9. Christine Hitch, Guymon, Okla., February 16, 1977, to author, HCHP; Laura B. Hamner, "Light 'n Hitch," radio broadcast, KGNC, Amarillo, Texas, October 12, 1958, Panhandle-Plains Museum, Canyon, Texas.

10. Personal interview with Ladd Hitch, August 3, 1976; Journal of Christine Hitch, April 20, 1940.

11. Personal interview with Ladd Hitch, August 3, 1976; personal interview with Clarence Alexander by author, January 6, 1977, HCHP.

12. Personal interview with Clarence Alexander by author, January 6, 1977; personal interview with Bud Perkins by author, January 5, 1977, Guymon, Okla., HCHP.

13. Ladd Hitch, Guymon, Okla., February 20, 1978, to author, HCHP.

14. Hamner, "Light 'n Hitch" broadcast.

15. Hitch, "Recollections of the Dirty Thirties"; Hitch Ledger Book, pp. 54–55.

16. Volta Torrey, *Wind-Catchers: American Windmills of Yesterday and Tomorrow,* pp. 121–29. The author's family installed a Wincharger about 1941 and experienced the problems as well as the promises of wind-powered electricity.

17. Journal of Christine Hitch, April 19, 1940.

18. Ibid., April 3, 5, 1940.

19. Ibid., April 3–5, 9, 1940.

20. Ladd and Lala Moores Hitch, Guymon, Okla., February 20, 1978, to author, HCHP.

21. Personal interview with Ladd Hitch, August 3, 1976; Hitch, "Recollections of the Dirty Thirties."

22. Ladd Hitch, Guymon, Okla., February 14, 1943, to Henry C. Hitch, HCHP.

23. Personal interview with Ladd Hitch, January 3, 1977.

24. Christine Hitch, Guymon, Okla., February 16, 1977, to author, HCHP.

25. Ibid.; Personal interview with Ladd Hitch, January 3, 1977.

26. Ibid.

27. Ibid.; Bond and Egan, *A History of Beaver County,* vol. 2, pp. 628–29, 457.

28. Personal interview with Ladd Hitch, January 3, 1977.

29. Chrisman, *Lost Trails of the Cimarron,* pp. 68–69; *Indian Chieftain* (Vinita, Okla.), June 30, 1892, p. 2; *Blackwell Morning Tribune,* April 4, 1931; *Chickasha Daily Express,* September 18, 1900; *Frederick Enterprise,* July 25, 1907.

30. *Oklahoma Farm Journal,* vol. 11 (February 15, 1903), p. 2.

31. *Oklahoma Farmer-Stockman,* vol. 32 (October 25, 1919), pp. 43, 45.

32. *Daily Oklahoman* (Oklahoma City), January 16, 1916; *Oklahoma Farmer-Stockman,* vol. 41 (April 15, 1928), p. 8; *Cattleman* (Fort Worth, Texas), vol. 20 (June, 1933), pp. 14–15.

33. *Oklahoma Farmer-Stockman,* vol. 51 (March 15, 1938), p. 7;

Ranchman (Tulsa), vol. 1 (May, 1941), p. 13; telephone conversation with Ellis Freeney, manager of the Oklahoma Cattlemen's Association by author, October 4, 1977, Oklahoma City, notes in HCHP.

34. *Northwest Oklahoma Cattleman* (Woodward, Okla.), vol. 4 (February, 1949), pp. 12–13.

35. *Daily Leader* (Guthrie), January 19, 1895; personal interview with Christine Hitch, August 6, 1976.

36. *Alva Review-Courier,* March 24, 1950; quoted in *Northwest Oklahoma Cattleman,* vol. 5 (April, 1950), inside front cover.

37. *Northwest Oklahoma Cattleman,* vol. 4 (October, 1949), pp. 1, 20.

38. Ibid., vol. 4 (December, 1949), pp. 10–11, 12.

39. Ibid., vol. 4 (July, 1949), pp. 8–9.

40. Ladd Hitch, Guymon, Okla., February 20, 1978, to author, HCHP.

41. *Northwest Oklahoma Cattleman,* vol. 7 (July, 1952), p. 4; personal interview with Ladd Hitch, January 3, 1977.

42. Personal interview with Christine Hitch, August 3, 1976; journal of Christine Hitch, April 5, 1940.

43. Personal interview with Christine Hitch, August 3, 1976; personal interview with Orville Nash by author, January 5, 1977, Guymon, Okla., HCHP; minutes of finance and building committees, church archives, Methodist Episcopal Church, Guymon, Okla.; *Guymon Daily Herald,* January 6, 1953; Gruebbel, *A History of Victory Memorial United Methodist Church of Guymon, Oklahoma,* p. 7.

44. *Old Timers News* (Keyes, Okla.), June, 1976, p. 4; minutes of board of directors meetings, No Man's Land Historical Society, April 3, 1939–October 3, 1951, No Man's Land Museum, Goodwell, Okla.

CHAPTER 9

1. *Oklahoma Cowman* (Oklahoma City), vol. 6 (January, 1966), p. 3.

2. Dyke Ballinger, Beaver, Okla., August 27, 1900, to William Jenkins, Secretary of Oklahoma Territory Papers, Oklahoma Historical Society, Oklahoma City.

3. *Guymon Herald,* March 3, 1910. Green, *Land of the Underground Rain,* pp. 62–80; Donald E. Green, "Irrigation: Making the Thirsty Plains Blossom," *Drovers Journal* (Kansas City, Mo.), vol. 100 (December, 1972), pp. 96–97.

4. *Guymon Herald,* March 10, 1910, October 13, 1910.

5. Personal interview with Ladd Hitch, August 3, 1976.

6. Personal interview with Henry C. Hitch, LLL.

7. Hamner, "Light 'n Hitch" radio broadcast.

8. Hitch, "Recollections of the Dirty Thirties"; *Amarillo Daily News,* August 27, 1955.

9. Hitch, "Recollections of the Dirty Thirties."

10. When my father arrived to settle in the Lone Mound community of the southeastern Texas Panhandle (Collingsworth County) in December, 1921, he inspected a feedlot on the Walter Darlington Ranch. The twenty-five-acre lot was enclosed by hog wire, as well as barbed wire. The ranch was feeding out about five hundred yearling heifers with grain sorghum heads and ear corn grown on local farms and harvested by hand. The feed was forked from wagons into wooden feed bunks. Then one man worked his way slowly down each trough tediously chopping up the heads and ears with a hatchet before turning the stock into the pen. In 1931, H. W. Stanton, who owned both a farm and a small milling plant, constructed a feedlot on the north side of Lubbock, Texas. Such feeding operations, however, were rare on the southern Great Plains at that time. Green, *Fifty Years of Service to West Texas Agriculture,* p. 52; personal interview with Lewis Green by author, May 14, 1977, Wellington, Texas, in author's possession.

11. Personal interview with Ladd Hitch, August 3, 1976; Schlebecker, *Cattle Raising on the Plains, 1900–1961,* pp. 205, 223.

12. Kenneth Frantz, Guymon, Okla., April 5, 1977, to author, HCHP.

13. Ibid.; personal interview with Ladd Hitch, August 3, 1976.

14. Personal interview with Ladd Hitch, August 3, 1976; personal interview with Juanita Reedy by author, August 2, 1976, Guymon, Okla., HCHP.

15. Personal interview with Juanita Reedy by author, August 2, 1976.

16. Personal interview with Ladd Hitch, August 3, 1976.

17. Ibid.; financial statement of Henry C. Hitch for 1958, HCHP.

18. Hitch, "Recollections of the Dirty Thirties."

19. *Cattleman,* vol. 47 (June, 1960), p. 54.

20. Hamner, "Light 'n Hitch" radio broadcast, copy of questionnaire completed by Henry and Christine Hitch for Laura B. Hamner, ca. 1958, HCHP.

21. Green, *Fifty Years of Service to West Texas Agriculture,* pp. 52–53, 125–26.

22. *Checkerboard Service* (St. Louis, Mo.), October–November, 1960, p. 10.

23. David L. Wheeler, "The Origin and Development of the Cattle Feeding Industry in the Southern High Plains," *Panhandle-Plains Historical Review,* vol. 49 (1976), p. 87; Jerry Sinise, "Feedlots Expansion in the Southwest," *Oklahoma Cowman* vol. 9 (October, 1969), p. 33.

24. *Checkerboard Service,* October–November, 1960, p. 10. "H. C. Hitch, Jr., Helmsman of Panhandle Feeding," *Oklahoma Cowman,*

vol. 10 (September, 1968), p. 18; Ladd Hitch, Guymon, Okla., February 20, 1978, to author, HCHP.

25. Ladd Hitch, Guymon, Oklahoma, February 20, 1978, to author; personal observations of author.

26. Personal interview with Ladd Hitch, January 3, 1977.

27. Personal interview with Bud Perkins.

28. Personal interview with Orville Nash; Roy P. Stewart, *Country Boy in Russia* (Oklahoma City: Oklahoma Publishing Co., 1956), HCHP.

29. Christine Hitch, Guymon, Okla., June 22, 1971, to Erma Walker Monesmith, HCHP.

30. Ibid.

31. Nomination of Christine Hitch for Oklahoma Mother of the Year, HCHP; personal interview with Melvin Ridley by author, January 7, 1977, Guymon, Okla., author's notebook, HCHP.

32. Hitch family newspaper clippings file, HCHP.

33. Ladd Hitch, Guymon, Okla., February 20, 1978, to author; personal interview with Joyce Hitch Gray, January 7, 1977; Joyce Hitch Gray, Guymon, Okla., January 12, 1977, to author, HCHP; Christina Gray, "Love versus Motivation" (typewritten MS, n.d.), HCHP.

34. Telephone conversation with Christine Hitch by author, February 11, 1978, Guymon to Edmond, Okla.; Ladd Hitch, Guymon, Okla., February 20, 1978, to author.

35. Personal interview with Ladd Hitch, August 4, 1976; *Amarillo Sunday News-Globe,* December 31, 1967.

36. *Guymon Daily Herald,* December 31, 1967.

37. Personal interview with Tom Pugh by author, January 6, 1977, Texhoma, Okla.

38. Joyce Hitch Gray, Guymon, Okla., January 12, 1977, to author, HCHP.

39. *Oklahoma Journal* (Midwest City), December 31, 1967, clipping, HCHP.

EPILOGUE

1. "H. C. Hitch, Jr., Helmsman of Panhandle Feeding," *Oklahoma Cowman,* vol. 8 (September, 1968), p. 18; Ferdie Deering, "30,000 Acre Homestead," *Oklahoma's Orbit* (Oklahoma City), July 19, 1964, p. 15; personal interview with Bud Danner by author, January 5, 1977, Guymon, Okla., HCHP.

2. "H. C. Hitch, Jr., Helmsman of Panhandle Feeding," p. 19.

3. *Guymon Daily Herald,* November 14, 1967, June 20, 1969; Jerry Sinise, "Feedlots: Expansion in the Southwest," *Oklahoma Cowman,* vol. 9 (October, 1969), p. 42; Donald A. Brown, "Mastering No Man's

Land," *Wichita Farm Credit Letter* (Wichita, Kans.), Fall–Winter, 1977, p. 4; newspaper clippings file, HCHP.

4. Personal interview with Orville Nash by author, January 5, 1977, Guymon, Okla., HCHP.

5. Clippings file, HCHP; *Record Stockman* (Denver, Colo.), May 23, 1974, pp. 1–2.

6. "H. C. Hitch, Jr., Helmsman of Panhandle Feeding," pp. 19–20. I spent a couple of days with O. C. ("Cotton") Furnish and Joe Fitzgerald "on their rounds" in the summer of 1976.

7. Brown, "Mastering No Man's Land," p. 7.

Bibliography

A NOTE ON SOURCES

The Henry C. Hitch Papers, now in the archives of the Oklahoma Heritage Association in Oklahoma City, constitute the single most important collection for this work. The papers contain letters, ledgers, memoirs, items relating to land and financial transactions, newspaper clippings, interviews, and other such materials. Other primary sources include: Homestead Applications and Final Certificates of the Beaver City Land Office, Record Group no. 49, National Archives, Washington, D. C.; *Kansas Tract Books,* copies in Kansas State Historical Society, Topeka, Kansas; *Oklahoma Tract Books,* copies in Oklahoma Historical Society; materials relating to Oklahoma Territory in Record Group no. 828, microfilm roll no. 3, National Archives; minutes of the Board of Directors meetings of No Man's Land Historical Society, No Man's Land Museum, Goodwell, Oklahoma; the Methodist Episcopal Church archives, Guymon, Oklahoma; the Thompson B. Ferguson Collection, Western History Collections, University of Oklahoma, Norman; files of the Secretary of Oklahoma Territory, Oklahoma Historical Society, Oklahoma City; the William G. DeLoach Diary, Southwest Collection, Texas Tech University, Lubbock, Texas; files of the Amarillo Office of the Soil Conservation Service, National Archives, Washington, D. C.; United States Census Bureau, Manuscript Census of 1870, Greene County, Missouri, and Manuscript Census of 1850, Bradley County, Tennessee, National Archives, microfilm copies in Oklahoma Historical Society, Oklahoma City; and Last Will and Testament of James K. Hitch, will no. 653, District Court Clerk's Office of Texas County, Guymon, Oklahoma.

In addition, many useful pieces of information were gleaned

from nonbyline news items appearing in *Northwest Oklahoma Cattleman* (Woodward), the *Oklahoma Cowman* (Oklahoma City), *Oklahoma Farmer-Stockman* (Oklahoma City), the *Ranchman* (Tulsa), and the *Oklahoma Farm Journal* (Oklahoma City). These publications may be found in the main library of Oklahoma State University, Stillwater.

GOVERNMENT DOCUMENTS

Collins, G. P., and W. G. Hill. *Prices Received by Oklahoma Farmers, 1910–1957.* Oklahoma Agricultural Experiment Station Bulletin No. P-297. Stillwater, Okla.: Oklahoma Agricultural Experiment Station, 1958.

Texas General Land Office. *Abstract of all Original Land Titles Comprising Grants and Locations to August 31, 1942.* Austin: Texas General Land Office, 1942.

U.S. Bureau of the Census. *United States Census Report, 1900.* Washington, D.C.: U.S. Government Printing Office, 1902.

———. *United States Census Report, 1910.* Washington, D.C.: U.S. Government Printing Office, 1913.

———. *United States Census Report, 1920.* Washington, D.C.: U.S. Government Printing Office, 1922.

———. *United States Census Report, 1930.* Washington, D.C.: U.S. Government Printing Office, 1932.

U.S. Department of Agriculture. *United States Census of Agriculture, 1935.* Washington, D.C.: U.S. Government Printing Office, 1936.

BOOKS

Billington, Ray Allen. *Westward Expansion.* 3d ed. New York: Macmillan Co., 1967.

Bogue, Allan G. *From Prairie to Cornbelt: Farming on the Illinois and Iowa Prairies in the Nineteenth Century.* Chicago: Quadrangle Books, 1968.

Bond, Pauline, and Gladys Egan, eds. *A History of Beaver County.* 2 vols. Beaver, Okla.: Beaver County Historical Society, 1970, 1971.

Chrisman, Harry E. *Lost Trails of the Cimarron.* 2d ed. Denver: Sage Books, 1964.

————. *Fifty Years on the Owl Hoot Trail.* Chicago: Sage Books, 1969.

Dale, Edward Everett. *The Range Cattle Industry: Ranching on the Great Plains from 1865 to 1925.* 2d ed. Norman: University of Oklahoma Press, 1960.

Emmett, Chris. *Shanghai Pierce: A Fair Likeness.* Norman: University of Oklahoma Press, 1953.

Faulk, Odie B. *Dodge City: The Most Western Town of All.* New York: Oxford University Press, 1977.

Fite, Gilbert C. *George N. Peek and the Fight for Farm Parity.* Norman: University of Oklahoma Press, 1954.

————. *The Farmers' Frontier, 1865–1900.* New York: Holt, Rinehart and Winston, 1966.

Franklin, Jimmie L. *Born Sober: Prohibition in Oklahoma, 1907–1959.* Norman: University of Oklahoma Press, 1971.

Gibson, Arrell M. *Oklahoma: A History of Five Centuries.* Norman: Harlow Publishing Company, 1965.

————, ed. *Frontier Historian: The Life and Work of Edward Everett Dale.* Norman: University of Oklahoma Press, 1975.

Green, Donald E. *Land of the Underground Rain: Irrigation on the Texas High Plains, 1910–1970.* Austin: University of Texas Press, 1973.

————. *Fifty Years of Service to West Texas Agriculture: A History of Texas Tech University's College of Agricultural Sciences, 1925–1975.* Lubbock: Texas Tech University Press, 1977.

Gruebbel, Mrs. R. A. *A History of Victory Memorial United Methodist Church.* Guymon, Okla.: Victory Memorial United Methodist Church, 1973.

Hamlin, James D. *The Flamboyant Judge.* Canyon, Texas: Palo Duro Press, 1972.

Hoag, W. Gifford. *The Farm Credit System: A History of Financial Self-Help.* Danville, Ill.: Interstate Printers and Publishers, 1976.

Hofsommer, Donovan L. *Katy Northwest: The Story of a Branch Line Railroad.* Boulder, Colo.: Pruett Publishing Co., 1976.

Johnson, Vance. *Heaven's Tableland: The Dust Bowl Story.* New York: Farrar, Straus and Co., 1947.

McCarty, John L. *Maverick Town: The Story of Old Tascosa.* Norman: University of Oklahoma Press, 1946. New ed., 1968.

McCoy, Joseph G. *Historic Sketches of the Cattle Trade of the West and Southwest.* Washington, D.C.: Rare Book Shop, 1932.

McReynolds, Edwin C. *Oklahoma: A History of the Sooner State.* 2d ed. Norman: University of Oklahoma Press, 1964.

Malone, Bill C. *Country Music, U.S.A.* Austin: University of Texas Press, 1968.

Nelson, Oliver. *The Cowman's Southwest, Being the Reminiscences of Oliver Nelson.* Edited by Angie Debo. Glendale, Calif.: Arthur H. Clark, 1953.

Owen, Jennie Small, compiler, and Kirke Mechem, editor. *The Annals of Kansas.* 2 vols. Topeka: Kansas State Historical Society, no date of publication.

Rainey, George. *No Man's Land.* Enid, Okla.: privately printed, 1937.

Richardson, Rupert N. *Texas: The Lone Star State.* 2d ed. Englewood Cliffs, N.J.: Prentice-Hall, 1958.

Rister, Carl Coke. *No Man's Land.* Norman: University of Oklahoma Press, 1948.

Rulon, Philip Reed. *Oklahoma State University—Since 1890.* Stillwater: Oklahoma State University Press, 1975.

Savage, William W., Jr. *Cowboy Life: Reconstructing an American Myth.* Norman: University of Oklahoma Press, 1975.

Schlebecker, John T. *Cattle Raising on the Plains, 1900–1961.* Lincoln: University of Nebraska Press, 1963.

Shirk, George M. *Oklahoma Place Names.* Norman: University of Oklahoma Press, 1965.

Stewart, Roy P. *Country Boy in Russia.* Oklahoma City: Oklahoma Publishing Co., 1956.

Sullivan, Vicki, and Mac R. Harris, compilers. *Index to the 1890 Oklahoma Territorial Census for the Counties of Kingfisher, Payne and Beaver.* Oklahoma City: Territorial Press, 1977.

Tait, Samuel W., Jr. *The Wildcatters: An Informal History of Oil Hunting in America.* Princeton: Princeton University Press, 1946.

Torrey, Volta. *Wind-Catchers: American Windmills of Yesterday and Tomorrow.* Brattleboro, Vt.: Stephen Greene Press, 1976.

Tucker, Lee, ed. *Second Annual Old Timers News Year Book.* Keyes, Okla.: Old Timers Publishing Co., 1977.

Webb, Walter P. *The Great Plains.* Boston: Ginn and Co., 1931.

ARTICLES

Brown, Donald A. "Mastering No Man's Land," *Wichita Farm Credit Letter* (Wichita, Kans.), Fall–Winter, 1977, pp. 3–7.

Dale, Edward Everett. "The Frontier Literary Society," in *Frontier Historian: The Life and Work of Edward Everett Dale.* Edited by Arrell M. Gibson. Norman: University of Oklahoma Press, 1975, pp. 152–66.

Davis, Moita D. "Boss Neff," *Chronicles of Oklahoma,* vol. 26 (Summer, 1948), pp. 159–73.

"Do You Have Cattle to Sell?" *Oklahoma Farmer-Stockman,* vol. 47 (September 1, 1934), p. 4.

Deering, Ferdie. "30,000 Acre Homestead," *Oklahoma's Orbit,* Oklahoma City (July 19, 1964), pp. 8–9, 15.

Flood, Francis A. "The Dust Bowl Is Being Tamed," *Oklahoma Farmer-Stockman,* vol. 50 (July 1, 1937), p. 3.

Floyd, Fred. "The Struggle for Railroads in the Oklahoma Panhandle," *Chronicles of Oklahoma,* vol. 54 (Winter, 1976–77), pp. 489–518.

Gates, Paul W. "Homesteading in the High Plains," *Agricultural History,* vol. 51 (January, 1977), pp. 109–33.

Gould, Charles N. "The Beginnings of the Panhandle Oil and Gas Field," *Panhandle-Plains Historical Review,* vol. 8 (1935), pp. 24–35.

Gracy, David B., II. "A Preliminary Survey of Land Colonization in the Panhandle-Plains of Texas," *Museum Journal* (Texas Tech University), vol. 11 (1969), pp. 50–79.

Green, Donald E. "Irrigation: Making the Thirsty Plains Blossom," *Drovers Journal* (Kansas City, Mo.), Special Centennial Edition, vol. 100 (December, 1972), pp. 96–98.

———. "Beginnings of Wheat Culture in Oklahoma," in *Rural Oklahoma.* Edited by Donald E. Green. Oklahoma City: Oklahoma Historical Society, 1977, pp. 56–73.

"H. C. Hitch, Jr. Helmsman of Panhandle Feeding," *Oklahoma Cowman,* vol. 10 (September, 1968), pp. 18–20, 40.

Holladay, Jeff. "The Great Panhandle 'Exodus' Furor." *Orbit Magazine* (Oklahoma City), June 19, 1977, pp. 6–8.

Kinchen, Oscar. "The Squatters in No Man's Land," *Chronicles of Oklahoma,* vol. 26 (Winter, 1948–49), pp. 385–98.

Lambert, C. Roger. "The Drought Cattle Purchase, 1934–1935: Problems and Complaints," *Agricultural History,* vol. 45 (April, 1971), pp. 85–94.

Logsdon, Guy. "The Dust Bowl and the Migrant," *American Scene* 12, Gilcrease Institute, Tulsa (1971).

May, Irvin, Jr. "Welfare and Ranchers: The Emergency Cattle Purchase Program and Emergency Work Relief Program in Texas, 1934–1935," *West Texas Historical Association Year Book,* vol. 47 (1971), pp. 3–19.

Neff, Boss. "Memoirs," in *Old Timers News Year Book.* Edited by Lee Tucker. Keyes, Okla.: Old Timers Publishing Co., 1976. Pp. 94–100.

Richards, O. H. "Early Days in Day County," *Chronicles of Oklahoma,* vol. 26 (Autumn, 1948), pp. 313–24.

Sinise, Jerry. "Feedlots Expansion in the Southwest," *Oklahoma Cowman,* vol. 9 (October, 1969), pp. 33, 42.

Spears, J. R. "Story of No Man's Land," *Chautauquan,* vol. 10 (October–March, 1889–90), pp. 176–80.

Stewart, Roy P. "Henry C. Hitch and His Times," *Chronicles of Oklahoma,* vol. 50 (Spring, 1972), pp. 41–64.

Tucker, Lee. "The Big Snow of 1918–19," in *Second Annual Old Timers News Year Book.* Edited by Lee Tucker. Keyes, Okla.: Old Timers Publishing Co., 1977. Pp. 15–16.

Wheeler, David L. "The Origin and Development of the Cattle Feeding Industry in the Southern High Plains," *Panhandle-Plains Historical Review,* vol. 49 (1976), pp. 81–90.

Woodram, Robert A. "Road Building in the Panhandle," *Second Annual Old Timers News Year Book.* Edited by Lee Tucker. Keyes, Okla.: Old Timers Publishing Co., 1977. Pp. 9–10.

NEWSPAPERS

Amarillo [Texas] Daily News
Beaver [Oklahoma] Herald
Cimarron News (Boise City, Okla.)
Guymon Daily Herald
Guymon Herald

Indian Chieftain (Vinita, Oklahoma)
Panhandle Herald (Guymon)
Texhoma [*Oklahoma*] *Times*

UNPUBLISHED WORKS

Brush, William L. "The Early History of Seward County." M.A. thesis, University of Wichita (Kansas), 1954.

Hamner, Laura B. "Light 'n Hitch." Radio broadcast over KGNC, Amarillo, Texas, October 12, 1958. Transcript in Panhandle-Plains Museum, Canyon, Texas.

Harder, Jesse. "Wheat Production in Northwestern Oklahoma, 1893–1932." M.A. thesis, University of Oklahoma, 1952.

Hitch, Charles A. "Charlie." "Memoirs." Typewritten copy in Henry C. Hitch Papers, ca. 1946–47.

Hitch, Ladd. "Recollections of the Dirty Thirties." Typewritten copy in Henry C. Hitch Papers, 1977.

Nall, Garry L. "Agricultural History of the Texas Panhandle, 1880–1965." Ph.D. dissertation, University of Oklahoma, 1972.

Risinger, Hurshal H. "Social and Economic Study of Texas County." M.A. thesis, University of Oklahoma, 1937.

LETTERS

(All in the Henry C. Hitch Papers)

Becton, Agnes Langston, Orlando, Fla., October 8, 1977, to author.

Frantz, Kenneth, Guymon, Okla., April 5, 1977, to author.

Gray, Joyce Hitch, Guymon, Okla., February 21, 1977, to author.

Hitch, Christine, Guymon, Okla., August 10, 1976, to author.

Hitch, Christine, Guymon, Okla., February 16, 1977, to author.

Hitch, Christine, Guymon, Okla., March 2, 1977, to author.

Hitch, Christine, Guymon, Okla., April 20, 1977, to author.

Hitch, Christine, Guymon, Okla., February 20, 1978, to author.

Hitch, Ladd, Guymon, Okla., February 20, 1978, to author.

Hitch, Lala Moores, Guymon, Okla., February 20, 1978, to author.

Price, Marjorie Hitch, Orlando, Fla., March 1, 1977, to author.

TELEPHONE CONVERSATIONS
(Notes in Henry C. Hitch Papers)

Cannedy, Jerry, and author, Oklahoma City, December 27, 1977.

Freeney, Ellis, and author, Oklahoma City, October 4, 1977.

Hitch, Christine, and author, Guymon–Edmond, Okla., June 18, 1977.

Hitch, Christine, and author, Guymon–Edmond, Okla., February 11, 1978.

PERSONAL INTERVIEWS
(In Henry C. Hitch Papers unless otherwise stated;
all interviews conducted by the author unless otherwise stated)

Alexander, Clarence, January 6, 1977, Guymon, Okla.

Baker, Artemus "Artie," June 3, 1968, Pecos, Texas. In Southwest Collection, Texas Tech University, Lubbock, Texas.

Danner, Bud, January 5, 1977, Guymon, Okla.

Fitzgerald, Joe, August 7, 1976, Guymon, Okla.

Furnish, O. C. "Cotton," August 5, 1976, Guymon, Okla.

Gray, Joyce Hitch, August 5, 1976, Guymon, Oklahoma.

Green, Lewis, May 14, 1977, Wellington, Texas. In author's possession.

Hall, Mary Hitch, August 4, 1976, Guymon, Okla.

Hitch, Christine, August 3, 1976, Guymon, Okla.

Hitch, Christine, August 4, 1976, Guymon, Okla.

Hitch, Christine, August 5, 1976, Guymon, Okla.

Hitch, Christine, January 4, 1977, Guymon, Okla.

Hitch, Christine, January 6, 1977, Guymon, Okla.

Hitch, Christine, January 7, 1977, Guymon, Okla.

Hitch, Henry C., ca. 1965, Guymon, Okla., by Jane Hensley. Original in Jane Hensley's possession, Guymon. Copies in Henry C. Hitch Papers and Living Legend Library, Oklahoma Christian College, Oklahoma City.

Hitch, Henry C., ca. 1967, Guymon, Okla., by John Gray. In

Living Legend Library, Oklahoma Christian College, Oklahoma City.
Hitch, Ladd, August 1, 1976, Guymon, Okla.
Hitch, Ladd, August 3, 1976, Guymon, Okla.
Hitch, Ladd, August 4, 1976, Guymon, Okla.
Hitch, Ladd, January 3, 1977, Guymon, Okla.
Knight, John, August 4, 1976, Stratford, Texas.
McDaniels, E. E., August 6, 1976, Guymon, Okla.
Nash, Orville, January 5, 1977, Guymon, Okla.
Perkins, Bud, January 5, 1977, Guymon, Okla.
Pugh, Tom, January 6, 1977, Texhoma, Okla.
Reedy, Juanita, August 2, 1976, Guymon, Okla.
Ridley, Melvin, January 7, 1977, Guymon, Okla.

Index

Panhandle Pioneer

Penrose, William H.: 11
Pens (cattle): 31, 32, 36, 41; for rodeo, 137; *see also* corrals, stockyards
Perkins, Bud: 163, 180, 222–23
Perkins, Okla.: 232
Perryton, Texas: 186
Petroleum: *see* oil, natural gas
Phillips Petroleum Company: 208–209
Phoenix, Ariz.: 109, 210
Physicians: 46, 70, 88, 103, 104
Pierce, Shanghai: 70
"Pioneer Days" celebration: 172–75, 227
Pittman, A. E.: 158
Platt, Jeremiah: 39
Playa lakes: 51, 52; *see also* Texas Lake
Pleasant Valley School: 76, 103
Plow: 31; disk, 121; purchase of, 147
Population: of No Man's Land, 18, 25; of Texas County, 170
Populists: 25, 192
Post, Wiley: 164
Powell, John Wesley: 57
Pratt County, Kans.: 78, 144
Prescott, Ariz.: 78
Price, Hickman: 144–45
Price, Karick: 231, 232
Price, Marjorie Hitch: 136, 186, 200; birth of, 98, 99; childhood of, 102, 103, 105, 126; education of, 103, 163; and fire, 128; in Great Depression, 148; marriage of, 163; and orange groves, 180–81; and move to Coldwater, 190; children of, 231; and death of husband, 232
Price, W. K. ("Dub"): 231
Price, W. K., Jr.: 186, 223; marriage of, 163; orange-grove business of, 180–81; and move to Coldwater, 190; children of, 231; death of, 231–32
Production Credit Association: credit for ranchers, 157–59; and Henry Hitch, 180; cattlemen's offices in, 193
Production Credit Corporation: *see* Production Credit Association
Progressive Farmer: 96, 204
Prohibition: 10, 36, 65, 77, 87
Prowers County, Kans.: 78
Public Land Strip: 3; *see also* No Man's Land
Pueblo, Colo.: 11, 85
Pugh, Tom: 233–34
Pugh, M. W.: 204, 205

Quarantine of cattle: 64–65
Quinlan, D. C.: 204
Quinn, R. B. ("Dick"): 25, 204; and

cattlemen's association, 191–92

Radios: 141, 163, 182–83, 190, 222, 241
Railroads: 27–29, 31, 32, 46, 47, 55, 84, 85, 88, 109, 169; link Panhandle to Kansas City, 60–61; Rock Island, 64, 65, 87; on Hitch land, 142; in Panhandle, 168–69; *see also* Rock Island Railroad
Rainey, George: 16
Rainfall: 35, 52, 57, 151, 168; conservation of, 154
Ragland, Carl: 75
Ranchers: 27; platting of ranches into farms by, 117–18; bankruptcy of, 118; *see also* cattlemen, ranches
Ranches: 210; beginnings of Westmoreland, 31–34; beginnings of Hitch, 34–35; of John Hittson, 32; change in ownership of, 43; Diamond Tail, 55; Taintor, 111; Atkinson, 129, 130; Stonebraker-Zea, 161; Anchor D, 205; *see also under names of ranches*
Ranchman: 193
Range rights: 12, 14
Rankin, David: 210
Rattlesnakes: 126
Real estate firms: 90, 133, 218; *see also* land, land claims
Reconstruction Finance Corporation: 156; *see also* Regional Agricultural Credit Corporations
Record Stockman: 240
Reedy, Cecil: 212, 216–17
Reedy, Juanita: 212
Reeves, Henry: 46
Regional Agricultural Credit Corporations (RACC): credit for ranches by, 156–58; bureaucracy of, 157–58
Reiman, Ernest A.: 15
Report on the Lands of the Arid Region: 57
Republican party: 190–91
Reser, E. F.: 45
Respective Claims Committee: 18, 19–20
Richfield, Kans.: 205
Ridpath, John Clark: 96
Riffe, G. W.: 114
Rister, Carl Coke: 5
Rizley, Ross: 165, 180, 190–91
Riverside, Okla.: 17
Roberson, C. A.: 107
Roberts, W. L.: 204
Robertson, J. B. A.: 205
Robertson, J. D.: 61

9 780806 146737